Charming Cadavers

Women in Culture and Society
A series edited by Catharine R. Stimpson

CHARMING CADAVERS

HORRIFIC FIGURATIONS OF THE FEMININE IN INDIAN BUDDHIST HAGIOGRAPHIC LITERATURE

Liz Wilson

THE UNIVERSITY OF CHICAGO PRESS

CHICAGO AND LONDON

Liz Wilson is assistant professor of religion at Miami University (Ohio).

The University of Chicago Press, Chicago 60637
The University of Chicago Press, Ltd., London

Printed in the United States of America
05 04 03 02 01 00 99 98 97 96 1 2 3 4 5

ISBN: 0-226-90053-3 (cloth)
0-226-90054-1 (paper)

Library of Congress Cataloging-in-Publication Data

Wilson, Liz.
Charming cadavers : horrific figurations of the feminine in Indian Buddhist hagiographic literature / Liz Wilson.
p. cm. — (Women in culture and society)
Includes bibliographical references and index.
1. Woman (Buddhism) 2. Women in Buddhism. I. Title.
II. Series.
BQ4570.W6W55 1996
294.3'378344—dc20 95-52000
CIP

♾ The paper used in this publication meets the minimum requirements of the American National Standard for Information Sciences—Permanence of Paper for Printed Library Materials, ANSI Z39.48-1984.

Contents

Foreword

"This book," Liz Wilson writes of *Charming Cadavers: Horrific Figurations of the Feminine in Indian Buddhist Hagiographic Literature,* "is my attempt to describe what I find so repugnant about making women into [revolting] things . . . , things to be looked at rather than persons with whom to converse" (p. xiv).

Writing for both general and scholarly audiences, Wilson has succeeded brilliantly, pungently, and engrossingly in her effort. The specific "horrific figurations of the feminine" that she anatomizes appear in exemplary narratives of the Buddha and Buddhist saints, the "awakened ones." Although composed over a millennium ago in India and Buddhist South Asia (about ten to twelve centuries after the time of the Buddha), these stories still circulate in the Buddhist world. They are a vital part of a pan-Buddhist, global religious and literary genre. They have some parallels to Christian hagiographies. Both genres, for example, feature women who mutilate themselves in order to deter sexual assault and rape. However, the Buddhist narratives have their unique themes and functions.

One of the functions is to dramatize and encourage a key Buddhist practice—that of contemplating the foulness of the body as a means of cultivating celibacy and detachment from the social world. Wilson argues that narratives dramatizing this practice are enmeshed in gender. In them, women represent transience and death. They personify the corrupt, corrupting social order that seekers of liberation must renounce. The more revolting the women seem to be, the more revolting the social order that is metaphorically linked to them becomes. To be sure, some women are lovely without, but even the loveliest are vile, foul, and putrefying within. They reek of impermanence, disease, suffering, and sexual folly, be the aim of sexuality the production of heirs or the gratification of lust. To see through the specious charms of women is to achieve insight into the essence of the human predicament. Freedom from the yearning for sensual gratification and from suffering and death are possible for those who learn to see all women as walking corpses.

Many hagiographies feature the Buddha or male meditators who move from being an eye that observes women to an enlightened "I" that abjures them. Women play a subordinate role in these tales, serving mainly as mute, anonymous objects of the male gaze. When a woman is the subject of the story, the narrative strategy blocks her from attaining authentic subjectivity. Adapting the insights of feminist film theory into how female spectators adopt the "male gaze," Wilson argues that Buddhist hagiographics showcase female subjects who have learned to imitate male conventions of looking. Such women internalize the male gaze through the instructions of male teachers, learning to see themselves as objects.

Wilson clearly respects the grand achievements of Buddhism. Respect, however, is no bar to pointed questions. Often witty and ironic, this student of hagiography is no hagiographer. What, she wonders, determines which characters are permitted agency, consciousness, and speech? Why are they more often male than female? Why are women conscious, not of themselves as agents, but of men's consciousness to them?

Not surprisingly, given her boldness, learning, and intellectual energy, Wilson has entered the debate, now a century old, about women and Buddhism. Has Buddhism, in all its complexity, with all its developments, helped to liberate women? To oppress them? Or both? Wilson suggests that a broad cross-section of Buddhist literature "encourages men to see women (and women to see themselves) through the gendered 'I' of a subject position that is clearly marked as masculine" (p. 193). Even the achievements of the celebrated Buddhist nuns whom she studies are minimized not only by their institutional subordination but by the literary conventions through which their words and deeds have been represented. Given her conclusions, it is hard for Wilson to support a conventional history of Indian Buddhism that emphasizes a gradual decline in "androcentric thinking" in the millennium after the death of the Buddha and "a gradual movement from gender-based discrimination to a mode of apprehension in which gender becomes irrelevant" (p. 193).

Charming Cadavers has life and dash. I encourage thoughtful people to converse with it now.

Catharine R. Stimpson

Preface

This book may not be suitable for younger or more sensitive readers. It may shock you, and if it does, it will have its intended effect. Spread out before you in the pages that follow are graphic literary images of dead and dying women—images created by Buddhist authors to teach stark lessons about the nature of the body and the folly of lust. I find these images revolting, just as their authors intended. But there is, in my revulsion, a feminist dimension beyond what those who composed these grisly stories may have intended me to feel.

I can recall very vividly the day about five years ago when I read in a commentary on the *Dhammapada* (an immensely popular compendium of the Buddhist path) a disturbing story that made me begin to call myself a feminist. This tale that woke me from my prefeminist slumber was a description of a man named Yasa whose life story mirrors that of the Buddhas ("awakened ones"): he was born to wealth, luxury, and sensual pleasure but, at a decisive watershed moment in his life, gave it all up. Yasa literally ran away from home one night when he saw that he could no longer enjoy himself in the women's apartments of his palatial home. The lassitude he saw in the bodies of women asleep in the harem disgusted him; the harem suddenly seemed like a charnel field strewn with bodies frozen in rigor mortis. Yasa, as it turns out, saw the women of his harem in this way because of his past-life conditioning: in a previous life he had recoiled in horror while cremating a pregnant woman's dead body. This man's story disturbed me, when I first read it. I did not know why it bothered me so much; I only knew that there was something creepy about it that called for further attention. Soon I found that Yasa's story was in no way an aberration. It was rather typical, in fact, of a genre of stories composed ten to twelve centuries after the time of the Buddha that reproduce in literary form the experience of Buddhist meditators who achieve liberation through the contemplation of revolting things.

My disgust at reading Yasa's story differed from the disgust that set Yasa free from his delusional attachment to a life of luxury because it was mediated through my growing awareness that all the revolting things I had encountered in my perusal of this genre were female things. This book is my attempt to describe what I find so repugnant about making women into things of this sort, things to be looked at rather than persons with whom to converse. My work poses questions that have rarely been asked of Buddhist literature, questions like:

- In representing people as objects of meditation, in what ways do Buddhist authors endow these representations with subjectivity?
- Are the people thus represented depicted as conscious agents with access to speech?
- Are they constituted as subjects who think, act, and speak only under certain conditions (and what are those conditions)?
- If their consciousness is, as Sartre would say, consciousness of themselves as perceived by others, will their voices and their actions also be constrained by this awareness of self-as-constituted-by-other? What kind of agency results from this derivative form of subjectivity?

I have written this book for the general reader, and with that audience in mind I have tried to let the stories I tell speak for themselves as much as possible. There is, of course, an editorial overvoice that is mine, just as there are editorial overvoices that have shaped the particular versions of the stories I tell in this book. But I have taken care to delegate quotations from the original languages of my sources, technical discussions, and surveys of scholarly literature to notes at the end of the text. I have also delegated material on the dating and sectarian affiliations of my sources and their place within the history of Indian Buddhism to an appendix.

Many people helped me with the difficult task of shaping this book so that it would speak to both scholars and nonscholars. Special thanks go to Charlie Hallisey and Lee Siegel, who read the manuscript for the University of Chicago Press and offered crucial advice on how to frame the project for a dual audience. Wendy Doniger plied me with apt Indian and European parallels and reminded me at every turn of the wider Indo-European context in which my materials are situated. Frank Reynolds helped me to see the richness of the Buddhological tropes at work in the stories I tell here and directed the dissertation out of which this book developed. David Gitomer's work on Sanskrit literary theory and recommended readings were crucial for the framing of the project, as were Larry Sullivan's writings and class lectures at the University of Chicago Divinity School. The late Ioan Culianu helped me to develop a feminist method for interpreting my materials. Without his mentoring and his work in the history of fashion and bodily adornment, I could not have written this book.

I am grateful to Clair Carty, Lee Horvitz, and Lisa Sommer for their wisdom and friendship, to James Lynn for his help in preparing the manuscript for publication, and to Miami University for providing me with a research appointment that enabled me to revise chapter 5.

Earlier versions of portions of this book have appeared in the *Journal of Feminist Studies in Religion* 11, no. 1 (1995): 41–80; *Union Seminary Quarterly* 48, nos. 3–4 (1994); and *Religious Reflections on the Human Body,* edited by Jane Marie Law (Indiana University Press, 1995), and are reprinted with permission.

It is common for many Buddhists to dedicate any merit they may receive from ritual performances to the well-being of the dead. If there be any merit to what I have done here, I would like to dedicate it to my mother, Jane Wilson (1934–1990), and Ioan Culianu (1950–1991).

Note on Terminology

Many of the terms used in this work exist in both Pāli and Sanskrit forms. Some of these terms are best left untranslated because there is no satisfactory English equivalent. In the interest of stylistic consistency and avoiding unnecessary confusion for the nonspecialist reader, it was necessary to choose between the Pāli and the Sanskrit when using these terms without translation. I have given preference to the Sanskritic forms of such terms (even though this work deals extensively with Pāli texts) since many of the most untranslatable Buddhist terms have become well known to English speakers in their Sanskrit forms (such as the term "nirvana").

Introduction

Encountering Death

Biographies of the Buddha place a vivid realization of the inevitability of old age and death at a crucial moment in the life of the founder. Living the pampered life of a prince intentionally shielded by his father from the realities of life, Gotama reportedly took a series of chariot rides that led him away from the sheltered environment of the palace. He saw during these outings a wizened old man, a sick man panting and shaking with fever, and a dead man. Learning from the charioteer that old age, sickness, and death are intrinsic to the human condition, Gotama was filled with agitation. One biography suggests that the prince was physically overcome with faintness when he saw the dead man and had to support himself by leaning against the pole of the chariot in which he was riding.[1]

Alarmed at these signs of the inevitable decay that begins with birth and ends in death, the prince marveled that people can enjoy themselves knowing the inevitability of death. That these are the rather naive words of one who has just had the scales fall from his eyes is clear. At some level we all know that death is, in the words of Gerard Manley Hopkins, "the blight man was born for," but that hardly stops us from savoring the pleasures of life.[2] In his later career as a teacher, the Buddha recognized the extent of human sanguineness with regard to old age and death and found ingenious ways to impart a vivid sense of realism and a concomitant sense of urgency to people oblivious of the blight they were born for.

Confrontation with death and decay looms large in the history of Buddhism.[3] While acknowledgment of the fact of death and reflection on the transformative mysteries of death figure prominently in other Indian religious traditions like Hinduism, Buddhism distinguishes itself among Indian traditions in the extent to which meditation on death and the transience of the human condition is linked with spiritual progress.[4] One of the lessons that the Buddha is said to have taught again and again in his capacity as head of the monastic order (*sangha*) is the utter perversity of pursuing sexual gratification when the human body, in its natural state, emits substances as foul as those emitted by putrefying corpses.[5] That living bodies are comparable to walking corpses was a lesson that Gotama learned with his own eyes in the harem just before he renounced the world. Waking up in the women's apartments in the middle of the night, one version of the Buddha's story explains, Gotama noticed the saliva dripping from half-opened mouths and the rigor-mortis-like postures of the sleepers and suddenly had a vision of the harem as a charnel field strewn with corpses. This vision of beautiful women ravaged by death so agitated Gotama that he left home immediately to seek a path that leads beyond birth and death.

In his later career as teacher and head of the male monastic order, the Buddha helped those monks troubled by sexual desire to see the perversity of yearning for bodies that are riddled with corruption. There were special places in ancient Indian cremation grounds where the bodies of paupers and executed criminals were left to rot; it was to those charnel fields, Buddhist hagiographies report, that members of the early *sangha* were sent by the Buddha so that they could contemplate the foulness of the body.[6] The Buddha reportedly urged his monks to visit charnel fields in order to contemplate the various kinds of disfiguration to which rotting corpses are subject. On one occasion, when a monk found that even in the charnel field he was troubled by lust, it is said that the Buddha went with that monk to the cremation ground and conjured up an attractive young female body for the man to feast his eyes upon. The Buddha then used his psychic powers to turn that alluring body into a worm-infested corpse.

The Buddha reportedly told love-smitten monks cautionary tales that explicitly compare attractive women to flesh-eating ogresses and other demonic beings who take on human forms in order to seduce and devour men. These tales suggest that monks would do well to view feminine charms as deceptive appearances covering corrupt, decay-ridden bodies. When an ogress wants to devour a man, she presents a deceptively attractive human facade that fools the unwary victim. Like the false form assumed by a demonic man-eater, the outer form of dress, ornaments, and cosmetics covering a woman's body constitutes a false facade that is as perilous to a man as the human guise of an ogress. Failure to see through the specious charms of human women, these cautionary tales suggest, is comparable to perishing at the hands of a terrible ogress or other demonic feminine being.

With such a strong sense of men's vulnerability to women's charms, it is not surprising that representations of the Buddha show him having grave reservations about allowing women to take ordination as nuns. He finally did so, we are told, on the condition that women accept a set of special rules that subordinate women to men within the monastic assembly.[7] Nuns were, for example, asked to show respect for monks by bowing to them, although the only gesture of deference required of men in the *sangha* is that a junior monk should bow to his seniors. "Any nun," Nancy Falk explains, "no matter how long she had been in the *sangha,* must treat any monk, even the rudest novice, as if he were her senior."[8] Falk has argued that it is no surprise that the order of nuns should have eventually disappeared from many Buddhist countries by the end of the first millennium. Subordinated to men from the beginning by special rules, women had few opportunities for leadership within the *sangha,* less prestige than monks because of their circumscribed leadership roles, and therefore less support from the lay community. When hard times came, the order of nuns was more susceptible to economic deprivation and eventually died out for lack of support.

Object Lessons

This book argues that the subordination of women to men within Buddhism as it developed in India and South Asia during the first millennium of the Common Era has a larger dimension that has not been articulated by scholars. My analysis of literary conventions used in Buddhist hagiographic literature shows women frequently represented as objects of meditation whose sole function in the narratives in which they appear is to lead to the edification of the male subjects who observe them. In a broad cross-section of hagiographic literature, male protagonists become Arhats, or "worthy ones," through viewing dead, dying, or disfigured female bodies. By viewing women as object lessons on the folly of desire, the men in these narratives thereby achieve the state of spiritual liberation that is characterized by the eradication of desire and thereby become worthy of veneration and emulation. Women are subordinated to men in this literature in that they are consistently made subservient to men by the very structure of narratives in which they appear. The women who serve as objects for the edification of men are, for the most part, anonymous. When they are given names, they are nevertheless scarcely endowed with anything comparable to the full subjectivity of the male protagonists in these narratives. It is always the man who sees and the woman who is seen, the man who speaks and the woman who is spoken about. The roles are not reciprocal. There is little possibility in these narratives for an intersubjective exchange of equals between the male subjects and their female meditation-objects, for the women are represented largely without consciousness, voice, or agency. My analysis suggests that these narratives, in constituting women as mute objects of the male gaze, express an androcentric Buddhist ethos that gives priority to the experience and perspective of male subjects. Because the body of literature I analyze cuts across sectarian and scholastic lines and includes a variety of Buddhist traditions, I argue that the objectification of women for the edification of men is truly a pan-Buddhist theme.

This book suggests that Buddhist women living in South Asia in the first millennium of the Common Era were subordinated to men not so much by rules that enshrine male privilege and circumscribe women's rights but by representational practices that would have made it difficult for a woman to imagine herself following in the footsteps of highly revered Buddhist saints. In influential hagiographies that were (and for the most part still are) repeated in sermons and enacted in performances throughout the Buddhist world, men achieve liberation from suffering by learning to see through the specious charms of women. These hagiographies tend to represent entrapment in *saṃsāra*—the painful cycle of birth and death—as a male dilemma while gendering *saṃsāra* itself as feminine, as a prison in which women are the agents of incarceration. It would have been difficult, I believe, for South Asian women to imagine themselves participating as active agents in the drama of salvation as it is represented in these tales. Cast in the active but negative role of a temptress charged with keeping male observers in a state of delusion, a Buddhist woman hearing a hagiographic sermon might well imagine herself playing a more positive role only when she is at her most passive. When, through death or serious illness, she has lost all control over her bodily functions, her charms will at last be revealed for what they really are. No longer a potential temptress, she will be transformed into a redemptress capable of liberating male observers from the bonds of *saṃsāra.*

There are a number of hagiographies redacted by South Asian Buddhists during the first millennium of the Common Era in which women are clearly the heroines, but I believe that they support rather than challenge my thesis that male subjectivity prevails in this body of literature. In them, nuns instructed by male mentors view their own aging bodies as objects of contemplation or, if too vain to objectify themselves in that way, view female phantasms that are magically conjured up by the Buddha for their edification. Cataloging the deterioration of their own bodies or viewing with horror the dying bodies of female phantasms, these nuns may be said to regard the female body from the perspective of a male subject. Their meditation experiences do not constitute a female equivalent of what monks do in charnel fields. These women, like their male mentors and other monks whose stories are told here, contemplate only female bodies, not the decaying bodies of men. Feminist film theorists have shown how women, while watching a movie shot from a male point of view, will adopt a male subject position and objectify the women on screen in order to identify with the movie's male protagonist. I believe that many South Asian Buddhist women learned to identify against themselves in order to see the world from the perspective of their male heroes. Despite the fact that South Asian Buddhists clearly appreciated tales with women protagonists, these stories of Buddhist heroines ultimately reinforce the message of female subservience found in the men's stories since in them the point of view associated with the male subject is reinforced and shown to be normative for all.

Was the Buddha a Feminist?

As Jonathon Walters has documented in an article on women in the Theravāda tradition, the earliest students of the role of women in Buddhist history tended to credit the Buddha with the liberation of Indian women.[9] Turn-of-the-century Pāli scholars such as Caroline A. Foley (later Mrs. C. A. F. Rhys Davids) and Mabel Bode, like many nineteenth-century Orientalists, regarded Buddhism as a radically egalitarian reform movement. Challenging those pre-Buddhist institutions that gave certain men privileged access to spiritual power, the Buddhism reconstructed by these scholars embraced a more democratic spiritual ideal that included those previously excluded, especially women and the lower castes. Foley argued that Buddhism placed women on an equal footing with men by offering a genderless ideal of the renouncer as "an asexual rational being."[10] I. B. Horner, encouraged by Mrs. Rhys Davids to produce a monograph on the subject, argued in 1930 that Buddhism brought women equality, autonomy, and respect unprecedented in pre-Buddhist India:

> Under Buddhism, more than ever before, [a woman] was an individual in command of her own life until the dissolution of her body, and less of a chattel to only be respected if she lived through and on a man. . . . What Gotama did for women shines as a bright light in the history of freedom. . . . Buddhism became not only an antagonist of Brahmanism [the early Indian religion out of which Hinduism developed] and a revolt against the caste system, then beginning to draw India into its clutches, but also an attempt to promote the cause of rights for women, for which in a spirit which was startlingly modern the women themselves were beginning to fight.[11]

That early Buddhism was championed, at the turn of the century and into the 1930s, as a progressive movement while Brahminical (or early Hindu) institutions were vilified as oppressive to women should come as no surprise to students of nineteenth-century Orientalism. The identification of more "advanced" religio-cultural systems against the backdrop of those deemed less advanced is a rhetorical strategy that permeates nineteenth-century discourse about Asia and the Middle East. Groups and institutions that did not threaten colonial interests were often favorably compared to those that did challenge colonial supremacy.[12] In the case of early twentieth-century British scholars writing about India, it was only natural to champion a religion that was all but defunct in India and vilify one that was, through the work of Indian activists such as Mahātma Gandhi, becoming increasingly intertwined with the Indian Independence movement. But to assert that Buddhism was not androcentric simply because it treated women better than early Hinduism did, as Walters aptly puts it, is to offer a hypothesis that cannot be verified without determining just how badly women actually fared under the auspices of Hinduism.[13]

Since the 1970s, the role of women in Buddhist history has re-emerged as a topic of interest to many scholars. Although different in significant respects, modern studies of Buddhist women's history evidence many of the same preoccupations and presuppositions that guided the groundbreaking work of the early Pāli school of Buddhist studies. Once again (as is inevitable, I believe), the history of Buddhism is made to reflect the concerns of the scholars reconstructing it. In the work of Foley, Bode, and Horner, the early history of Buddhism is seen to anticipate the struggle for suffrage by women in the West. These authors are anxious to show that Buddhist women themselves struggled for full participation in the life of the community; their arguments are cast in terms of women's "rights," access to the public sphere, and other issues pertinent to women fighting for full participation in democratic society. With the rise of the second wave of the women's movement in the late 1960s and throughout the 1970s, a new feminist agenda emerged in Buddhist studies. Having been granted access to the public sphere, women in the sixties and seventies found themselves restricted by unstated assumptions and discriminatory "glass ceilings." Recognizing that women can be granted full legal privileges and still be barred from enjoying them because of stereotypical assumptions about how women behave, the advocates of second-wave feminism set about changing society's image of the feminine. Representations of women deemed exploitative and demeaning were exposed and their authors censured as a means of liberating women from the stereotypes that oppress them. In her monograph on images of the feminine in Mahāyāna Buddhism, Diana Paul reflects such guiding concerns.[14]

Like many contemporary scholars of Buddhist women's history, I have been influenced by the women's liberation movement of the 1960s and 1970s. Like them, I consider the images of women in Buddhist literature worthy of close scrutiny, believing that they are as decisive as the actual powers and privileges accorded to women. But unlike those contemporary scholars who regard the history of Buddhism as a gradual movement away from the misogyny of early Buddhist literature, I am unable to give later forms of Buddhism such as the Mahāyāna a clean bill of health with regard to sexism.[15] Harsh condemnations and exploitative figurations of the feminine in which women undergo mortification for men's edification abound in those texts (such as the *Lalitavistara* and other Sanskrit biographies of the Buddha) which proclaim in their colophons their allegiance to the Great Vehicle, as well as those that show Mahāyānist influence but belong to other canons. Explicit arguments against the importance of gender in path progress coexist, in Mahāyāna texts, with vicious tirades against women.[16]

Claimed by the Theravāda school as their scriptural foundation, the Pāli *Nikāyas* (collections of discourses of the Buddha) are as ambivalent as Mahāyāna texts with regard to the spiritual capacities of women. On the one hand, the Mahāyānist view that gender distinctions cease to exist when understood from the perspective of emptiness is not absent from the Pāli *Nikāyas*. For example, in the *Saṃyutta Nikāya* an interchange between Māra, archenemy of the Buddhist order, and the nun Somā begins with Māra challenging the ability of a woman, with her "two-finger wit," to achieve the status of a sage. Somā responds by suggesting that femininity means nothing when mindfulness and insight are established, concluding that Māra should go tempt someone deluded enough to distinguish male and female.[17] On the other hand, another passage from the same text declares womankind the corruption (*duṭṭha*) of the celibate life.[18] Elsewhere in the *Nikāyas*, women are repeatedly blamed for the downfall of men and explicitly linked to the premature decline of the Buddha's teachings.

The focus of this study, however, is not so much the perceived character of women but rather how disgust-inspiring representations of women figure in the religious achievements of members of the men's monastic order. My sample is a broad cross-section of hagiographic literature redacted in India and Buddhist South Asia after the reign of the Indian emperor Aśoka (third century B.C.E.) in which repulsive figurations of the feminine lead to the edification of prominent monks.[19] In hagiographic texts representing a variety of scholastic affiliations, including Mahāyāna and Hīnayāna schools (such as the Theravāda), appealing female bodies become edifying objects of contemplation through death, disfiguration, and sleep so deep that it resembles death.[20] Within each of these three basic scenarios there are various permutations. Thus women who die may die in a variety of ways. Some fall ill and die; some grow old, fall ill, and die; and some die suddenly without any signs of old age or disease. After death, their corpses may burst open with putrefaction, wither away with desiccation, or shrivel up in the flames of the cremation fire. Placing macabre figurations of the feminine at crucial moments in the hagiographies of leading members of the *sangha,* the redactors of post-Aśokan texts show the power of horror to promote insight into the Dharma, or the teachings of the

Buddhas. In addition to linking grotesque figurations of the feminine with the lofty spiritual attainments of their subjects, the redactors of these hagiographies frequently suggest, in editorial asides, that such grisly scenes can have salutary consequences for all who listen to the tales of the lives of the saints. Horrific figurations of the feminine instantiate the Buddha's teachings in such a graphic and compelling manner that only a fool would be oblivious to the lessons about life and death that they teach.

The female objects of meditation at the heart of this book are curious creatures. They are teachers who taught noted monks (and who continue to teach, as their stories are repeated by Buddhists today). But in their role as teachers they do not utter a single word. What they have to teach is not what is on their minds but what is going on in their bodies. As Sartre points out in his discussion of what it feels like to be the object of another's gaze, the person being observed by another will remain a mere object, a fixture in the mental universe of the other, unless he or she can return the gaze of the other and make the other an object in his or her own universe of meaning.[21] But the dead, dying, or unconscious women who appear in the pages to follow are incapable of returning the gaze of their male observers. Since they are never given the capacity to return the gaze that surveys them, they cannot assert their own status as conscious subjects.

In thinking about the role that dead, dying, and disfigured women play when they serve as objects of meditation for saints and those who hear and repeat their tales, I have found Elaine Scarry's *The Body in Pain* to be a useful resource.[22] In this meditation on the role of bodily alterations in instantiating abstract, disembodied ideals, Scarry focuses on the many spheres of life in which altered bodies are made to serve as display boards that instantiate and thus confer facticity on abstractions whose truth is otherwise difficult to demonstrate. Although Scarry's analysis of torture, war, circumcision, and other forms of marking the body does not involve a systematic consideration of gender, it does comment on the frequency with which women's bodies are drafted into the service of ideological instantiation.[23] Her argument supports the work of art historians like John Berger and sociologists like Erving Goffman who argue that the female form is constantly called upon to embody abstract ideals for (and to sell goods and services to) the spectator.[24]

The gruesomely transformed female bodies that appear in post-

Aśokan hagiographic literature instantiate three principles that, while characteristic of all conditioned phenomena, are not always easy to discern. In the eyes of one with insight, all phenomena are impermanent (Sanskrit, *anitya;* Pāli, *anicca*), characterized by dis-ease or suffering (Sanskrit, *duḥkha;* Pāli, *dukkha*), and without any abiding essence (Sanskrit, *anātman*; Pāli, *anatta*). Horrifically transformed women make these three features of conditioned things emphatically visible for those who have a tendency to reify what are only transient, essenceless phenomena. With their aging, dying, bleeding, and putrefying bodies, they body forth the truths of the Dharma that many people have to see with their own eyes to believe.

While altering the perceptual world of the observer, grotesque figurations of the feminine are also associated with dramatic changes in behavior. For monks troubled by sexual desire, horrifically transformed female bodies serve as object lessons on the folly of lust. But seeing the ills to which flesh is heir also alleviates another problem that threatens the commitment of Buddhist renouncers to their monastic vocation, and that is the desire to produce heirs. Chapter 1 explores the sociology of celibacy in its South Asian context and suggests why the desire for sexual gratification and the desire to reproduce pose such a threat to the life of the *sangha.*

Chapter 2 describes various forms of meditation by which insight into the nature of *saṃsāra* may be achieved through developing a salutary sense of aversion toward impermanent things, particularly the body. I argue that Buddhist constructions of the body capitalize on Brahminical concerns about bodily impurity, but in Buddhist texts Brahminical discourse is used selectively, for distinctly Buddhist purposes. Brahminical discourse focusing on the filth that leaks from the anus, mouth, nostrils, and other bodily apertures is echoed in Buddhist scripture and meditation literature. The body is constituted in Buddhist literature as a leaky, sievelike container that is constantly sullied by the defiling substances that flow from every orifice. But where Brahminical discourse advocates closing off the apertures of the body through purificatory rites, the sacrality that Brahminical discourse promises the practitioner of purificatory rites is achieved by Buddhists through recognizing that bodily closure is impossible. Like a boil so filled with pus that it leaks in nine places, the body described in Buddhist discourse is a wound with nine holes that neither merits nor is amenable to ritual purification.[25] Although it should certainly be cared for—that is, washed and clothed, just as one cleans and bandages a wound—there is no point in fussing over the body since it is a wound that will never heal.

Chapter 2 also introduces the reader to some of the literary methods that post-Aśokan writers and redactors use to evoke a salutary sense of aversion toward carnal pleasures. Analyzing Pāli, Sanskrit, and Tamil Buddhist texts, I argue that Buddhist authors and redactors were masters at subverting accepted literary conventions in order to communicate the folly of desire. Post-Aśokan Buddhist texts use unconventional literary methods such as the blending of erotic and repulsive imagery to suggest homologies between carnal pleasure and carnage, bedrooms and battlefields, bliss and bondage—homologies that persuade the sensitive reader or listener of the rapacity of the sex act and the perversity of sexual desire.

Chapter 3 focuses on Pāli hagiographies that climax in repulsive figurations of the feminine. Several of these hagiographic narratives take place in the women's apartments or harem. Through the appearance of death in the midst of deep sleep, the erotic space of the harem suddenly comes to resemble a charnel field strewn with dead bodies. Other hagiographies are set in the charnel field itself. These narratives echo the Buddhist meditative practice of going to charnel fields to contemplate uncremated corpses in various stages of decay and disfiguration. They recall the typologies found in meditation manuals: there are worm-infested bodies that teach the lesson that the human body is a repository of parasitic creatures, there are festering corpses that show the natural putridity of the body's interior, as well as other types of dead bodies with other lessons to teach. One woman has had her appendages cut off and is deposited in the charnel field along with her detached body parts. She resembles the type of corpse that meditators are likely to find after a battle, an execution, or an animal attack in the jungle; meditators must partially reassemble such corpses for the purposes of meditation.

These hagiographic retellings of prominent monks' meditative experiences do more than simply illustrate the successful use of techniques described in meditation manuals. They also innovate. They feature, for example, "fresh" cadavers—the bodies of women who have died quite recently, bodies too well preserved to serve as objects of contemplation. In these latter accounts, cremation is used to transform the charming cadaver into a charmless tangle of burnt limbs. Hagiographic depictions of charnel ground meditations are also innovative in their very premise. While meditation manuals suggest that it is a bad idea for a monk to look at a dead woman's body because he might find it arousing, post-Aśokan hagiographies combine arousing and disgusting stimuli in ways practitioners of aversion therapy might approve of: alluring women die sudden, spectacular, and disgusting deaths that sicken the beholder just at that moment when he is most vulnerable to the charms of women. These narratives suggest that the path to wisdom is not always the path of prudence; sometimes the path of prurience—in which desire is encouraged only to be subverted in the end—is much more efficacious.

Chapter 4 reflects on the similarities between Māra, the god of death and enemy of renouncers, and the Buddha as "fishers of men." Both Māra and the Buddha are depicted as using guileful methods to foster allegiance to the way of life they represent, and neither one is averse to using the enticing bodies of beautiful young women as a lure for men susceptible to lust. Māra captures his victims by offering them such flesh-baited hooks that deliver death instead of gratification. Through the provisional encouragement of sexual desire, the Buddha occasionally mimics Māra, baiting the "hook of the Dharma"[26] with female flesh that is intended to deceive the unwary. But the Buddha ultimately subverts the sexual desire that he encourages by the strategic use of repulsive figurations of the feminine.

Seeing Through the Gendered "I"[27]

In the narratives analyzed in chapters 1–4, the women whose bodies burst open with putrefaction, wither away with desiccation, or shrivel up in the flames of the cremation fire do not typically occupy the position of literary subjects. With one notable exception, the stories in which they appear are not *their* stories but those of the monks who apprehend them as objects of contemplation. These grotesquely transformed women are merely objects of the male gaze, solutions to the male dilemma of how men may be liberated from the captivating charms of women. Chapter 5 presents post-Aśokan Pāli hagiographies of nuns who do occupy the subject position. These are accounts of genuine female subjects, but they are curiously self-reflexive subjects who achieve insight into the Dharma by observing their own bodies (or those of magical doubles) undergoing grisly transformations. Many of the nuns whose excellence in monastic training brought them recognition and inclusion in hagiographic anthologies are women whose preferred form of meditation is self-contemplation. Such women often comment on how old age has wrecked the former beauty of their bodies and turned every eye-catching feature into an occasion for disgust. Nuns are often represented, in hagiographic anthologies, as if standing before the mirror. They survey their aged flesh and catalog with pride the wrinkles and cataracts and sagging breasts that make them less likely to turn men's heads now that time has made them perfect exemplars of the truth of the Dharma. By turning their gaze in the direction which androcentric convention compels them to look in order to achieve the insight of an awakened subject, these female subjects inevitably interact with themselves as objects.

My reading of post-Aśokan hagiographies suggests that those nuns who saw themselves from the point of view of their male observers had the best chance of being recognized by their peers for their perspicacity and insight into the Dharma; the stories of such self-objectifying women were likely to be remembered and included in hagiographic anthologies. Those nuns who went out of their way to make sure that their true inner nature was clearly conspicuous and not hidden from the male gaze were singled out for special appreciation by the monastic assembly. There is a tale, for example, of an attractive young nun named Subhā who gouged out her eye and gave it to a man who was smitten with the beauty of her eyes. Subhā's self-disfiguration had a (predictably) spectacular effect on her deluded admirer; she gave that man an education the likes of which only the Buddhas can give. She made the abstractions of Dharma come alive for him by bodying forth the words of the Buddhas in her own flesh.

Subhā also managed to arrest an unwanted sexual overture that bordered on sexual assault (in that her admirer had followed her to an isolated place and cornered her there, using physical force to prevent her escape). This Buddhist tale of self-disfiguration as self-defense bears striking resemblances to medieval Christian accounts of women who disfigure themselves in order to repulse potential rapists (a trope within Christian hagiography that Jane Tibbetts Schulenberg has dubbed "the heroics of virginity").[28] In both the Buddhist and the Christian accounts, women keep potential rapists at bay by making themselves abhorrent to their assailants. That they do so at great cost to their own physical integrity (and are lionized by their hagiographers in some disturbing ways that elide their bodily suffering) is a significant and (to feminists) troubling feature of both Buddhist and Christian hagiographic traditions.[29]

But there is a more interesting dimension to the comparison that emerges when we consider the fact that both Buddhist and Christian hagiographic traditions lionize women who gouge out their own eyes to repulse the gaze of their assailants. Subhā resembles those sainted Christian women like Saint Brigid of Kildare and Saint Lucy of Syracuse who, their hagiographers tell us, avoided unwanted marriages and preserved their virginity by sacrificing their own organs of sight. As we explore the ways that hagiographic literature represents the actions of sainted Buddhist and Christian women, the eye that is so dramatically gouged out serves as an icon of a distinctly female way of seeing. What better image to represent the blinders that restrain the female gaze (subject, as it is, to the derivative forms of subjectivity that exist for it in the empire of the male gaze) than the eyes that these women removed so that they might see (and be seen) as good Buddhist and Christian women?[30]

CHAPTER ONE

Celibacy and the Social World

What makes a man to wander,
What makes a man to roam,
What makes a man to wander,
And turn his back on home?

Lines from a song by Max Steiner
in the film *The Searchers*

Shock Therapy

It can be a momentous and shocking experience when one sees the world through the eyes of a renouncer for the first time. Especially when one has formally renounced the social world in joining a monastic order but has lost or not yet achieved a sense of commitment to monastic life. Indian Buddhist hagiography is full of climatic scenes of transformation in which worldly, dissatisfied renouncers—especially lovesick monks and vain nuns—become serious, committed renouncers when they suddenly perceive the truth of the Dharma or cosmic order displayed in the world. Such breakthroughs are described as searing, mind-jolting experiences. They are denoted in Pāli and Sanskrit by the term *saṃvega* and other derivatives of the Sanskrit root $\sqrt{vij}$, meaning "to tremble or shudder with excitement or fear." Because they involve seeing with deep emotion, the Indian art historian Ānanda Coomaraswami refers to *saṃvega* experiences as instances of "aesthetic shock." These experiences certainly are, as Coomaraswami's terminology suggests, primarily associated with seeing rather than with hearing. But the agitation of *saṃvega* occurs primarily when the Dharma one has *heard* becomes the Dharma one *sees*. *Saṃvega* thus might be rendered as "the agitation of recognition," or, in more popular parlance, an "aha experience."

Sometimes it is the sight of beautiful things, like the body of a Buddha or a place of pilgrimage, that causes the shock of recognition.[1] But usually, the state of *samvega* is brought on by the sight of things that incite pity, things that convey the ideas of impermanence and suffering. Because the cremation ground is a repository of corpses and thus a mute testimony to the impermanence of all human life, it is the site of many *saṃvega* experiences described in post-Aśokan hagiographies. Members of the *sangha* spent time in the charnel fields of cremation grounds practicing a meditation technique called the meditation (*bhāvanā*) on foulness (Sanskrit, *aśubha;* Pāli, *asubha*) in which the meditator contemplates corpses in various stages of decay.[2] This form of meditation is praised by the Buddha of the Pāli canon and discussed at length in doctrinal compendia such as Buddhaghosa's *Visuddhimagga.* According to Buddhaghosa—the fifth-century commentator who is often considered the premier spokesman of monastic Buddhism—the meditator should go to a cremation ground and select a corpse in one of ten stages of decay, from a corpse bloated with putrescence (*uddhumāta*) to a skeleton (*aṭṭhika*).[3] Each of the ten stages has a characteristic foulness that serves as an antidote to the one of ten types of attraction to physical form.[4] For example, the bloated corpse suits those who are particular about the shapes of bodies; discolored corpses are recommended for those who are attentive to the complexion of the skin.

Cultivating a sense of foulness is especially recommended for those of a passionate disposition.[5] But Buddhaghosa warns would-be meditators not to go rushing off to view just any corpse they should happen to hear about. They should first ascertain the sex of the corpse, as it could be a hindrance to their chastity to contemplate the body of someone of the opposite sex, especially one that is newly dead.[6] Because such a body could cause untoward thoughts (literally, "writhing," *vipphandana*), Buddhaghosa states that monks should avoid using female bodies as objects of meditation, as nuns should avoid using male bodies.[7]

But if the hagiographic tradition of the post-Aśokan period is any indication of actual practice, it appears that many monks did not heed Buddhaghosa's warning. Stories in which prominent monks contemplate dead women with salutary results at watershed moments in their monastic careers appear quite frequently, even in commentaries that are attributed to Buddhaghosa himself. And what's more, a number of these stories show the Buddha lending his authority to this practice by commandeering dead women's bodies and orchestrating experiences of aesthetic shock around them.

Why would the redactors of these post-Aśokan hagiographies give pride of place to a practice that holds such risks for the meditator? This deviation from the council of prudence calls for a reflection on the vagaries of desire and the value of temptation in overcoming desire.[8] The structure of many of these stories suggests an analogy with aversion therapy.[9] Just as aversion therapists initially encourage inappropriate desires only to eradicate them by introducing painful, noxious stimuli, so these monks' encounters with bodies of the opposite sex are experiences that arouse the desire of the monk only to subvert it in the end. In one, a lovesick monk goes to see the object of his affection only to find that she has been dead for three days and her body is bloated with putrescence. In another, the Buddha evokes an aha experience in a lust-ridden monk by conjuring up an apparition of a lovely young woman that stirs the monk's desire; the Buddha then uses his psychic powers to transform the spectral woman into a worm-infested corpse.

Hagiographies that climax in horrific figurations of the feminine are extremely graphic; they assault the senses like an open wound. The reader or listener cannot help but recoil from the stark images of decaying beauty these stories present. Through this visceral experience of revulsion, one can achieve an existential awareness of the first Noble Truth (Pāli, *ariya-sacca;* Sanskrit, *arya-satya*) of Buddhism: the dis-ease or dissatisfaction that dogs even the most pleasurable sensations. By acting on the body as a site of knowing, these stories persuade the reader or listener that there is no gainsaying the cardinal truths of Buddhism. The effect of such stories on the sensitive reader or listener may approximate the transformative power of contemplating decaying corpses in the cremation ground. What Buddhaghosa says of the charnel ground meditator may well be said of those who listen to tales of men transformed by encounters with bodily corruption: "Because he sees so many corpses, his mind is no longer subject to the power of lust."[10]

Horrific Figurations of the Feminine

As objects of sexual desire, women are often seen as obstacles in the celibate path of the monk, sensual stumbling blocks to be avoided at all costs. The Buddha of the Pāli canon frequently advocates avoiding women altogether. For example, when the Buddha's personal attendant Ānanda asked, shortly before the Master's death, about how one should behave toward women, the Buddha reportedly answered: "You should avoid their sight, Ānanda." "But what if we do see them, Blessed One? What are we to do then?" The Master replied: "Do not speak to them, Ānanda." "But what if we do speak to them, Blessed One?" "Then you must watch yourself, Ānanda."[11]

Although avoiding the opposite sex is recommended, the monastic community must rely on the lay community for its material support, and such dependence requires that monks and nuns live in close proximity to lay households. For monks who regularly gather alms from door to door and accept invitations to eat in lay households, avoiding women altogether is out of the question. Thus avoidance is impractical as a strategy for subduing desire. But avoiding women may also be as ineffective as it is impractical. Avoidance certainly reduces the opportunities for a monk to act on sexual urges, but it does not necessarily protect his mind from lustful thoughts. The stories of aesthetic shock analyzed here suggest that in order to vanquish sexual desire, the enemy must be encountered, engaged, and exposed as a cause of suffering. In this pursuit, encounters with beautiful women are extremely useful to the renouncer, offering him a field in which to engage and overcome his desire. Like the young women who shared Gandhi's bed during his controversial "experiments in celibacy," tempting female bodies may be drafted into the service of male celibacy.[12]

Because all bodies harbor the signs of foulness within, anyone's body can be used as an object lesson on foulness. But one finds few post-Aśokan accounts of women experiencing aesthetic shock while viewing male bodies.[13] There is, to my knowledge, only one post-Aśokan tale of a male body causing an aha experience in a woman, and it involves the disciple Ānanda—a man who is depicted as closer to women than any other man in the early *sangha,* a man whose identification with women is so complete that he calls himself a "womanly" (*mātṛgrāma*) man.[14] The relative absence of male objects of contemplation is as conspicuous as the presence of the male gaze in this literature. From the number of narratives in which alluring female bodies serve as sources of insight for sexually frustrated monks, it is clear that these post-Aśokan narratives have the suppression of male sexual desire as one of their primary goals.

It is crucial to recognize, however, that lust is not simply a carnal weakness, but a sign of spiritual impoverishment, social engagement, mental delusion, and moral turpitude. To invoke a psychoanalytic trope, sexual desire is overdetermined, caused by a variety of conditions that are not conducive to liberation. Thus before exploring literary strategies for suppressing sexual desire, it is necessary to understand why lust impedes the disciplined life of the *sangha.* The following sections situate the place of the Buddhist renouncer within the Indian milieu and indicate some of the distinctively Buddhist values associated with celibacy.

Celibacy in the Life of the *Sangha*

Celibacy (Pāli, *brahmacariya;* Sanskrit, *brahmacarya*) is essential to the homeless life of poverty and freedom from social obligations praised by the Buddha and his early followers. Defined as one who goes forth from home to homelessness (*agārasma anagāriyan pabbajati*), the early Buddhist renouncer (Pāli, *pabbajita:* "one who has gone forth") was the antithesis of the householder tied down by family and possessions. Like the largely celibate cowboy heroes of American Westerns who delight in making their home on the range, early Buddhist renouncers are represented as free agents enjoying a blessed release from domestic entanglements.[15] Similes that contrast the free wandering life of the holy vagabond with the householder's lack of autonomy are found repeatedly in the *Sutta Nipāta,* a collection of verses that contains some of the earliest poetry composed by Buddhists in India. For example, the "Discourse on the Rhinoceros Horn" (*Khaggavisāṇa Sutta*) in the *Sutta Nipāta* is a poem in praise of the celibate life that warns of the filial and social obligations that entrap the householder. The state of being single that celibate renouncers enjoy is compared to the strong, durable horn of a rhinoceros and the freedom of a deer wandering in the forest:

> Affection for children and wives is like an entangled, overgrown bamboo grove; being unentangled like the new bamboo tip, wander single as a rhinoceros horn. Untrapped like a deer in the forest who grazes here and there at will, the wise man is intent on autonomy [*seritaṃ,* cognate with "self-will"]: wander single as a rhinoceros horn.[16]

From the perspective of these mendicants who renounce their land, property, and familial life, the wealthy householder with many sons to carry on the family lineage is caught in a web of social obligations that permit him no freedom; he is like a deer caught in a trap. The impoverished but autonomous renouncer stands in stark contrast to those whose lives are devoted to the acquisition and maintenance of wealth, power, and heirs. With no obligations save those taken on out of compassion and no constraints on movement, the renouncer wanders through the world like a dancer moving gracefully through space (while the rest of us plod along gravity-bound and preoccupied with our obligations to others).

Monks ordained by the Buddha in the sixth century B.C.E. led a seminomadic existence in which nomadism was equated with a salutary escape from the suffocating closeness of the social world, with its endless web of family and friendship obligations. Wandering the countryside for at least eight months of the year (the monsoon season being a time of retreat in which renouncers avoided the muddy, impassable roads out of compassion for the worms and other creatures likely to be trampled underfoot), the renouncer was said to enjoy freedoms that those bound by the duties of childbearing and breadwinning can hardly imagine: the leisure to spend days in meditation and study, the ability to travel at will in search of wholesome environments and accomplished teachers, and the freedom of propertylessness, of having nothing to take care of (beyond the minimal care of the body that is necessary for the pursuit of the deathless state of nirvana such as daily begging rounds in search of food). Householders can never know such freedom.

The homeless life was quintessentially a wifeless life, for the early monks of the primitive monastic community. And so it is today, among most of the Buddhist communities of South and Southeast Asia (see fig. 1).[17] Although monasteries were eventually established and Buddhist renouncers settled into cenobitic communities, the ideal of the nonmarried renouncer remains at the core of monastic life in South Asia. Higher ordination (*upasampadā*) in the Buddhist *sangha* dissolves familial and matrimonial ties.[18] If one is married at the time of ordination, that bond is dissolved; spouses are thereafter referred to as "former" spouses. If one is not married at the time of full ordination, one renounces the possibility of marriage.[19]

Early Records of the Celibate Life

The circumstances that led the Buddha to promulgate and modify rules concerning celibacy are given in the first portion of the *Suttavibhaṇgha*

Figure 1. This contemporary image from an illustrated edition of the *Dhammapada* printed in Taiwan shows a monk cutting himself off from the matrimonial and filial ties that bind a householder to continued experience of *saṃsāra.* He sits under an auspiciously decorated hand, which represents the teaching of the Buddha.

section of the monastic code (*Vinayapiṭaka*).[20] The first episode described in the *Suttavibhaṅgha,* where a monk named Sudinna impregnates his former wife, shows that forsaking the bond of marriage was not always an easy task. Sudinna's family was dead set against his practice of *brahmacariya* and they conspired to lure him off his celibate path long enough to produce a male heir. Sudinna's story raises a number of themes that are essential for understanding the role of celibacy in

Buddhist monastic life. In fidelity to the storytelling traditions that communicate the fundamental values of the Buddhist path in narrative form, I will now narrate the story of Sudinna, noting the issues it raises for the study of celibacy in Indian Buddhism.

> Sudinna, the son of a wealthy merchant, hears the Buddha teaching and thinks: "So far as I understand the teaching taught by the Lord, it is no easy matter for a householder to practice *brahmacariya*, complete and undefiled and polished like a conch shell. I'd like to cut off my hair and beard, put on the yellow robes, and wander forth from home into homelessness [*agārasma anagāriyaṃ pabbajituṃ*]. May the Lord let me wander forth."[21]

When Sudinna asks for ordination, the Teacher directs him to obtain the consent of his parents. They, however, are reluctant to give their consent since Sudinna and his wife have not yet produced an heir. A battle of wills then ensues, a battle that plays on the idea of renunciation as a kind of death—a death to the social world that leaves grieving relatives in its wake. Sudinna's parents tell him that they would be desolate at his death and simply cannot abide the thought of his going forth into the homeless life. "I will die here, or go forth," replies Sudinna, who lies down on the ground and begins a hunger strike.[22] After abstaining from seven meals, Sudinna appears to be quite serious. His friends inform Sudinna's parents that they will be able to see him again if he goes forth, but if they continue to withhold their consent, he will die. Given no other option, they agree to Sudinna's going forth into the homeless life, and Sudinna goes off to the jungle after receiving ordination.

Not long afterward, there is a famine in the village on which Sudinna depends for his alms. He returns to his hometown and begins to beg alms at his parents' home, offering them the opportunity to gain merit and relieving less wealthy families of the burden of maintaining him during a food shortage. Sudinna's father seizes this golden opportunity to win his son back to the householder's life. He shows him the stacks of gold that are his inheritance and explains to him that if he returns to the life of a layman, he can enjoy pleasure and earn merit at the same time.[23] But the monk replies that he is delighted with the celibate life and advises his father to sink all his gold in the Ganges River, where it will do the least harm.[24]

At this juncture, Sudinna's former wife asks the monk what celestial nymphs he intends to win through his practice of celibacy.[25] Sudinna tells her: "I do not practice *brahmacariya* for the sake of celestial nymphs, sister."[26] When she hears her former husband call her "sister" (*bhagini*), a form of address appropriate for a person with whom one has no sexual relationship, Sudinna's former wife realizes the gravity of the situation, faints, and falls to the floor.[27]

After the failure of his father and former wife, Sudinna's mother renews the effort at persuasion. She begs him to produce a son so that the family's property will not go to another clan for lack of an heir. Rather surprisingly, Sudinna agrees to impregnate his former wife (the commentary explains that the monk believes his family will leave him alone once he has produced an heir).[28] She is brought to him in the forest during her fertile period, wearing the ornaments that were his favorites when they were together as man and wife. After having sex on three occasions, she conceives and gives birth to a son who is called Bījaka, or "seed" (a fitting name for a boy brought into the world to carry on the ancestral line).

Meanwhile, Sudinna becomes filled with remorse over his actions. The melancholy state of his mind proclaims itself in the jaundiced, haggard appearance of his body, which provokes comments from his fellow monks and leads to Sudinna's confessing his actions before the Buddha. The Teacher declares intercourse an offense entailing "defeat" (*pārājikā dhammā*)[29] and rebukes Sudinna in no uncertain terms:

> It would have been better, confused man, had you put your male organ inside the mouth of a terrible and poisonous snake than inside the vagina of a woman. It would have been better, confused man, had you put your male organ inside the mouth of a black snake than inside the vagina of a woman. It would have been better, confused man, had you put your male organ inside a blazing hot charcoal pit than inside the vagina of a woman.[30]

Several themes emerge from this story. First, it dramatizes the tension that existed, in the early days of the monastic community, between the goals of that community and those of the society from which it drew its numbers. Most of the sixty men who joined the *sangha* during the first months of its existence were married men who left wives and families behind. The *Vinayapiṭaka* records the disapproval of some of the distinguished families of Magadha who lost their sons to the *sangha:* "That monk Gotama is on a path which takes away people's children.

That monk Gotama is on a path which makes widows. That monk Gotama is on a path which destroys families."[31] Initially, men were ordained by the Buddha without obtaining familial consent. Parental consent was later required at the request of the Buddha's father, who objected to the ordination of his youthful grandson, Rāhula, without the approval of himself or Rāhula's mother. With the establishment of the order of nuns (*bhikkhunī sangha*), women were allowed to join the order provided they first obtained the consent of their husband and their parents—a reflection of the more limited autonomy accorded to women in Indian culture during this period.[32] But even when admission into the *sangha* was restricted to those who had obtained some form of consent, the case of Sudinna suggests that consent was not always freely given. Those who joined the *sangha* clearly left grieving loved ones in their wake.

In joining the *sangha,* Sudinna has abandoned his ties to the world and is no longer compelled to carry out familial obligations. But the young monk still feels obligated to perform matrimonial duties so that the family patrimony may be passed down to the next generation. Brahminical culture invests the uninterrupted succession of sons with a profound religious significance beyond the mere perpetuation of the family line: having a son to perform the proper rituals assures the father of a place in the world of the ancestors (*pitṛ loka*) at death.[33] The fate of the father in the next world (as well as that of *his* ancestors) depends on the ritual activity of the son, who is the double of the father in this world.[34] Sudinna was faced with the difficult choice of committing an offense against his ancestors or committing an offense entailing his own defeat (*pārājika*) as a monk.[35]

Sex and the Social World

Sudinna's story demonstrates that the social dimensions of sexuality are not to be underestimated. Filial piety, not raging lust, led this monk down the primrose path to defeat. As Peter Brown has noted, modern notions of sexuality as a brute physical instinct can obscure what is at stake in the repudiation of sexual activity in the ancient world. In discussing the celibacy of ascetic early Christian men living in the Egyptian desert, Brown warns:

> There is no doubt that our own experiences of sexuality and that of the early hermits overlapped at some points: "The devil changed him-

> self into an Ethiopian maiden whom I had once seen in my youth in the summertime picking reeds, and came and sat on my knee." But if we go on to ask what was the precise meaning of sexuality in the overall life of such men, then we get an answer that is both less modern and more serious. The woman stood for all that was most stable and enveloping in the life of men. When a man dreams of his wife, Artemidorus wrote, he is usually thinking of his job: "The woman stands either for the profession of the dreamer or for his business obligations."[36]

Because sexual desire is not only a biological instinct but also an eminently social instinct, the mastery of sexual desire is of paramount importance to the Buddhist renouncer.[37] Celibacy looms large among the strategies for social disengagement because it safeguards the renouncer from matrimony, reproduction, and the transmission of patrimony—in a word, from the ties that bind one to the perpetuation of life in the social world. Christian encomiums to virginity also emphasize the repudiation of social bonds and the liberation thereby experienced. The Desert Fathers tradition, for example, links fornication with reproduction, labor, and drudgery in recounting the following episode in the life of a celibate desert hermit:

> Abba Olympios of the Cells was tempted to fornication. His thoughts said to him, "Go, and take a wife." He got up, found some mud, made a woman and said to himself, "There is your wife, now you must work hard in order to feed her." So he worked giving himself a great deal of trouble. The next day, making some mud again, he formed it into a girl and said to his thoughts, "Your wife has had a child, you must work harder so as to be able to feed her and clothe your child." So he wore himself out doing this, and said to his thoughts, "I cannot bear this weariness any longer." They answered, "If you cannot bear such weariness, stop wanting a wife." God, seeing his efforts, took away the conflict from him and he was at peace.[38]

The Church Father Tertullian predicted that "on the day of our great exodus, children will be a great handicap to those that bear them. . . . At the sound of the angel's trumpet, the widows will leap forth lightly, easily able to endure any distress or persecution with none of the heavy baggage of marriage in the womb or at their breasts."[39]

As a society of renouncers, the *sangha* offers its members an autonomous identity gained through the repudiation of social ties, especially kinship and conjugal relations. Whether leading a peripatetic existence as the first monks ordained by the Buddha were said to have done or living a less nomadic existence in the cenobitic communities that eventually developed in South Asia, Buddhist renouncers enjoy liberties that those bound by the duties of childbearing and breadwinning can hardly imagine. The work of Louis Dumont, who has characterized the essence of post-Vedic Indian religions as a dialogue between the renouncer and the man in the world, underscores what is at stake for the Buddhist renouncer in remaining chaste.[40] The typical Indian renouncer is an autonomous being, a free agent who discovers himself as an individual by stepping outside the structures of the social world, such as those imposed by familial and caste duties. In contrast to the renouncer, Dumont's "man-in-the-world" lacks individuality as it is understood in the West. Like the Brahminical householder whose wife and progeny are extensions of himself just as he is the extension of other, more encompassing selves, the identity of the man-in-the-world is a composite structure of encompassed and encompassing relations. To invoke the language of the *Puruṣa Sūkta*—an early Indic account of creation out of the body of a primordial man Puruṣa—where the renouncer as an integral autonomous being may identify with the entire cosmic body of the primordial man, the man-in-the-world can only identify with a limb of the cosmic giant, an encompassed position within the body politic.[41] Steven Collins has argued that Dumont's description of the Indian renouncer as an individual outside the social world illuminates certain strands of Buddhist and Christian monasticism more readily than classical Hinduism, where renunciation either has a specific location within the social world or entails continued ritual activity, the result of which is the perpetuation of the social world.[42] Although it is probably pointless to try to ascertain whether Buddhist renouncers approach Dumont's ideal type more perfectly that do their Hindu counterparts, Collins's assertion highlights one of the questions that will occupy our attention below: is it possible to pursue otherworldly goals from within a specific social location?[43]

Members of the *sangha* are free to go back to the social world at any time, although in the Pāli canon this decision is described as a regression, a "turning back to the lesser" (*hīnāyavattati*). Buddhist monastic literature maintains, like Saint Paul, that "it is better to marry than to burn."[44] The practice of *brahmacarya* is deemed superior to noncelibate lifestyles, but concessions to human weakness must be made. Texts advise the smitten or lovesick renouncer who cannot continue to practice *brahmacarya* happily to renounce the practice formally. What cannot be done, what leads to expulsion from the *sangha,* is precisely what Sudinna did: to resume sexual relations without first renouncing one's vocation as a renouncer.

Scholars have traditionally characterized the Buddhism of the Pāli canon as more otherworldly and monastic in orientation than that of the Mahāyāna *Sūtra*s, which are seen as catering to a more popular, worldly audience. With the development of the Mahāyāna ideal of the *Bodhisattva,* conventional wisdom has it, householding came to be regarded as an acceptable alternative if not a superior way of life to the path of those who strive to become Arhats through monastic training, now deemed an inferior way (*hīnayāna,* or "Lesser Vehicle") to that of the *Bodhisattvas.*[45] However, this view has come under much criticism in recent years. It is becoming increasingly clear that the *Bodhisattva* path described in the Mahāyāna *Sūtra*s is a monastic path, and that the Mahāyāna tradition must be seen as a movement originated largely by and for monks, and not a lay movement as previously thought.[46] But the question operative in Buddhist texts from a wide range of traditions is not the intrinsic superiority or inferiority of either way of life—since that is a given in a hierarchical system—but rather the possibility of practicing both at once. It is the issue raised by the debate over whether Hindu renouncers are "real" world-renouncers or not: is it possible to renounce the world from within a specific social location? A surprising number of Buddhist texts originating in different parts of the Indian Buddhist world under the auspices of different schools answer this question with a resounding "no," and in that negation one can perhaps discern an affirmation of Buddhism's distinctiveness via-à-vis competing ideologies.[47]

Householder's Hell

For example, the *Mahāvastu,* a biography of the Buddha produced by the early Mahāyānist Mahāsaṇghikā school, has the *bodhisattva* utter this pointed condemnation of the householder's life: "Now this householder life is constricting [*saṃbādho*]. One must go forth to an open space; it is not possible for one to practice the utterly disciplined, utterly irreproachable, pure, clean *brahmacarya* while staying in a house. I will go forth from home to homelessness."[48] The *Mahāvastu* paints an anxious picture of the home as a claustrophobia-producing space. The constriction under which the would-be renouncer chafes at home is indicated by the use of the term *saṃbādha* in the passage above; *saṃbādha* denotes an oppressively close place such as the vagina or womb. Thus the plight of a would-be renouncer at home is akin to the constriction of the fetus in the womb, a space that is conventionally described in Buddhist as well as Hindu texts as extremely tight and disgustingly impure. The comforts of hearth and home cause the renouncer great discomfort. The safety and privileges of the home can make one a prisoner, for the life of domesticity impedes movement, imposes myriad obligations, and makes *brahmacarya* difficult. In the *Mahāvastu,* as in the Pāli canon, disengagement from the social world through the semi-nomadic life of a celibate renouncer is described in expansive terms suggestive both of physical freedom and moral autonomy.[49] If the life of the renouncer is, as Steven Collins has suggested, lived in the somewhat utopian space of a society of renouncers, the life of a householder is lived in the dystopian space of the home, a space that is as cramped and oppressive as the womb.[50]

While indicting the life of the householder, the *Mahāvastu* nevertheless devotes a great deal of attention to the domestic situation of the *bodhisattva* and gives pride of place to stories about the *bodhisattva*'s wife Yaśodharā. We learn from this text what early Pāli texts ignore (even if they are, as I indicate below, informed by many of the same oral traditions that served as sources for the Sanskrit biographies): the *bodhisattva*'s youth, education, royal training, courtship, and marriage. We see the *bodhisattva* and Yaśodharā as husband and wife in many previous lives. However, in each life the *bodhisattva* leaves Yaśodharā behind, as this is what *bodhisattva*s must do and what Gotama has done so many times before.[51] The *Mahāvastu* lavishes a great deal of attention on Gotama's family, but not necessarily in order to elevate the institution of marriage or to paint a glowing picture of family life. The virtues of Gotama's family are enumerated to show how much the *bodhisattva* gave up in going forth from home to homelessness, thus inspiring other heroic acts of renunciation:

> And monks, it was not when he was worn down with debility [*parijuññena parijūrṇo*] that the *bodhisattva* went forth from home into the homeless state, but when he was in the peak and perfection of

> youth. Again monks, it was not when he was worn down by debilitating disease that the *bodhisattva* went forth from home into the homeless state, but when he was in the peak and perfection of health. Again monks, it was not when he was worn down by loss of wealth that the *bodhisattva* went forth from home into the homeless state, but he left behind him a vast array of riches. Again monks, it was not when he was worn down by the loss of relatives that the *bodhisattva* went forth from home into the homeless state, but he left behind him a vast group of relatives.[52]

The Buddha as a Family Man

The *Mahāvastu* is not anomalous in giving pride of place to the very worldly structures that the *bodhisattva* must renounce. Post-Aśokan literature, in both Sanskrit and Pāli, is replete with stories about the Sakya clan, the extended family the renouncer left behind on the evening of the Great Departure. We learn, for example, of how Yaśodharā and other members of Gotama's family assume semimonastic lifstyles after Gotama left the palace in search of wisdom. This concern that the family should "pray together" even if they no longer stay together raises an interesting question: to what extent do the Buddhas reconstitute conjugal and filial bonds under the banner of renunciation? For the literatures evolving during this period, the Great Departure that signals the *bodhisattva*'s break with the social world is often complemented by a Great Return in which the awakened Buddha returns to his native town and teaches the Dharma to the family he left behind. As John Strong has demonstrated, the awakened Buddha is often seen to exercise a charismatic allure that is irresistible to his family of birth.[53] They join him as converts en masse. Such stories reconstitute the family that was sundered at the Great Departure. The paradox of the renouncer turned family man need not detain us so long as it is recognized that the utopian family of the *sangha* is the redemptive model for such worldly families as that headed by the Buddha. Familial relationships need not be completely severed by the renouncer as long as such relationships are reconfigured to resemble the utopian family of the *sangha.*

Evidence from every category of Indian Buddhist literature may be found to support the view that the *sangha* is held together by a variety of pseudofamilial ties. Kinship structures are reduplicated within the *sangha* in a variety of ways. In the *Gotamī Apadāna* of the *Khuddaka*

Nikāya, a highly composite *Nikāya* in which very old materials and materials of a distinctly post-Aśokan flavor are combined, the Buddha is represented as a mother who gives her monastic children the milk of liberative teachings. Medieval Sinhalese commentators were very enamored of this image of the Buddha as mother, as Richard Gombrich's translation of a commentary on a Sinhalese biography of the Buddha indicates:

> "The Buddha is like a mother." Our holy king Buddha, teacher of the three worlds, who is so described, is like a mother to the inhabitants of the three worlds. Should it be asked how the Buddha is similar to a mother: Any mother who is giving milk to her children, fearing lest bad disease and affliction befall them, does not consume noxious, unwholesome food, but takes food and drink fitted to making her milk wholesome. In the same way our holy Buddha does not do the ten bad deeds (such as killing) which are like taking unwholesome food. . . . Further, a mother, when any disease or affliction has befallen her babies, who cannot drink medicine, herself consumes the medicine which is hard to consume because of its unpleasant harsh, bitter flavor, and makes her babies drink the milk which arises with the efficacy of that medicine's essence. . . . In order to make the children, namely the people capable of being trained, who were afflicted with the disease of moral defilement, drink the draught of ambrosial milk [of the Dharma, the Buddha] seized and carried them with the arm of compassion, held them on the hip of kindness, looked at them with the eye of his knowledge of inner potential, took them by the mouth of their individual characters, proffered the breast of his sweet voice endowed with eight qualities, opened the lips of their ears, gave them inside the mouth of mental process the milk of immortal doctrine, and putting on the tongue of wisdom the sweet flavour of the five joys, . . . healed all the diseases of moral defilement and brought them to the painless diseaseless state of nirvana.[54]

Although this commentary suggests that it is the beings of the triple world that are the children of the Buddha, a look at the aforementioned *Gotamī Apadāna* makes it clear that it is the men and women of the *sangha* who are truly the Buddha's children, for they alone suck the milk of the teaching directly from its source. The *Gotamī Apadāna* is a dialogue between the Buddha and Gotamī Mahāpajāpatī, the foster mother who raised him when the *bodhisattva*'s own mother died seven days after his birth. In her old age, Gotamī Mahāpajāpatī became a nun in her son's monastic order. In these words to the Buddha, spoken at the end of her life, Gotamī Mahāpajāpatī contrasts the Buddha's present role as her spiritual mother with her own former role as the *bodhisattva*'s wet-nurse and nurturer:

> I nurtured your physical body [*rūpakāyo*], well-gone one, but this flawless Dharma-body [*dhammatanu*] of mine was nurtured by you.
>
> I suckled you with milk
> which momentarily quenches thirst.
> From you I drank the milk of the Dharma [*dhammakhiraṃ*],
> continually at peace.[55]

Where Gotamī Mahāpajāpatī gives her foster son a mortal human body, he gives her something more lasting—the eternal body of the Dharma. This eternal body of the Dharma is precious indeed: it is not only the body of teachings that issue from the lips (or rather, breasts) of the Buddhas but also the most subtle and rarified form in which Buddhas exist.[56] Those who imbibe this body of truth can themselves become Buddhas, and thus it is a very transcendental gift that Gotama offers his mother. Where her milk quenches thirst only temporarily, leaving the child hungry within a few hours, the Buddha's milk quenches thirst and hunger forever. The Dharma is an elixir of immortality, a substance of the highest nutritive essence, in contrast to mothers' milk, which leads to renewed hunger and therefore reinforces the link between desire and the rest of the factors of dependent arising (Pāli, *paṭicca-samuppāda;* Sanskrit, *pratītya-samutpāda*) that keep one bound to *saṃsāra*.[57] In this text, it seems, the Buddha's spiritual role as mother of the *sangha* is made clear in contrast to and devaluation of worldly motherhood and worldly nourishment.[58] Since the nurturing that takes place in families cannot terminate suffering altogether, one should seek the milk of the Dharma that one imbibes at the breast of the Buddhas in the bosom of the *sangha*—a milk that quenches the thirst for continued becoming once and for all. The comparison with *saṃsār*ic family life is only there as a foil for the contrast.

Likewise with fatherhood, only here the devaluation is more subtle and fraught with paradox. In the first four *Nikāya*s, the emphasis is on the Buddha as father: the Dharma is seen as patrimony, the monk as son (*buddha-putta*), and the *sangha* as lineage (*buddha-gotta*). The spiritual patrimony of the Dharma is contrasted with the householder's wives, children, slaves, and material wealth, all of which constitutes the patrimony that the householder bestows on his son. This worldly patrimony imprisons the recipient in a seamless web of social obligations. In the language of contemporary Western psychology, the worldly patrimony robs the individual of an internal locus of control where the spiritual one restores it.

Father Knows Best

While Gotama Siddhartha walked the earth, he behaved toward his biological sons in the manner of a true Brahminical patriarch, disposing of his progeny as he saw fit. Like the *bodhisattva* of the *Vessantara Jātaka* who gives away his entire family along with his material wealth in an act of sacrificial liberality, the prince who leaves the palace on the eve of the Great Departure disposes of his patrimony by renouncing it.[59] In reconstituting his family at the Great Return, the Buddha does not resume the role of householder. But he does exercise the patriarchal privilege of the lord of the house in constituting a *dharm*ic family under his care as an otherworldly father. When his son Rāhula went to the awakened Buddha to ask for his inheritance, the Buddha suggests that this worldly inheritance will bring him only suffering.[60] He might well have thrown Rāhula's gold into the river where it would do the least harm, as Sudinna suggested his father do with the legacy his father offered him. But instead the Buddha proposes that Rāhula receive a different sort of legacy from him. The paternalistic father of Rāhula knows best; he insists that his son partake of the only patrimony that a loving father would offer his son—the Dharma. The householder's wealth of wives, sons, and possessions is deemed an albatross around Rāhula's neck, just as Rāhula, whose name connotes "bondage," was a fetter to the would-be renouncer who fathered him. It is because the Buddha is endowed with the authority of a Brahminical patriarch to dispose of the wives, sons, and wealth that are his extended self in any way he sees fit that the Buddha refuses to give his son Rāhula the patrimony he requests.

If the Buddha is something of a family man, he is also something of a home wrecker, as the negative reaction of the Sakya clan in the aftermath of Rāhula's ordination suggests. The charisma that the Buddha achieves by leaving the world makes the Buddha an irresistible fisher of men, a snatcher of husbands and fathers from their social locations, a man who leaves widows and orphans in his wake. In his zest for bestowing the otherworldly patrimony on his half brother Nanda, the Buddha takes on a somewhat demonic guise, as I will demonstrate in chapter 4. First the Buddha shanghais Nanda to a monastery *(vihāra)* on the morning Nanda was to be doubly initiated into the social world by being consecrated as king and marrying the beautiful princess Janapāda Kalyānī. Then the Buddha uses Nanda's lack of assertiveness to cause him to be ordained. Soon, however, the reluctant monk is ready to renounce the practice of *brahmacariya* and return to the world to marry Janapāda Kalyāṇī, visions of whose tearful face he cannot banish from his mind. At the conclusion of this story and in other episodes like it, the Buddha saves the wayward monk from his own desires by mimicking Wicked Māra (Māra Pāpimā), the god of death who fishes for men in crafty ways that appeal to their basest instincts in order to captivate their higher instincts. Where Māra seduces people with tempting forms as a hunter lures the unsuspecting prey into his clutches, so the Buddha likewise preys on the weakness of Nanda's flesh in order to captivate the wayward monk's mind. Just as Māra's lure of choice is the female form, so the Buddha often baits his traps with the bodies of alluring young women—in the case of Nanda, the bodies of 500 celestial nymphs (*apsarāses*). But who is this Wicked Māra whom the Buddha stoops to imitate and thereby conquer? A brief profile of Māra as the enemy of liberation will shed light on the philosophical and mythological dimensions of celibacy in the life of the *sangha* and on the methods used in monastic circles to fight Māra and promote *brahmacariya.*

Māra and His Minions versus the Sons and Daughters of the Buddha

It is impossible to understand the value of celibacy in monastic Buddhism without situating sexual desire within the larger doctrinal framework that holds desire or craving (*tṛṣṇā,* literally, "thirst") for pleasures of the senses responsible for continual rebirth and endless suffering. The four Noble Truths (Pāli, *catuḥ ariya sacca;* Sanskrit, *catuḥ ārya satya*) of Buddhism are: suffering, the origin of suffering, the abolition of suffering which is the state of nirvana, and the path that leads to nirvana. They have often been compared to a medical diagnosis, by which analogy suffering is the condition, craving the cause, the abolition of craving the cure, and the Eightfold Path the treatment plan.[61] This analogy with medicine is supported by recent work on the decisive role of Buddhists in the systematization of classical Indian medical theory and by the many parables and epithets that liken the Buddha to a skilled physician. It is also useful in that it allows us to render the first Noble Truth (Sanskrit, *duḥkha;* Pāli, *dukkha*), for which there is no close English synonym, with the etymologically faithful translation "dis-ease." The dis-ease of life is caused, according to the Buddha of the *Saṃyutta Nikāya,* by "that craving that leads back to rebirth, characterized by infatuation with pleasure, finding delight in this and that: namely, the craving for sensual delight, the craving to be born again, and the craving for existence to end."[62]

In the Buddhist context, sexuality must be seen not as a sin but as a signifier—namely, the sign of an untamed[63] mind that is greedy for sensual gratification because unaware of the ills to which all flesh is heir. Because it is associated with ignorance, sexual desire has its locus in the head or the heart (the word *citta,* identical in Sanskrit and Pāli, denotes both) as much as in the genitals. What Brown suggests of the Desert Fathers tradition, which also emphasizes the renunciation of all social bonds, applies here as well: sexual desire is seen as a base instinct that causes humans to behave like animals, but it is also seen as an indication of one's mental state. Many ascetics in the Desert Fathers tradition knew the value of desire as a "seismograph"[64] of the soul that illuminates the obscurities of the inner self, and therefore they frequently chose not to ask God to relieve them of their lust.[65]

As the Lord of Sensual Desire (Kāma-Adhipati), Māra holds all ignorant, untamed creatures under his sway. Just as the Hindu god of love (Kāma) makes it his mission to incite cupidity, captivating even austere renouncers like Śiva with his flower-tipped arrows, so Māra delights in inciting sexual desire and the dystopian instincts it unleashes in the sons and daughters of the Buddha.[66] Cosmologically speaking, Māra is the Lord of the Realm of Desire (*kāma loka* or *kāma dhātu*), the lowest of the three divisions of the cosmos. All beings who perpetuate their existence within the Realm of Desire are his subjects, including six classes of gods and "the world below with its recluses and brahmins, its princes and peoples."[67]

But Māra is also the god of death, as his name ("Death") indicates. And because all beings in the threefold cosmos are subject to death, they are all Māra's subjects. Thus the entire Triple World (Pāli, *tebhūmaka dhamma;* Sanskrit, *tribhūmika loka*) is under Māra's sway, including the rarified beings who occupy higher cosmic levels within the Realm of Form (*rūpaloka* or *rūpadhātu*) and the Formless Realm (*arūpaloka* or *arūpadhātu*). As the god of death, Māra destroys the life of all creatures in his power. Māra is not only the death that comes at the end of life, however. All of the aggregates (Pāli, *khandhas;* Sanskrit, *skandhas*) or constituent elements that constitute human beings (namely, matter, mind, perceptions, volitions, and consciousness) are themselves under the sway of decay and death. The death that is the continual arising and ceasing of these constituent elements is called the aggregate-Māra (Pāli, *khandha*-Māra; Sanskrit, *skandha*-Māra). Thus Māra's deadly grip is felt even in the transitory nature of our bodies and mental lives. The only beings who escape Māra's deadly grip are Buddhas, who belong to no *gati* (category of being, literally, "going") within any cosmic realm due to the cessation of their desires.

Legend suggests that Māra is loath to let the Buddhas out of his reach. According to the *Buddhacarita,* a highly developed poetic account of the life of the Buddha that will be discussed more fully below, Māra and his minions attempt to dissuade Gotama Siddhartha from his goal on several occasions, both before and after the *bodhisattva*'s awakening to Buddhahood. When the *bodhisattva* had sat down at the foot of the Bodhi-tree and stated his intention to awaken in that place, Māra sent a ferocious army of ghouls led by his three sons, Confusion (*vibhrama*), Excitement (*harṣa*), and Pride (*darpa*), to attack Gotama.[68] This ferocious army is easily rebuffed, and the *bodhisattva* begins the night-long meditations that constitute his awakening as a Buddha. Then, after the newly awakened Buddha immerses himself in a form of meditation lasting several weeks, Māra again goes on the offensive in the hope of preventing the Buddha from teaching others what he has learned. This time, Māra introduces a new strategy: he sends his three daughters, Lust (*rāgā*), Thirst (*tṛṣṇā*), and Discontent (*aratī*), to persuade the Buddha. First, Lust attempts to lure the Buddha back to the householder's life using thirty-two means of seduction (such as longing glances and dishabille), while Thirst and Discontent use verbal means of persuasion, appealing to filial duty and the like. All this time, the Buddha remains self-absorbed, not speaking to them. So the three daughters of Māra next attempt to trick the Buddha by appearing before him as young women renouncers eager to take refuge in him.

Again, he remains as if asleep. They then decide to assume the forms of older women, thinking (according to one version of this tale) that such forms will incite the Buddha's pity.[69] Māra's daughters become decrepit old women stooped over with age. Again, there is no response. But when they attempt to resume their youthful forms, the daughters of Māra find that they cannot do so. Hoisted by their own petards, they go hobbling off to their father pleading for help: "'O father, lord of the realm of Desire, restore us to our own forms.' His daughters were dear, but he was not able to overcome the power of the Buddha. So their father said to them. 'Go to him for refuge [*saraṇaṃ gacchata*].'"[70] Although the Buddha has only frozen Māra's daughters in forms of their own making, his act turns them into display boards for revealing the truth of the Dharma that governs all of *saṃsāra,* including Māra and his minions. Māra has no power to reverse the effects of impermanence now so graphically displayed by Lust, Thirst, and Discontent. Thus the daughters of Māra must take refuge in the Buddha, who is the overlord of Māra by virtue of his insight into the laws governing *saṃsāra.*

No one, to my knowledge, has ever attempted to connect this act of taking refuge in the Buddha on the part of Māra's daughters with the founding of the nuns' order (Pāli, *bhikkhunī sangha;* Sanskrit, *bhikṣunī sangha*). But several facts support making such a connection. First, there is the fact that Māra's words to his daughters echo those of novices taking ordination in the *sangha.* The words that Māra uses when telling his daughters to take refuge in the Buddha are used today in the formula of taking refuge in the Three Jewels of Buddha, Dharma, and *Sangha* spoken by novices at their ordination ceremonies: "I go to the Buddha for refuge."[71] The second piece of evidence in support of my argument is the tendency to cast all human women in the role of Māra's daughters; scriptural passages attributed to the Buddha indicate that human women are essentially minions of Māra. For example, the Buddha of the *Aṇguttara Nikāya* explains that "womankind [*mātugāmā*] is entirely the snare of Māra [*pāso Mārassa*]."[72] Moreover, just as the Buddha stopped Māra's daughters in their tracks by making them confront the loss of beauty and physical decrepitude that comes with age, so too among human women who became nuns during the post-Aśokan period it would appear that reflection on the ravages of old age was a common form of meditation. As will be seen in chapter 5, the inspired utterances of the advanced nuns recorded in the *Therīgāthā* and the

Therī-apadāna are full of allusions to the ways in which old age destroys beauty. This is a lesson that some younger nuns reportedly resisted. These nuns, like Māra's daughters, had to be shown the ravages of old age by the Buddha himself, though his use of magical powers. In the hagiographic narratives included in commentaries on the *Dhammapada* and *Therīgāthā,* there are many stories about how the Buddha chastises vain women by causing beautiful young female phantasms to age and die before their eyes. The insight acquired through viewing gruesome figurations of the female body allowed these women to become leaders of the *bhikkhunī sangha.* Thus the symbolic processes by which vanity is eradicated in the *bhikkhunī sangha* echo the magical processes by which Māra's daughters were brought into submission by the Buddha: both emphasize the decay (*jarā*) of physical form as demonstrated by disgust-inspiring figurations of the feminine.

Who's Afraid of Māra's Daughters?

Scenes of sexual temptation, like that of the Buddha by Māra's daughters, abound in Brahminical and Hindu mythology. Whenever a demon or ambitious human gains too much spiritual power through sacrifice or austerity, the balance of power in the universe is threatened. The gods' favorite method for chastising uppity demons or human sages is to send down *apsarās*es or celestial nymphs (see fig. 2) to disturb their meditation. This divine sex offense almost always succeeds; it is the gods' best defense against those whose celibate practices threaten the balance of power. Few ascetics are able to resist the charms of the *apsarās*es, and in spilling their seed, they squander a precious source of spiritual power.[73]

Now not every leitmotiv of these non-Buddhist stories is to be found in Buddhist scenes of sexual temptation. For example, the loss of semen appears to be of lesser concern to Buddhist renouncers (although not without significance). Semen loss is more likely to be viewed as a symptom of an untamed mind than as a cause of physical enervation. But whatever the differences between Buddhist and Hindu tales of sexual temptation, both clearly feature the renouncer as the besieged party who stands to lose all in losing his self-control.

After his awakening, however, the Buddha is no longer susceptible to the onslaughts of temptresses. He can no longer be tempted, since his craving has ceased entirely. The attempted seduction by Māra's

Figure 2. An *apsarās* or celestial nymph with her maid. Reproduced by permission from Ananda Coomaraswamy, *History of Indian and Indonesian Art* (New York: Dover Publications, 1985; orig. pub. 1927).

daughters is in fact a literary device for highlighting the ironic reality of temptation: to one who is truly awakened, scenes of temptation have a decided propensity for inciting aversion. This connection between liberation and aversion is well established in the *Nikāya*s, as this passage from the *Saṃyutta Nikāya* indicates:

> And what, monks, is the cause of liberation? Passionlessness [*virāga*] is the answer. I say, monks, that passionlessness is causally associated with liberation. And what, monks, is the cause of passionlessness? Aversion [*nibbidā*] is the answer. I say, monks, that aversion is causally associated with passionlessness. And what, monks, is the cause of aversion? The absolute knowledge of things as they really are [*yathābhūtañāṇadassana*] is the answer. Monks, I say that the absolute knowledge of things as they really are is causally associated with aversion.[74]

Perhaps if the daughters of Māra had not brazenly attempted to seek refuge in him, the Buddha would have kept his absolute knowledge of things as they really are to himself. Instead, he imprisons them in forms true to the reality of impermanence: withered old bodies hardly adequate to the task of seduction.

If all women, as the Buddha reportedly said, are Māra's snares, lures by which Māra controls men, then all women play the role of daughters of Māra, using sexual and verbal appeals to dissuade the renouncer from his goal. In hoisting the mythological daughters of Māra by their own petards, the Buddha illustrates an important method of resistance against all womankind as daughters of Māra: the viewing of repulsive transformations of the female body as a defense against the onslaughts of the opposite sex.

Such transformations need not be magically induced. As the backfired seduction attempted by Māra's daughters would suggest, the minions of Māra will often reveal their true nature when left to their own devices. Sooner or later, all of Māra's daughters will decay and die. A renouncer has only to recognize the ravages of impermanence in every alluring body. The next chapter explores South Asian conceptions of the body, showing how tales of dead, dying, and mutilated women provide the spectator with decisive lessons in what Buddhists regard as the true nature of the body.

CHAPTER TWO

"Like a Boil with Nine Openings": Buddhist Constructions of the Body and Their South Asian Milieu

The grave's a fine and private place,
But none, I think, do there embrace.

Andrew Marvell, "To His Coy Mistress"

The Ambiguous Status of Cremation-Ground Meditation

The practice of contemplating corpses in the cremation ground is not for everyone. The Buddha, according to tradition, made the contemplation of foulness (*asubhabhāvanā*) optional for members of the *sangha* after its unsupervised practice led many members of the early community to commit suicide. In the *Saṃyutta Nikāya*'s pithy version of the story, the Buddha taught the monks to contemplate the foulness of corpses in the cremation ground and then went away for a fortnight of solitary meditation. When he returned, he noticed that the *sangha* had considerably diminished in his absence, and so he asked his personal attendant Ānanda what had transpired in his absence. The monks, Ānanda explained, had mastered the meditation on the foul, but with their insight came disastrous consequences:

> As to this body, they fretted about it, felt shame and loathing for it, and wanted to kill themselves. As many as ten monks did so in a single day; even twenty, thirty of them killed themselves in a single day!
>
> Would the Blessed One please teach some other method, so that the order of monks might be established in knowledge?[1]

The Buddha has Ānanda summon the monks and then teaches them another meditation technique, that of mindful breathing (a form of meditation that focuses on the intake and exhalation of breath as examples of the ebb and flow characteristic of all conditioned existence).

In the Pāli *Vinaya,* a more elaborate version of the tale appears as an account of the occasion that led the Buddha to establish the precept against killing. This story suggests that murder—both invited and uninvited by the victims—resulted from the unsupervised practice of contemplating corpses. As in the other account, here the Buddha goes away after teaching the meditation technique, leaving the monks to practice on their own. As they meditated on the foulness of the body, the monks' bodies became loathsome to them, as shameful as a garland of dogs' or snakes' corpses would be to a freshly washed young dandy.[2] The miserable monks then contrived in various ways to die. Some committed suicide; others found a monk named Migalaṇḍika and convinced him to take their lives.

Unfortunately, this Migalaṇḍika became a mass murderer, deluded by the belief that he could help his fellow monks cross to the other shore by slitting their throats. At first, Migalaṇḍika killed only those who asked him to do so in exchange for their bowls and robes (the only units of exchange allowed to members of the *sangha,* for whom possessions are forbidden). The killing would have stopped there because Migalaṇḍika, while he was cleaning his bloody knife in the river, became terribly remorseful about what he had done. But at that moment, a minion of Māra came walking on the water toward him, announcing that bringing other monks across the ocean of *saṃsāra* by slaying them is a meritorious act, a deed to be repeated, not repented.[3] So Migalaṇḍika went from monastery to monastery and from cell to cell, taking the lives of any monks he encountered, up to sixty in one day. Then, as in the *Saṃyutta Nikāya*'s account, the Buddha returns to find his *sangha* decimated, learns the cause from Ānanda, and immediately assembles the monks and teaches them mindfulness in breathing.

Such accounts suggest the ambiguous status of *asubhabhāvanā* in Buddhist history. On the one hand, cremation-ground meditation is a somewhat marginal practice, undertaken by ascetically inclined members of the *sangha* at their option. Spending each night in a cremation ground is one of the austerities known collectively as the *dhutanga* (Sanskrit, *dhutāṅga*).[4] Richard Gombrich, noting that the Buddha of the

Pāli canon frequently dismissed austerities as misguided deviations from the middle path, describes the *dhutanga* as the outer limit "to what the Theravādin tradition will sanction by way of mortifying the flesh."[5] On the other hand, the *dhutanga* are symbolically central to the Buddhist tradition, even if somewhat marginal as practices. Several of the thirteen *dhutanga,* such as wearing cast-off rags sewn together into a robe and begging for alms, are virtual emblems of the *sangha* in Theravāda communities. For example, at the end of Theravāda ordination ceremonies, members of the *sangha* are instructed in the ascetic customs known as the four "resorts" (*nissaya*): begging for alms, wearing robes made from cast-off rags, dwelling at the foot of a tree, and using fermented cow urine as medicine (as opposed to more palatable medicines like molasses and honey).[6] There is no denying that the Buddhist emphasis on moderation militates against extreme asceticism. But the *dhutanga,* according to commentators such as Buddhaghosa, are moderately ascetic practices used to cultivate a disciplined outlook characterized by equanimity, vigor, and contentment. The goal is not to mortify the flesh but to help the practitioner cultivate the central Buddhist goals of restraint in thought, deed, and word.

As for the centrality or marginality of cremation-ground meditation as one of the *dhutanga,* the case is much the same. The stories that describe the contemplation of foulness leading to suicide and murder terminate with the teaching of mindfulness in breathing as a substitute for *asubhabhāvanā.* Pursuing the logic of this substitution, we discover that mindfulness in breathing is the chief meditative practice (*mūlakammaṭṭhāna*), the most fundamental of all meditative exercises.[7] Mindful breathing incorporates aspects of cremation-ground meditation in its emphasis on the body and its impermanence. The early stages of the exercise entail mindfulness of the body; later stages involve mindfulness of the impermanence of all conditioned things. Steady attention to the inhalation and exhalation of breath leads the meditator to achieve insight into the arising and cessation of all phenomena. Thus, minding the breath, like dwelling in cremation grounds, entails awareness of the decay that is the natural condition of all composite beings.

Aversion and Liberation

If the practice of haunting cremation grounds in search of foul objects of contemplation is not something that all Buddhists or even all members of the *sangha* are expected to engage in, developing a sense of aversion toward impermanent things is nevertheless considered an essential prerequisite for liberation.[8] The aversion that comes from seeing the world as it really is (*yathābhūta*) leads to passionlessness and hence to liberation, as the passage in the *Saṃyutta Nikāya* cited above suggests.[9] This progression from aversion to passionlessness to liberation suggests that aversion is an attitude that conduces to liberation but is not necessarily an end in itself. As an antidote to passion, aversion is a necessary preliminary, a prerequisite for liberation. In his *Bag of Bones: A Miscellany on the Body,* the contemporary Theravāda monk Khantipālo suggests that meditation on the repulsiveness of the body should be seen as a "bitter medicine" that may be discontinued once greed for bodily pleasures has been alleviated.[10]

Although all elements in the chain of dependent origination (Pāli, *paṭicca-samuppāda;* Sanskrit, *pratītya-samutpāda*) are to be regarded as impermanent and dissatisfying, the Buddha of the *Saṃyutta Nikāya* singles out four elements in particular as examples of how one should cultivate a healthy sense of aversion toward transient phenomena. These are the four sustainers (*āhārā*): food, sense contact, volition, and consciousness. One should regard taking food and drink with the same horror that parents, having run out of provisions while crossing a vast jungle, would experience at the prospect of having to eat their only child.[11] Likewise, one should view the other sustainers of psychophysical existence with aversion. Sense contact (Pāli, *phassa;* Sanskrit, *sparṣa*) should be understood as the constant biting of insects on the suppurated hide of a cow, volition (*cetanā*) as a pit of coals into which one is being pushed by force, and consciousness (Pāli, *viññāṇa;* Sanskrit, *vijñāna*) as the torture of a prisoner repeated throughout the day. By regarding the four sustainers in this way, one becomes master of one's mind and senses.

In the *Visuddhimagga,* Buddhaghosa gives pride of place to reflection on the loathsomeness (*paṭikūla*) of food. In his comprehensive treatment of the theme, he turns the daily alms round into an occasion for developing a salutary sense of aversion not only toward food but toward all manner of dirty, disagreeable things associated with obtaining and eating food. A monk setting off on an alms round should attend to a variety of unpleasant sights and smells on the way. Noting lizard droppings on the floor of the monastery and bird droppings on the monastery door, he should also observe that the threshold is stained by mucus and saliva and the bodily wastes of sick novices who have relieved themselves just outside the door. "Like a jackal approaching a cremation ground," the monk cannot avoid repugnant things if he is to eat.[12] He must cross over vile-smelling cesspools full of decomposing matter. Flies light on his skin and his begging bowl. People may fill his bowl with stale and putrid foods. Should he receive choice, tasty foods (as is likely to be the case, since lay supporters earn merit by giving the *sangha* high-quality food in generous portions), the sensual appeal of such foods can be decreased by mixing everything together into a uniform paste.[13]

But no food remains appealing once the monk begins to eat. Buddhaghosa asserts that the process of eating sullies even the finest foods because in the mouth they are mixed with saliva and ground into a "highly disgusting state like dog's vomit in a dog's feeding trough."[14] Traveling to the stomach, this miasmic paste undergoes a digestive process that reminds Buddhaghosa of refuse decomposing in a cesspool "at the gate of a village of outcastes [*caṇḍālagāmadvāre*]."[15] Cooked by the body's heat in the stomach like a boiling pot of rice, food is transformed into urine, excrement, sweat, mucus, and so on.[16] These bodily effluvia pollute the apertures through which they flow such that no amount of washing can purify them.[17] From the necessity of having to eat like a vulture in the cremation ground comes the necessity of having to excrete like a pariah. Even the food one eats in pleasant, convivial gatherings is ejected in shameful solitude:

> At the time of eating, one eats with many people around; but at the time of discharging, one goes off alone and expels what has become excrement, urine, etc. Eating, one is high spirited and joyful on the first day. But when relieving oneself on the second day, the nose is plugged up, the face is distorted, and one is shamefaced with loathing. . . . Thus the Ancient ones said:
>
> Exquisite food and drink, food hard and soft,
> By one opening they enter in, by nine they flow out.
> Exquisite food and drink, food hard and soft,
> One eats with others but hides oneself when excreting it.
> Exquisite food and drink, food hard and soft,
> One eats joyously but is disgusted when defecating.
> Exquisite food and drink, food hard and soft,
> It all becomes putrid [*pūtika*] in one night's time.[18]

Thus from start to finish, there is nothing attractive about taking nourishment. Those who attend to these repugnant facts, Buddhaghosa concludes, will achieve mastery over their senses and over the realm of material form: in this way, they will escape Māra's deadly clutches.

Ways to Discern the Body's Foulness

While the body is only one among many impermanent, ultimately dissatisfying phenomena, it is a good focus for cultivating aversion because it is relatively easy to discern the body's transience and thus to develop aversion toward it. The Buddha of the *Saṃyutta Nikāya* notes that while mental processes are much more impermanent than physical form, it is in observing "this body, product of the four great elements" that untrained people are able to feel aversion.[19]

Buddhist scriptures present a wide variety of meditations that focus on the body.[20] Many involve mindful awareness of everyday activity—mindfulness of breathing, of the modes of deportment such as standing and sitting, of routine activities such as talking, eating, resting, sleeping, and so forth. Others are analytic in nature. The body may be broken down into its four material elements: earth/solidity, water/fluidity, fire/heat, and air/movement. Such analytic exercises are particularly beneficial for overcoming a sense of self (Pāli, *attan;* Sanskrit, *ātman*). In the *Majjhima Nikāya,* the analysis of the body into its four material elements is likened to the quartering of an ox; once the ox is so divided, the generic concept of "flesh" militates against a recognition of the individuality of the ox.[21]

Perhaps the most central form of analytic meditation on the body is one that owes much to the experiences of Buddhist monks as physicians. Recent studies of the early history of Indian medicine underscore the importance of Buddhist and other non-Brahminical healers in the development of Indian medical theory. Heterodox healers, with their relative (but as we shall see, certainly not absolute) indifference to Brahminical purity strictures, contributed to anatomical theory through their empirical approach to healing and their use of dissection.[22] Praised as a uniquely Buddhist practice, the meditation on mindfulness of the body (*kāyagatāsatibhāvanā*) is essentially an exercise in anatomical analysis that combines the insights of meditation and medical practice. In the course of the meditation, the body is broken down into its thirty-two constituent parts, including internal organs such as the heart, the liver, the spleen, and the kidneys.[23] The various component parts of the body are described in a detailed, clinical fashion that would no doubt be useful to physicians.[24]

A central point in the pursuit of mindfulness of the body is to cultivate tranquillity through awareness of the body's loathsomeness (*paṭikūlamanasikāra*).[25] Thus Bhikkhu Khantipālo notes that the first five items in the list of thirty-two bodily constituents are all things that consist of dead matter:

> It is a remarkable thing that the first five parts on this list—the "person" we see—are all dead! Hair of the head and body lives only at its roots; we see dead hair. Nails that we see are dead nails; the quick is painful and hidden. The teeth, all that is visible, are dead, and their tender living roots we only experience painfully from time to time. Outer skin is dead—horrible if it was not, for it is sensitive enough already. The living skin is more painful.
>
> So when we get excited about a visual form—someone else's body—we are stimulated by impressions of what has died already. Strange to be excited by what is dead on the outside and dying within![26]

For each of the thirty-two parts of the body, Buddhaghosa specifies five forms of loathsomeness to be apprehended. Taking the first of the thirty-two parts of the body, the hair of the head, as an example, Buddhaghosa explains:

> In color, these hairs are loathsome (*paṭikūlā*). They are also loathsome in shape, in scent, in origin, in range. For, seeing anything of the color of hair in a nice bowl of gruel or rice, people get disgusted and say, "It's mixed with hair; take it away!" Thus hairs are loathsome in color. People eating at night and feeling with their hands a fiber of the swallow-wort or the rush of the shape of hairs, likewise become disgusted. This is loathsomeness in shape. The smell of hair untouched by preparations such as oil pomade, essence of flowers, and so on, is very disgusting. Even more disgusting than that is the smell of hair when thrown into the fire. Hairs indeed may not be loathsome in color or shape, but are certainly loathsome in smell. A baby's excrement is the color or turmeric and is like a pile of turmeric in shape; the swollen corpse of a black dog tossed onto a trash heap is of the color of a ripe palmyra fruit, and is like a perfectly rounded drum in

> form, with teeth resembling jasmine buds. Just as these things may not be loathsome in color and in form but are certainly disgusting in smell, so also hair may not be loathsome in color or shape, but it's certainly disgusting in smell. And as curry leaves growing in an unclean spot by a village are repulsive and therefore not eaten by the people of the town, so also hairs that have come into being on account of pus, blood, urine, excrement, bile, phlegm, and so on, are repulsive. Such is their loathsomeness as regards origin. And these hairs arise in the heap of [the body's other] thirty-one component parts like a mushroom springing up in a dung heap. Like a vegetable shoot growing in the cemetery . . . hairs are highly repulsive because they grow in unclean places. This is their loathsomeness as regards range.[27]

Perhaps it is because this meditation technique can be used for cultivating both insight and tranquillity that the Buddha of the *Nikāya*s praises *kāyagatāsatibhāvanā* as the sine qua non of liberation: "Those who experience mindfulness of the body experience deathlessness. Those who do not experience mindfulness of the body do not experience deathlessness."[28] Or perhaps the preeminence of *kāyagatāsatibhāvanā* is due to the fact that so many other forms of meditation are also exercises in mindfulness of the body. In the *Kāyagatāsati Sutta,* the Buddha explains that mindfulness of the body can be achieved in a plethora of ways. The liberative state of mindfulness of the body is won not only by those who engage in analytic reflection, mentally dissecting the body into its component elements and parts, but also by those who contemplate the various types of dead bodies in the cremation ground and by those who are mindful of the body in everyday activity.

Anatomy and Impurity in Brahminical Thought

It is important to examine Buddhist views of the body against the backdrop of Brahminical concerns about bodily purity and pollution. Preoccupation with the boundaries of the body, the bodily orifices, and substances that are emitted from them is a hallmark of Brahminical culture.[29] Such concerns are also evident to varying degrees in Zoroastrianism and Judaism.[30] Among those who have explored religious concepts of purity and pollution, Mary Douglas has distinguished herself by proposing an elegant theory that illuminates a remarkably wide range of cases with a small number of explanatory principles.

In an essay on the abominations of Leviticus, Douglas argues that anything violating the proper order of things is likely to be viewed as defiling. From the hybrid species of Leviticus to the monstrous, gargoylelike creatures that serve as Christian *exempla in malo,* it is clear that humans have deemed as impure or treated as taboo all manner of anomalous beings—beings who, like hermaphrodites confounding neat divisions of sex and gender, fill more than one classificatory niche. "Holiness," Douglas explains, "requires that individuals shall conform to the class to which they belong."[31] Like hybrid species and other beings that escape the classificatory niches to which all matter is assigned, dirt or pollution is simply anomalous matter, matter that is out of place.

This view of pollution helps us to understand why bodily emissions are so often seen as posing a threat to purity. Matter produced in the body and then discharged from the body defiles because it is both body and not-body. Emissions such as phlegm, snot, earwax, saliva, urine, and excrement are frequently considered polluting because they transgress the boundaries of the body. This concern with substances that violate the integrity of the body is evidenced in authoritative texts within the Hindu legal tradition (*dharmaśāstra*) such as *The Laws of Manu* (*Mānavadharmaśāstra,* also known as the *Manusmṛti*). Manu declares all orifices below the navel impure (*amedhyāni*), "as are the secretions that are expelled from the body."[32] Urinating, defecating, menstruating, ejaculating, eating, and sneezing are all occasions where transgressive matter threatens bodily purity. Manu mentions semen, blood, urine, excrement, snot, earwax, phlegm, tears, rheum, and sweat among the substances that defile the body.[33] The orifices through which these defilements flow should be cleaned with water, earth, or other purifying agents.[34] For example, Manu prescribes a ritual bath and the consumption of clarified butter (a highly refined, ritually pure milk product) for a person who has, through vomiting or diarrhea, violently spewed the contents of his or her body from either end of the digestive tube.[35]

According to Brahminical texts, the effort required to maintain bodily purity differs from person to person depending on social status, gender, and stage of life. Purity strictures are hierarchically calibrated, precisely tailored to suit a person's social location. Constant vigilance is required of Brahmins, members of the priestly caste that stands at the top of the caste hierarchy. According to the ancient myth of the sacrifice of the primordial man Puruṣa, the hierarchical divisions of the Brahminical (and later Hindu) body politic derive from the body of the cosmic man Puruṣa. Brahmins are Puruṣa's head, kings and warriors his arms, commoners his thighs and genitals, and servants his feet. Just as the dignity of the head appears self-evident in contrast to the humility of the buttocks and the subservient position of the feet, so the purity of Brahmins is constituted in contrast to less exalted "members" of Puruṣa's body. Because Brahmins are by nature more pure than members of other castes, they recover their purity more quickly when sullied by pollution: "A priest is pure ten days after (a death), a king after twelve days, a commoner after fifteen days, and a servant after a month."[36] But by the same token, Brahmins have more to lose in terms of purity than others, so they must guard the integrity of their bodies closely. Thus bodily purity is of most concern to Brahmins and others whose intrinsic purity is considered to be relatively high. Twice-born males—adult men belonging to the Brahmin, Warrior (*Kṣatriya*), and Commoner (*Vaiśya*) castes—have a great deal more at stake in terms of purity than do women and members of the servant (*Śudra*) caste. Adult women are seen as more amenable to pollution than men because their bodies entail major *irruptions biologiques* such as childbirth and menstruation for which seclusion and ritual purification are required: "One who has touched an Untouchable, a menstruating woman, anyone who has fallen (from his caste), a woman who has just given birth, a corpse, or anyone who has touched any of these objects, can be cleaned by a bath."[37] Likewise, members of the servant caste (and outcaste groups classified as "Untouchable" who are assimilated to the subservient position of *śudras*) are sullied by occupational impurity. They serve society by handling the defiled things that twice-born males should not touch. By disposing of excrement and corpses, washing clothes soiled by emissions such as menstrual blood, cutting hair, and the like, servants and outcastes dispose of the polluting wastes of the body politic and thus help to maintain the ritual purity of the social whole.

A Brahminicized Buddhism?

Buddhist discourse on the body reflects a marked concern with bodily emissions. In the *Aṅguttara Nikāya,* a number of similes focus attention on the orifices of the body and the substances they discharge. In one passage, Sāriputta describes his body as a faulty container, a vessel riddled with holes that dribble viscous liquids: "Just as, Lord, a man might attend to a cooking pot full of fat, riddled with holes, perforated all over, oozing and dripping, even so, Lord, I attend to this body of mine, riddled with holes, perforated all over, oozing and dripping."[38] Using an even more graphic metaphor than Sāriputta's, the Buddha compares the body to a festering pustule. With its nine oozing, spurting apertures (i.e., the ears, the eyes, the nostrils, the mouth, the urethra, and the anus that are the nine orifices of the male body), the body is like a boil with nine openings that emit putrid discharges:

> Imagine, monks, a boil that has been gathering for many years which might have nine open wounds, nine natural openings, and whatever might ooze out from this, foulness would certainly ooze out, stench would certainly ooze out, loathsomeness would certainly ooze out; whatever might be brought forth, foulness would certainly be brought forth; stench would certainly be brought forth; loathsomeness would certainly be brought forth.
>
> This boil, monks, is an apt metaphor for the body which is made up of the four great elements, begotten of mother and father, formed from a heap of boiled rice and sour gruel, subject to impermanence, concealment, abrasion, dissolution, and disintegration, with nine gaping wounds, nine natural openings, and whatever might ooze out from this, foulness would certainly ooze out. . . . Therefore, monks, you should be disgusted with this body.[39]

Pocked with nine open sores leaking putrid stuff, the body is like an infected wound that never heals.[40] Buddhaghosa alludes to the body-as-wound analogy in the above-mentioned meditation on the repulsiveness of food. Monks should think of putting on clothes as the bandaging of a wound and should regard eating food as taking medicine: "Then, putting on his undergarments as though covering a boil, fastening his waistband as though binding a bandage on a wound, putting on the outer garment as though covering a heap of bones, and taking out his bowl as though taking out a medicine jar, he arrives near the village gate."[41]

Just as an open wound must be cleaned and smeared with ointment, so the body with its suppurating apertures must be constantly washed and smeared with oils and perfumes. In the *Milindapañha,* the monk Nāgasena explains to King Milinda that "the body is not dear to those who have gone forth": renouncers regard the care of the body as a necessity comparable to the care of an arrow wound.[42] Knowing that the body is an affliction that requires constant nursing, efforts at enhancing the body's beauty through elaborate routines for the care and presentation of the body appear ludicrous. Thus the Buddha of the *Dhammapada* scoffs at those who vainly attempt to beautify the mass of wounds that is the body: "Look at this decorated image, an elevated mass of wounds. This diseased thing is highly fancied, [although] it's neither permanent nor stable."[43]

Buddhist discourse constitutes the body as a permeable, sievelike entity pocked with holes. Contemporary Buddhists have drawn on modern embryological theory to support this understanding of the body. In his reflections on the nature of the body, Bhikkhu Nyāṇamoli (a Theravādin monk known for his skill as a translator of Pāli scripture) alludes to contemporary embryological theory in describing the body as an open-ended digestive tube that develops out of a simple ring of cells: "A man's body is structurally simply a hollow ring. A hollow ring elongated into a hollow cylinder, with the inner portion lengthened and coiled; and above the upper orifice there bulges a head and between the upper and lower orifices the limbs stick out. The world passes in small portions through the ring, helped in by spoon and gulping, and out by pressure and paper."[44]

It is clear that both Brahminical and Buddhist discourse focus attention on the body's apertures and the substances emitted by them. But where Brahminical purity strictures reinforce the body's boundaries by offering ritual means for neutralizing the impure substances that violate those boundaries, Buddhist texts do not provide ritual correctives to counteract the miasmic secretions and excretions of the body. The wound that is the body will never heal; the body can never be made integral through ritual means. One could say that Brahminism (and hence Hinduism) sanctifies the body by closing it where Buddhism instrumentalizes the body by making its chronic lack of closure an object of meditation and hence a means of spiritual progress.

Although Hinduism sanctifies those bodies that are closed by means of ritual and yogic control, not every body is considered amenable to closure. Only twice-born male bodies are eligible for closure and the sanctification bodily closure brings. The bodies of women and outcaste groups, being permanently sullied by contact with bodily emissions, are not considered amenable to closure. In the *Visuddhimagga,* there are a number of occasions where Buddhaghosa uses caste-based images of occupational impurity to suggest the foulness of the body. Buddhaghosa frequently evokes disgust by comparing the inner body to a carrion-filled cesspool where outcastes defiled by handling impure things dispose of their waste. This image appears, for example, in his explanation of the repulsiveness of food.[45] Buddhaghosa revisits that vile swamp at a number of points in the *Visuddhimagga,* as in this passage describing the worms that dwell in the stomach:

> To these worms the stomach is their birthing room, bathroom, hospital, and cremation ground. Just as in the summertime when it rains in torrents various things that issue from the body (such as urine, dung, hide, bones, strips of sinews, saliva, snot, blood, and the like) are carried along by the water and fall into a pool by the gate of a village of outcastes [*caṇḍālagāmadvāre candanikāya*], . . . so there in the stomach the various kinds of things to eat and drink that were crushed by the pestle of the teeth . . . get mixed with families of worms and, sending up foam and bubbles, reach an absolutely vile, foul-smelling, disgusting state.[46]

Although the Buddha may not have been the social reformer he is often made out to be, nevertheless the teachings that are attributed to him emphatically deny that caste has any bearing on religious matters. Anyone, regardless of caste identity, who realizes the Dharma in body, speech, and mind wins the spiritual preeminence Brahminical texts accord only to men who are Brahmins by birth. Such a person is a "true Brahmin," unlike those who are Brahmins in name alone. What, then, are we to make of this village of outcastes? Why does Buddhaghosa speak so often of the dirty cesspools of socially marginal people (i.e., the pollution that even these benighted people will not tolerate within their borders)? Isn't the outcaste trope gratuitous, given that Buddhaghosa is tremendously resourceful in finding other ways to evoke a sense of religious horror?

In her analysis of Buddhaghosa's discourse on the body, Sue Hamilton suggests that this Brahminically educated commentator's concern with pollution has a distinctly Brahminical or Hindu flavor to it. In her view, Buddhaghosa's construction of the body as a mass of filth "is nothing more than the Brahmanization of Buddhist hermeneutics."[47] It seems to me, however, that Hamilton begs the question. The Buddha of the *Nikāya*s regularly uses familiar Brahminical terms to speak of bodily impurity.[48] A marked concern with the polluting effects of bodily secretions is evidenced in a variety of Buddhist scriptures, early and late. If this focus on bodily impurity is indicative of a Hinduized Buddhism, then I think we must regard Buddhism as Hinduized from the start.

It is certainly tempting to view Buddhists' preoccupation with emissions from the body as a reflection of their concern that people should stay in the places ordained for them by the caste system. Mary Douglas has argued that the physical body always serves as a cipher for the social body: "There can be no way of considering the body that does not involve at the same time a social dimension. Interest in its apertures depends on the preoccupation with social exits and entrances, escape routes and invasions. If there is no concern to preserve social boundaries, I would not expect to find concern with bodily boundaries . . . bodily control is an expression of social control."[49] People who fear the corruption of the social order tend to reinforce the boundaries of the body through rules of etiquette and ritual purity.[50] At the risk of gross oversimplification, one could say that in a truly classless society there would be nothing miasmic about belching or farting, nothing unseemly about picking one's nose at the dinner table.[51] Since Buddhist texts so clearly regard bodily emissions as polluting, it is plausible to suppose that Buddhist texts uphold the social hierarchy of the caste system.

Buddhaghosa, however, explicitly rejects a hierarchy of purity based on caste. In the following passage, he moves from an anatomy lesson highlighting the foulness of the body to a refutation of the view that some people are more polluted than others:

> The body is a construct of over 300 bones, jointed by 180 joints, bound together by 900 sinews, plastered over with 900 pieces of flesh, enveloped in a moist inner skin, enclosed by the outer skin, constantly dribbling and leaking like a cooking pot riddled with cracks and holes, inhabited by an assembly of worms, the haunt of diseases, the basis of painful states, continually oozing from the nine orifices like an old boil that's split open to the foundation, from both of the eyes eye-secretion trickles, from the ears earwax, from the nostrils snot, from the mouth food and bile and phlegm and blood, from the lower orifices excrement and urine, and from the 99,000 pores foul sweat seeps out, with black flies and the like drawn to it. The body, when untended with tooth sticks and mouthwashing and hair ointment and bathing and underclothing and dressing and so forth, would, judged by its repulsiveness, make even a king, if he wandered from village to village with his hair in a wild disorder, no different from a flower-

> scavenger or outcaste or what you will. So *there is no distinction between a kind's body and an outcaste's* in so far as its impure stinking repulsive foulness is concerned.[52]

Because we all have bodies like cisterns, one person cannot be more polluted than another just because that person handles excrement or other forms of bodily waste. No one whose stomach is a graveyard of worms is exempt from the polluting effects of handling carrion. So much for the view that Buddhaghosa has capitulated to the caste system. There is no denying that Buddhaghosa occasionally invokes the sense of religious horror that a caste Hindu feels at the prospect of intimacy with a polluted outcaste. But such appeals to Brahminical or Hindu sensibilities always appear in the service of Buddhist rhetorical purposes. For Buddhaghosa, there is no hierarchy of pollution and no such thing as occupational or caste-based impurity.

The preoccupation with bodily discharges evidenced in Buddhist scripture is better understood as an expression of minority group identity than as a capitulation to the caste system. Even a society with few class distinctions can still fear the transgression of its social boundaries from without. For such societies, a sense of bodily purity is useful, since maintaining bodily integrity helps to preserve the integrity of the group. The purity codes of minority groups like Diaspora Jews clearly help such peoples to maintain their cultural identity as members of a distinct group.[53] The same argument could be made for the *sangha*'s need to distinguish itself as a society of renouncers from the rest of the social world. In Douglas's terms, the Buddhist *sangha* is a high-group, low-grid society in which there is a strong sense of corporate identity and many clearly recognizable signs of belonging to or being excluded from the group, but relatively little emphasis on differentiation within the group.[54]

If a preoccupation with the apertures of the body is evident in Buddhist scripture, it is not because the renouncer maintains caste identity. It is, on the contrary, because the renouncer has abandoned caste in favor of a new identity. With each visit to the village of outcastes, Buddhaghosa attempts to persuade those who have opted out of the caste system to cherish and maintain their status as homeless renouncers. In the eyes of a renouncer standing outside it, the entire world of production and reproduction is nothing but a teeming cremation ground, and thus it is appropriate to use images of pollution to engender a sense of abhorrence toward that world. Even Mahāyāna thinkers such as Śāntideva are inclined to speak of the world as a cosmic cremation ground. In his *Bodhisattvacaryāvatāra,* a compendium of the Mahāyāna path, Śāntideva asks:

> Seeing a skeleton that does not even move, you are terrified,
> Why aren't you frightened by a walking corpse animated by a *vetāla*?[55]
>
> You are disgusted by skeletons in the cremation ground [*śmaśāne*],
> But you enjoy yourself in the cremation ground that is the village
> [*grāmaśmaśāne*] filled with walking crowds of skeletons![56]

While eliciting a sense of disgust at the foulness of the body, Buddhist images of bodily pollution also suggest the immanence of death in life. They depict the perpetual dying that is living in lurid images of putridity that convey the urgent necessity of renunciation. The normal emission of defiling substances from the apertures of the living body is, for example, equated with the emission of putrid matter from the apertures of a rotting corpse.[57] Reminders of human mortality that do not emphasize the putridity of the human body are often ambivalent. They can be read as exhortations to seize the day as well as arguments for self-restraint. The skeletons that adorned Egyptian banquet tables would suggest the former sentiment. Likewise, the festive atmosphere of contemporary Mexican Day of the Dead celebrations—children eating skulls made of sugar and other skeletal treats, adults drinking, eating, and listening to music in the cemetery—suggests a carpe diem spirit:

> If there is fear of death, it has been masked and in modern Mexico, appears in the guise of entertainment. . . . Only for very devout Catholics is this a time of mourning. There is no need to fear death in Mexico where the tendency is towards necrophilia rather than necrophobia.[58]
>
> Death in Mexico is usually personified as a woman. Often we portray her humorously, with scant respect. We show her as a sugar skull, and we eat her clean away. We show her as a skeleton, dressed in black and carrying a scythe. Or we show her dancing, in accordance with our sense of fun and jollity. . . . This is our way of showing that we love her, that we are not afraid of her.[59]

It would be difficult to imagine Buddhist images of the body's putres-

Figure 3. This figurine of a skeletal ice-cream vendor made by a contemporary Mexican artist demonstrates the lighthearted spirit of Mexican Day of the Dead imagery. Private collection.

cence evoking the lighthearted, ironic celebration of the immanence of death in life that one finds in Mexican Day of the Dead imagery (see fig. 3). While there is, as I will shortly suggest, a literary quality of ambiguity in some cremation-ground reveries, even these poetic exercises in ironic understatement ultimately leave no doubt as to the folly of seeking joy in the charnel house that is the world.

Desire and Loathing Strangely Mixed

The use of shocking and unconventional literary styles is a means of engendering a salutary sense of aversion that is frequently met with in Buddhist texts. Sanskrit literary theory draws clear distinctions between different types of aesthetic mood or sentiment (*rasa,* literally "sap," "flavor," or "taste") that authors should strive to convey through the use of prescribed similes, settings, and other literary conventions. The *Natya Sastra* (ca. second century C.E.), a textbook of dramatic arts, distinguishes four basic *rasa*s: the erotic (*śṛngāra*), the heroic (*vīra*), the violent (*raudra*), and the repulsive (*bībhatsa*). These aesthetic sentiments are like flavors, and it is the job of the author or playwright to produce a literary dish with a predominant *rasa* for the connoisseur to savor.

Certain combinations of *rasa*s are expressly forbidden by aesthetic theory as examples of bad taste (*virasa,* literally "tasteless"). The conflation of the erotic and the repulsive *rasa*s is one such forbidden combination. The literary critic Kṣemendra describes a verse in which the repulsive mood has eclipsed the erotic as being like "a bouquet of flowers that has been seasoned with garlic."[60] But there is no gainsaying the fact that Sanskrit authors were masters at whipping up strange concoctions of incongruous *rasa*s. For example, Sanskrit composers created weird combinations of antithetical aesthetic moods in their accounts of the ambivalent career of the Hindu god Śiva.[61] When this god who combines the opposed social roles of renouncer and householder takes Pārvatī as his wife, Śiva transforms the terrifying ascetic emblems that he wears as symbols of his world-renouncing austerity into conventional ornaments suitable for a world-embracing bridegroom. The skulls that adorn his head become a tiara, the ashes on his skin become sandalwood paste, his third eye becomes a precious gem. Thus Śiva calms the fears of his bride's apprehensive parents by transforming his ghastly ascetic appearance into the regal, sensually inviting appearance expected of him.

In the fifth act of his *Mālatīmādhava,* the celebrated Sanskrit playwright Bhavabhūti describes the love-play of female ghouls in a much-anthologized verse that combines the conventions of erotic and horrific representation:

> These shapely demonesses, their auspicious marital necklaces made of
> intestines, wearing earrings decorated with the red lotus hands of
> women,
> having hastily put on lotus-garlands made of hearts,
> Feeling refreshed wearing a saffron paste of blood,
> they unite with their lovers and drink the liquor of marrow grease
> from cups made of skulls, enjoying themselves immensely.[62]

Although an erotic poem should never depict death or be set in a cremation ground, this bacchanal takes place in a charnel field strewn with dismembered body parts. Indeed, Bhavabhūti's famous verse brims with death, dismemberment, and cannibalism. It depicts the sensual pastimes of demonic women through the use of conventions (such as descriptions of dress and ornamentation) normally reserved for high-class heroines in more auspicious settings.

Buddhist authors frequently portray eroticism in vulturesque settings—and with good reason. As Lee Siegel has argued, the aesthetic sentiment of peace (*śanta rasa*) can be elicited through the conflation of the erotic and repulsive moods.[63] Scenes where love blossoms in settings as unlikely as the outhouse or cemetery engender a liberative sense of the body's foulness. Although shocking in their graphic depiction of the perversity of sexual desire, such scenes convey doctrinal messages that are ultimately calming. In the *Maṇimēkalai,* a sixth-century Buddhist epic about a courtesan's daughter who renounces her hereditary occupation to become a Buddhist nun, the Tamil poet Cāttaṉār conflates the erotic and the repulsive moods in a grisly scene set in a cremation ground called (significantly) the "Cosmic Place." Cāttaṉār describes the feasting of dogs, vultures, and ghouls on human flesh as if it were the feasting of guests at a wedding ceremony:

> A boy named Cārṇkalaṉ went inside the Cosmic Place [*cakkaravāḷam*] all alone, thinking it was a well-fortified city. Instead he met with sounds proclaiming to people who love the body that it is only flesh, blood, and bones: there was the ceaseless, exultant howl of a jackal clutching in his jaws a corpse's foot decorated with red cosmetic paste, a lump of wormy decaying flesh. Then he heard the drawn-out shriek of a vulture piercing and consuming a naked mound-of-venus, the unrestrained howl of an evil dog who had snatched and torn apart a severed arm, stacked with bangles, and the crunch of the hungry kite seizing and eating beautiful, erect, young breasts adorned with sandal paste.
>
> These sounds served as the beats of the *muḻavam* drum played on a stage created out of white ashes from once-lovely bodies. A female ghoul gleefully mounted onto that stage. She did not ask herself, "What are these, clouds or a woman's tresses? Carp or eyes? Is this a *kumiḻ* flower ar a nose? Are these lips or *kavir* flowers? Teeth or

> pearls?" She did not show any mercy. Dancing with joy on her cloven feet, she gouged out the eyes of that head and ate them with insatiable glee.[64]

The *mu_lavam* drum, used in South Indian marriage ceremonies, suggests imminent sexual consummation.[65] But the poet has subverted the erotic mood, lingering on the dismembered parts of corpses as a lover fixates on favorite parts of the beloved's body. A naked mound-of-venus is "sexually" penetrated by the beak of a vulture. The erect, adorned breasts of a young woman are seized by a rapacious kite. As Paula Richman explains, Cāttaṉār has transformed the vocabulary of erotic love "into a catalogue of cannibalism."[66] "Each item consumed—the breast, the mound of venus, the arm with bangles—is an element found in the accounts of [Tamil] poets of a given heroine's beauty."[67] Turning classic Tamil poetic conventions on their head for Buddhist rhetorical purposes, Cāttaṉār parodies standard images of erotic love. The female ghoul gorges herself on dismembered parts of women's bodies that, in more auspicious circumstances, would remind poets and lovers of clouds, flowers, and gems. Cāttaṉār, like the feasting ghoul, rejects such delicate similes. In the cosmic cremation ground that is the world, Cāttaṉār suggests, sensual pleasure is necessarily vulturesque, sex always an exercise in necrophilia.[68] In the eyes of a renouncer, the conceits of poets and the yearnings of lovers are ludicrous category mistakes; only fools mistake walking corpses for paragons of beauty.[69]

Another cremation-ground scene with erotic overtones appears in the widely disseminated *Kusa Jātaka*.[70] In a former life, the Pāli version goes, the Buddha took birth as a wise but ugly prince named Kusa. Predicting that whatever bride his parents might find for him would run away at the sight of him and bring shame to the family, the ascetically inclined Prince Kusa attempts to circumvent his parents' plans. He fashions a golden image of an impossibly perfect young woman and tells his parents that if they can find a bride as beautiful as the statue, he will marry her.[71] Unfortunately for Kusa (and for the young woman herself) such a woman exists. Pabhāvatī, eldest daughter of King Madda, is so radiantly beautiful that, in a boisterous scene of mistaken identity, her hunchbacked nurse slaps the golden statue thinking that the young princess in her charge is somewhere she is not supposed to be.[72] A marriage between Kusa and Pabhāvatī is soon thereafter arranged.

Kusa's wise mother suspects that Pabhāvatī will not be happy once she sees the man she has married. So she arranges things so that Pabhāvatī only sees Kusa in a pitch black chamber at night, telling her that this nocturnal pattern is an old family tradition. When Pabhāvatī insists that she see her husband in the light of day, she is shown the prince's handsome younger brother instead of Prince Kusa. The stratagem, however, eventually breaks down when Pabhāvatī figures out why her marriage is such a strange one and demands to see her hideous spouse. As predicted, Pabhāvatī cannot stand the sight of Kusa; when she sees him she faints with terror, thinking he is a demon. As soon as Pabhāvatī recovers consciousness, she returns to her father's city.

The god Indra then intervenes in order to force Pabhāvatī back to Kusa. Using the name of her father, King Madda, he sends messengers to seven neighboring kings, promising each that Pabhāvatī will be his bride. All seven kings arrive at the capital city and are outraged at hearing that Pabhāvatī has been promised to all. Afraid that if he gives her to any one of the seven kings the others will wage war against him, King Madda in his Solomonic wisdom decides that all seven will have a piece of his daughter: "After rejecting the chief king of the entire continent, let her suffer the consequences of her coming home! I will kill her, divide her into seven pieces, and send one to each of the seven."[73]

When Pabhāvatī learns what her father has in store for her, she imagines the horrors to which her dismembered body will soon be subject. She visualizes the various body parts that will be tossed aside by their recipients and enjoyed by carrion-eating animals:

> These dark tresses of mine—hair that's soft to the touch and fragrant with the essence of sandalwood—will end up scattered in the middle of a cremation ground, carried off by the talons of vultures.
>
> These soft, downy arms with their red-tipped fingers, fragrant with the essence of sandalwood, will end up cut off and tossed aside by kings in the forest; seizing one, a wolf will go off wherever he pleases with it.
>
> My breasts that are shapely like the fruit of the date-palm and used to being rubbed with Benares sandalwood will end up with a jackal hanging on them like a little baby son hanging on his mother's breast.[74]

> My broad buttocks, so well massaged and used to a golden girdle, will end up cut off and thrown aside by kings in the forest; seizing them, a wolf will go off wherever he pleases.[75]

As in Cāttaṉār's *Maṇimēkalai,* so here the central conventions of erotic poetry are deftly subverted. This is no standard cataloging of feminine charms but a lurid anatomy lesson, a graphic description of a body cut into pieces and ravaged by carrion-eating animals. These animals, especially the jackal "nursing" at Pabhāvatī's breast, are portrayed as stand-ins for the human beings who might legitimately have enjoyed Pabhāvatī's body. Here no vulture penetrates Pabhāvatī's mound-of-venus as in the *Maṇimēkalai,* but sexuality is implicit in this flesh-eating frenzy. The seven kings who expected to marry Pabhāvatī have, in Pabhāvatī's envisioning of her fate, rejected the macabre substitutes that her father proposes to give them. The tender breasts and broad buttocks that she imagines these men to have coldly tossed aside have been seized and carried off by more appreciative admirers—the dogs, wolves, and jackals who, jealously guarding their precious booty from one another, secrete pieces of Pabhāvatī away to their lairs for later consumption.

Aside from the logic of the story itself, with its substitution of rapacious animals for human lovers, there are other reasons for regarding necrophilia as implicit in the necrophagy here. As O'Flaherty has demonstrated, the homology between food and sex that Lévi-Strauss has discussed at length plays an important role in Indian mythology.[76] There are a variety of Indic words derived from the root $\sqrt{bhuj}$ (e.g., the Sanskrit and Pāli noun *bhoga,* "enjoyment") that denote both eating and sexual gratification. Linguistically and stylistically, then, the story signals that Pabhāvatī has been debased in a most horrifying manner; she has become the contested sexual prize of rapacious carrion-eating animals.[77]

Cremation-ground reveries such as Cāttaṉār's and Pabhāvatī's show that literary moods (*rasa*s) used in resourceful and unexpected ways can serve to persuade the reader or listener to accept as true those ideas about the world that may not be intuitively obvious. By presenting alluring female bodies as food for worms, cremation-ground reveries enable Buddhist authors to comment with ironic wit and dark double entendre on the futility of beauty, the rapacity of the sex act, and the perversity of sexual desire.

Bliss and Bondage in the Harem

Buddhist authors working in Sanskrit were equally adept at combining incongruous literary conventions in order to communicate the folly of lust. In the Sanskrit biographies of the Buddha, a scene in which women in the *bodhisattva*'s harem are transformed by sleep so deep it resembles death suggests homologies between bedroom and cemetery, erotic disarray and life-threatening devastation. Although fully developed accounts of the harem scene apear in all the Sanskrit biographies (i.e., the *Mahāvastu, Lalitavistara,* and *Buddhacarita*), it is in the *Buddhacarita,* Aśvaghoṣa's celebrated biography of the Buddha, that these homologies are suggested with the greatest skill and subtlety.[78]

The time is twilight. The setting is a richly furnished chamber in one of the upper stories of the palace. When, according to an early established tradition, the prince's father Suddhodana had learned from the sage Asita that his son would become either a great ruler or a great renouncer, he was determined that Gotama should succeed him as king. To prevent the young man from renouncing his family, patrimony, and kingdom, Suddhodana kept his son sequestered from the harsh realities of life in a suite of sumptuous apartments where all kinds of sensual delights were provided:

> The king, reflecting that the prince should not see anything disagreeable that might upset his mind, assigned him a dwelling place from the interior quarters of which he was never to descend to the ground.
>
> Then in his quarters, which were white as flowing water in the autumn, like mansions in spaciousness, and equipped for pleasures suited to each season, he amused himself with the splendid music of singing-women.
>
> That palace was charmed like [the heavenly mountain] Kailāsa, with gold-rimmed tambourines beaten softly by the tips of women's fingers and with dances as enchanting as those of the most accomplished *apsarās*es.
>
> There the women delighted him with soft voices, languid gestures, amorous talk, playful revels, sweet laughter, curving of eyebrows and sidelong glances.
>
> Then, captured by women who were skilled in the prerequisites of

> love and invincible in the pursuit of pleasure, he did not descend from the height of his mansion to the ground, just as one who has earned merit does not descend from their heavenly mansion.[79]

Allusions to Mount Kailāsa and the heavenly *apsarās*es constitute the *bodhisattva*'s quarters as a heavenly place, a place where all desires are fulfilled. Like the gods whose days and nights are filled with the dancing and singing of heavenly nymphs, the prince is surrounded by beauty that is captivating.

At this point in the narrative, however, it has become clear that the *bodhisattva* is no longer under the sway of feminine charms. He has recently seen things that have left him stunned with sorrow and cognizant of his status as a prisoner in his own home. The prince had recently gone on an excursion, and although King Suddhodana had seen to it that all evidence of suffering—that is, the sick, the maimed, the old, and so forth—was removed from the *bodhisattva*'s path, the gods thwarted Suddhodana's plans by conjuring up for the prince the appearance of a wizened old man.[80] On subsequent outings, the sheltered prince saw a sick man, a corpse, and a man dressed as a monk who described himself as a "renouncer who, afraid of birth and death, left the home life for the sake of liberation."[81] Having seen the suffering that all flesh is heir to, the *bodhisattva* is anxious to follow the example of the renouncer.

He goes to his father hoping to attain Suddhodana's permission for him to leave home and wander as a renouncer. Hearing his son's request, King Suddhodana bursts into tears. He begs Gotama to delay renunciation until the end of his life, to do his duty as a son by taking the reins of power from his father's aging hands. Doing what is appropriate to someone at this early stage of life, Gotama must assume the responsibilities now borne by Suddhodana and thus allow Suddhodana to follow the spiritual path appropriate for his advanced age. It is the father, not the son, who should now be retiring from the world as a renouncer. But the *bodhisattva,* extremely agitated by what he has seen, is not prepared to wait for a more convenient time to renounce. He tells his father that it is wrong to restrain a man who is trying to escape a burning house. Moreover, Gotama argues, he will eventually be separated from his wife and parents through death. So why should he not separate himself from loved ones now through renunciation—the separation that puts an end to birth and death? The king, however, cannot abide the prospect of this premature separation from his son and heir. He will not grant his permission. When Gotama leaves his presence, King Suddhodana arranges even more choice pleasures for his son. But, since it is painfully evident to Suddhodana that the bonds of desire will not hold Gotama for long, the king also posts more guards around the prince's quarters to prevent him from leaving without permission.[82]

At the end of this trying day, just as the sun is setting, the *bodhisattva* retires to his quarters. He is in no mood to be captivated by feminine charms:

> Going to a chamber filled with incense of the finest black aloe and lit with glittering golden lanterns, he lay down on a splendid golden seat colorfully inlaid with diamonds.
>
> Then in the night women of distinction entertained with musical instruments this preeminent man who rivals the king of the gods just as troops of *asparās*es wait on the son of the Lord of Wealth on top of a moon-lit, snow-capped summit.
>
> But he was neither pleased nor excited by those excellent musical instruments, even though they were quite divine; since the desire of the virtuous one was to leave his home in search of the bliss of the highest goal [*paramārthasukhāya*], he did not rejoice.[83]

The Akaniṣṭha gods—divine supporters of the Dharma who are anxious to see the *bodhisattva* renounce the world—seize this opportunity to galvanize the *bodhisattva,* turning his resolve into action. They cast a magical sleeping spell over the women of the harem, causing a sea change into something exceedingly strange.

The description begins auspiciously enough. Verses 48–57 are rather straightforward depictions of beautiful women in a state of amorous indolence. In his description of women assuming playfully petulant attitudes and clutching their musical instruments in suggestive ways, Aśvaghoṣa employs standard images in the lexicon of erotic poetry.[84] One woman whose robe has fallen aside resembles "a river with lotuses being enjoyed by a straight row of bees"; another hugs her drum "as if it were her lover."[85] Verse 56 makes the musical-instrument-as-lover motif remarkably explicit: "Another young woman lay with her drum, whose decorative strap had slipped from her shoulder region, clutched between her thighs like a lover grown languid with the culmination of sexual pleasure."[86] But there is a subtle shift at verse 57: "Others, although in actuality large-eyed and fair-browed, showed no beauty with their eyes shut, like lotus-ponds with their flower buds closed at the setting of the sun."[87] With their beautiful eyes closed, the inherent beauty of these sleeping women is hidden away like the blossoms of the lotus at night. Their beauty is temporarily effaced, but in the morning their eyes will open and reveal their beauty again.

In verse 58, however, there is a suggestion that the sleeper being described will not awaken in the morning: "Another too had her hair loose and disheveled, and with the ornaments and clothes fallen from her hips and her necklaces scattered she lay like an image of a woman broken by an elephant."[88] With her clothes and ornaments scattered as if in postcoital disarray, this woman seems to fit the profile of an erotic heroine. Those who savor the amorous sentiment, however, will find that this verse leaves a bitter aftertaste. The carnal mood of the bedroom is marred by the suggestion of carnage carried by the last simile. In telling us that "she lay like an image of a woman broken by an elephant," Aśvaghoṣa introduces a conceit more appropriate to the battlefield, where elephants were used as weapons of war, than to the bedroom.[89] It is true that wild and sometimes pain-inflicting erotic abandon figures prominently in manuals of the erotic arts. In Vatsyayana's *Kāma Sūtra,* for example, biting and scratching are par for the course in the game of love.[90] But the scenario suggested by this simile is clearly more in accord with the canons of war-making than those of love-making.

What is indirectly insinuated through quiet subversions of good taste is stated more plainly in verse 60: "Others looked ugly, lying unconscious like corpses, with their ornaments and garlands broken to pieces, the fastening knots of their clothing undone, and their eyes motionless with the whites showing."[91] The next verse highlights the openness of the body—a motif that we have seen in cremation-ground reveries like Cāttaṉār's and will see again and again in hagiographic accounts of monks' real-life encounters with decaying corpses. This motif is not necessarily limited to poetry in the aesthetic mood of disgust. An open body, a body in which the orifices are displayed in the full view of the spectator, can be erotic in that it may invite penetration.[92] But this verse presents a scene that is anything but sensually appealing—the body of a woman who has lost control over her movement (and thus lost her allure) like someone on the verge of passing out from too much alcohol:

"Another lay as if sprawling in intoxication, with her mouth gaping open and saliva flowing out, and with her limbs spread out so as to show what should be concealed. Her beauty was gone, her form distorted."[93]

Only after more than a dozen verses have unobtrusively pushed the boundaries of good taste to their limits in suggesting the ambivalence of the scene are we told outright that this spectacle is meant to arouse the sentiment of disgust. Gazing on the scene before him in verse 63, the *bodhisattva* "was filled with contempt."[94] "Such," he concludes, "is the real nature [*svabhāvaḥ*] of women, impure [*aśuci*] and monstrous [*vikṛtaḥ*],[95] yet a man [*puruṣaḥ*], deceived by dress and ornaments, succumbs to passion for women."[96] Aśvaghoṣa's poetic rendering of the scene is a beautiful instantiation of the very point the *bodhisattva* is making here. In the early stages of the description of this hothouse scene, it really is difficult to distinguish between the erotic and the horrific, the sublime and the grotesque. The literary ornaments (*alaṃkāra,* "decoration," "embellishment") that Aśvaghoṣa uses to embellish the scene lead us to mistake sleep-death for erotic lethargy. Likewise, deceived by the outer beauty of the ornamented body, people mistake abject bags of filth for paragons of beauty. Deluded by the spell of specious beauty, people in the throes of passion imagine themselves kings while behaving like vultures.

Seeing these bodies contorted in sleep like stiffening corpses, the *bodhisattva* recognizes the perversity of seeking satisfaction in the body. These lovely young bodies have become "impure and monstrous," taking on the features of death in their unconscious state. Continual decay being the natural condition of all impermanent beings, this soporific body language transmits a profound message to the renunciant prince: *saṃsāra* is a charnel ground where pleasure is snatched from the teeth of death.

Where the other visions that lead Gotama to take a jaundiced view of the pleasures of *saṃsāra* occur some days prior to his leaving home, the harem vision occurs at a watershed point in the narrative, immediately preceding the Great Renunciation. The other shock-inspiring encounters with old age, sickness, and death have set the scene for this final vision by suggesting the transience and dis-ease of life. But it is not until he sees the harem as a charnel field that the *bodhisattva* realizes it is time to seek an end to death and birth. He calls for his horse, pays a brief visit to another part of the palace where he takes one last look at his sleeping wife and his son, and then, with the help of the deities who make sure that he escapes detection, flees the palace and takes on the emblems of a renouncer.

The Chinese version of the *Buddhacarita* (*Fo-sh-hing-tsan-king*, translated from the Sanskrit by Dharmarakṣa) lacks the poetic subtlety characteristic of Aśvaghoṣa's Sanskrit text but introduces some remarkably apt images of beauty as bondage. Some of the women of Gotama's harem, for example, resemble inhabitants of one of the many Buddhist hells where the form of torture symbolically reenacts the untoward behavior that led to incarceration in hell: "leaning and facing one another, or with back to back, or *like those beings thrown into the abyss, their jeweled necklets bound about like chains*, their clothes and undergarments swathed around their persons."[97] The jeweled necklaces the women wear to enhance their beauty have turned into chains around their necks. In the eyes of the *bodhisattva*, the harem has become a place of retribution where alluring women who captivate men are given a taste of their own medicine. Being bound around the neck by chainlike necklaces, the women are literally prisoners of their own beauty. The next verse suggests (although this may be an interpolation of the translator) the presence of torturers who assist the perpetrators in symbolic reenactments of their crimes: "grasping their instruments, stretched along the earth, even as those undergoing punishment at the hands of keepers, their garments in confusion."[98]

The Chinese text also gives added clues to the interpretation of Aśvaghoṣa's initial description of the harem as an erotic space. Like the tradition of composing verses that can be read in either of two opposed ways, Aśvaghoṣa's framing of the harem scene is full of artful double entendres.[99] The master poet's subtle blending of aesthetic sentiments is such a virtuoso performance that at times one is truly unable to distinguish heaven from hell, pleasure from pain, and erotic tumult from carnage on the battlefield. But in a clear signal that fallen garments, twisted limbs, and broken jewelry should not be understood as the dishabille of passionate women abandoning all sense of decorum, the Chinese text compares the disordered appearance of the women to that of a madman: "their mouths half opened or else gaping wide, the loathsome dribble trickling forth, their heads uncovered and in wild disorder, like some unreasoning madman's."[100]

In other Sanskrit biographies of the Buddha, treatments of the harem scene tend to be considerably more blunt, leaving no doubt as to the aesthetic sentiment that predominates in this hothouse setting. According to the *Lalitavistara,* the deities who have effected this sea change characterize the scene in asking Gotama this rhetorical question: "How can you find pleasure in the midst of this cremation ground [*śmaśāna-madhye*] in which you live?"[101] The *bodhisattva,* seeing that the harem is truly disgusting (*bībhatsām*), replies: "I really do live in the middle of a cremation ground."[102] Then, sighing with compassion, the *bodhisattva* cries: "Alas! This world is miserable! The weak are oppressed by pain. How can one find pleasure with a troop of *rākṣasīs*?"[103]

One may well ask whether Gotama's pity includes the "*rākṣasīs*" themselves or whether, like the sad little girl in Gerard Manley Hopkins's "Spring and Fall," it is really Gotama he mourns for.[104] The next line is not much help, as it is equally ambiguous: "Fools who are covered by the darkness of deep delusion take as virtues those nonvirtues that are the qualities of desire; like birds in the midst of cages, they find no way out."[105] In its reference to entrapment, this statement could either be describing women trapped in their own vanity, choking on pieces of jewelry that have turned into instruments of bondage, or men such as Gotama who fall prey to the captivating beauty of women. The thirty-two similes that follow, however, confirm that it is not the sleeping women but the foolish men deluded by such charming cadavers that incite the *bodhisattva*'s compassion:

> Then the *bodhisattva* again observed the women's apartments by means of *dharma*-vision [*dharmālokamukhena*] and bemoaned the fate of beings, lamenting with great compassion:
>
> Fools are dying here like prisoners in the place of execution.
> Fools are charmed here by decorated vases brimming with filth, idiots that they are. . . .
> Fools enjoy themselves here like pigs rolling in excrement.
> Fools bed down here like dogs in the midst of bones and blood.
> Fools fly in here like moths flying into the flames of lamps.
> Fools are trapped here like monkeys lured by filth.
> Fools suffer here like fish bound up together in a net.
> Fools are processed here like sheep lined up in slaughterhouses.
> Fools are suspended here like criminals impaled on a spike.
> Fools sink here like old elephants stuck in the mud.

Fools perish here like travelers whose ship has broken up on the ocean. . . .
Fools go round and round here like dogs tied on a leash.
Fools wither here like grass and trees drying up in the heat of summer. . . .
Fools, thinking only of sating themselves, are wounded here like true half-wits licking honey off the blade of a razor.
Fools are carried away here like tree trunks swept away by the current of a river.
Fools amuse themselves here like little children playing with their own urine and excrement.
Fools are controlled here like elephants pulled here and there by the driver's hook.
Fools are deceived here like true half-wits led by swindlers.
Fools lose the roots of virtue here like men squandering their money by gambling.
Fools are consumed here like merchants fallen prey to *rākṣasīs*.[106]

Saṃsāra as a Mantrap

Clearly, the harem is an image of *saṃsāra,* the cycle of birth and death in which all but Buddhas are entrapped. Like Cāttaṉār's cosmic cremation ground, it is a place that affords only vulturesque necrophagic pleasures. It is a place where people gobble up excrement as if it were liver pâté. It is a place of bondage where only the likes of the Marquis de Sade could find pleasure. There are many metaphors of bondage and entrapment in this passage—prisoners condemned to death, monkeys caught in a trap, fish caught in a net, aging elephants stuck in a swamp, and so forth. But who are the captives here? Doctrinally speaking, the answer is clearly all of us—women trapped by their own vanity and men beguiled by the semblance of feminine beauty. But I think there can be little doubt that in the thirty-two similes the prison/execution chamber of *saṃsāra* is gendered as feminine and its occupants are gendered as masculine. Just as Gotama's penthouse is a prison in which women are charged with the duty of holding him captive to their beauty, so *saṃsāra* is a prison in which women are the agents of incarceration.[107]

Grammatically, the subjects of all these similes are male (*te bālā,* "these fools").[108] But even if the noun "fools" was not gendered as male in the Sanskrit, the passage is full of intertextual signals, allusions to statements about female duplicity found in other texts that leave no doubt as to the power of womanly wiles to delude, entrap, immobilize, and destroy unwary men.[109] In the *Theragāthā*, for example, women are described as razor blades coated with honey.[110] In Aśvaghoṣa's *Saundarananda*, a monk uses various images of danger and entrapment in his attempt to dissuade a fellow monk who wishes to go back to his wife. He suggests that women are like poisoned creepers, like caves filled with snakes.[111] Deceptively dangerous, they lead their pleasure-intoxicated victims onto the path of transgression.[112] They have honey in their speech but the great poison *hālahala* in their hearts.[113] *Aṅguttara Nikāya* 3.68–69 is the locus classicus for Buddhist metaphors of women as mantraps.[114] In this passage, the Buddha alerts his monks to the dangers of what Lee Siegel has so aptly translated as "Māra's booby trap." Even men with hearts of granite are advised to avoid spending time alone with a woman because it is easier to outwit a demon or to be intimate with a venomous snake than to be impervious to the charms of womankind:

> Monks, if ever one could properly say that something is in all respects a snare of Māra [*samantapāso Mārassa*], one can surely say of women [*mātugāmaṃ*] that they are in all respects a snare of Māra.
>
> Have a conversation with a man holding a sword in his hand, or with a demon [*pisācena*], or sit down next to a snake whose bite is fatal, but never have a conversation alone with a woman![115]

Another way in which the similes constitute *saṃsāra* as feminine and entrapment in *saṃsāra* as a male dilemma is through allusions to the demonic power of women to deceive their victims through the power of illusion. The final simile in the *bodhisattva*'s thirty-two analogies mentions merchants who have "fallen prey to *rākṣasī*s." This refers to a genre of Buddhist horror stories (with distant echoes in the exploits of Sinbad the Sailor in the *Arabian Nights*) that relate how shipwrecked merchants marooned on an island populated by cannibalistic female ghouls are saved by a magical horse who is a Buddha-in-the-making.[116]

Marooned on Vampire Island

Redactions of this much-repeated tale of shipwrecked merchants have been preserved in a variety of contexts. The Buddha reportedly told the tale to different members of the *sangha* for different reasons. The Pāli recension found in the *Jātaka*s (*Valāhassa Jātaka*) is a flashback to the past told for the benefit of a monk who is dissatisfied with the life of celibacy on account of having been smitten by the sight of an adorned woman. With a preliminary warning that "these women that cause greed in men through their womanly wiles [*itthikuttavilāsehi*] and their form, sound, smell, savor, and touch are to be called ogresses [*yakkiniyo*]," the Buddha launches into a grisly cautionary tale of shipwrecked men devoured by guileful ogresses.[117]

A ship with 500 seafaring merchants wrecks off the coast of an island populated by *yakkinī*s (Sanskrit, *yakṣinī*s)—ambivalent, shape-shifting spirits associated with trees and rivers.[118] Although these *yakkinī*s are horrible demonic creatures with fangs and other features appropriate for eating raw human flesh, they take on youthful human forms when they see the merchants swimming to their island. Carrying spectral, psychically created children on their hips, they carry bowls of food to the shore and feed the merchants. These *yakkinī*s present themselves to the merchants as widows whose seafaring husbands have been gone three years and are presumed dead. When these seemingly young and beautiful women offer to become their wives (literally, "foot servants," *pādaparicārikā*), the 500 stranded merchants are more than happy to serve as their husbands.[119] But waking in the middle of the night, the leader of the merchants finds one night that his lover's body is cold to the touch. On investigating the matter, he discovers that she had slipped out of bed and gone off to gorge herself on the bodies of other shipwrecked men who are being kept like cattle in a building on the other side of the island. Using methods that are both ordinary and magical, it is the habit of these *yakkinī*s to entice the victims of shipwrecks using their feminine charms (*itthikuttabhāva*) and then, when another party of sailors arrives on the island, to throw the previous victims into a workhouse, bind them there with divine charms (*devasaṃkhalika*), and use them nocturnally as a food supply.[120] The leader, having ascertained their modus operandi, quietly alerts the rest of the men and suggests that they make their escape at once. Half of them are so intoxicated with pleasure that they are simply unable to leave their femmes fatales. But the 250 men who follow their leader's advice reach the mainland safely by riding on the back of a flying horse.

It is significant that the Buddha illustrates the dangers that women pose for renouncers by reference to demonic women who regularly attract their victims by magically altering their appearance. When human women are said to be traps that lead to the downfall of men, Buddhist philosophers and psychologists would insist that it is not women per se that endanger men but rather women as they *appear* to deluded men. If anything is Māra's snare, it is surely men's distorted, unreal perceptions of women.[121] The false form of a demonic woman is the perfect metaphor for this dangerously perfect, undecaying, dischargeless woman-as-perceived-by-man. It is only when an ogress, having assumed a false human form, is misapprehended by a man and thought to be human that she wields the kind of power that women are thought to have over men. Wise men, knowing the forms assumed by demonic females to be false appearances, do not fall into their power. But fools, taken in by appearances, become victims of these duplicitous, shape-shifting beings. Likewise, the power that human women wield over men is constituted entirely by the deluded vision of the men who perceive them.

But if these demonic women wield power over men only by virtue of men's misapprehension of them, it is also true that these ogresses are held culpable by those who composed the texts in which they appear. They—and the human women whose specious beauty exerts an analogous force in the minds of men—are depicted as agents of incarceration in the prison of *saṃsāra.* John Holt has noted the opposition between the male forces of Dharma and the female forces of *saṃsāra* in his reading of a Sanskrit version of the shipwrecked merchants' tale:

> The allegorical symbolism of 500 merchants setting off on a sea voyage in search of precious jewels is almost too obvious to explicate in a Buddhist context. Five hundred is a number used frequently in Buddhist texts, Mahāyāna and Hīnayāna alike, to designate the presence of the immediate disciples surrounding the Buddha. Sinhala and his 500 comrades searching for jewels represent the Buddha (the culture hero of the Sinhalese people) and the *sangha.* . . . The *rākṣasīs* represent their obstacles: the forces of *saṃsāra* that first seduce one by means of desire and lust before leading one down the path to being eventually consumed by them.[122]

There are, however, several versions of this story ripe for a feminist retrieval, versions in which there is much irony in the equation of women with man-eating demons. The tale was told all over South Asia, with many versions surviving in many languages. In a Newari recension of the *Siṇhalasārthabāhu Avadāna* composed in Nepal, the eponymous leader of the merchant group is the only one to escape.[123] The rest of the crew attempt to follow his advice. But as they are crossing the ocean on the back of the flying horse, they make the perennial fairy tale mistake of looking back when instructed not to do so. One by one, they turn their gaze to the *rākṣasī*s who are cooing terms of endearment and declaring the charms of their lovely young bodies (while actually flying in their hideous *rākṣasī* forms in hot pursuit). One by one, each merchant falls into the sea, only to be plucked up and eaten by his demon bride.

The *rākṣasī*s are afraid that the escaped merchant will spread the news of their vampire kingdom throughout the mainland and thus dry up their food supply. So they turn on their queen, Siṇhalasārthabāhu's former spouse, telling her that if she does not follow the merchant to the mainland and destroy him, they will eat her. She agrees to follow Siṇhalasārthabāhu home and devour him. Thus the queen of the *rākṣasī*s appears in Siṇhalasārthabāhu's native town with an infant at her breast, telling everyone in town about the heartless merchant Siṇhalasārthabāhu who seduced and then abandoned her. When the queen of the vampires and her spectral child appear before Siṇhalasārthabāhu's parents with the same story, they interrogate their son. He, of course, insists that she is a *rākṣasī* and that her baby was made by the power of illusion. Siṇhalasārthabāhu's parents are remarkably phlegmatic in their response. The father responds, "O Son, *all* women are *rākṣasī*s. Therefore, after forgiving her faults, you must love her."[124] In other words: "She may be a witch but she's *your* witch, young man."

This exchange reproduces something of the Indic cultural dialogue between homeless renouncers and householders remaining in the social world. Both parties agree that women have access to "demonic" powers of sweet persuasion. But in the worldly perspective of Siṇhalasārthabāhu's parents, women's character flaws are no excuse for avoiding one's responsibilities in the realm of production and reproduction. All women partake of the demonic, but in keeping women under the protection of fathers, brothers, husbands, and sons, their feminine wiles may be controlled.

In contrast to the outright misogyny (the devaluing of women) of this worldly perspective, the misogamy (devaluing of marriage) characteristic of the renouncer is not necessarily misogynistic. Wilson and Makowski make this point clear in their wide-ranging and perceptive study of antimarriage literature: "Misogamous ideals or those opposed to the rearing of children do not necessarily preclude the glorification of women, nor does the exaltation of marriage and childrearing necessarily entail the exaltation of women."[125] In the exchange of views between the young merchant and his parents, the parents aggrandize marriage but demonize women. Siṇhalasārthabāhu, on the other hand, evidently does not regard all women as demons but only *this particular* woman.

Wilson and Makowski also suggest that the ascetic misogamy of the renouncer resembles the hedonistic misogamy of the libertine in one crucial respect: the renouncer and the libertine share a countercultural disregard for societal norms like monogamy.[126] For the renouncer, the state of wifelessness is achieved through chastity. For the libertine, the state of wifelessness is achieved through what Wilson and Makowski, following late antique precedents, call promiscuous celibacy.[127] In a Sanskrit version of the shipwrecked merchants' tale found in the *Mahāvastu,* the queen of the *rākṣasī*s provides some pathetic embellishments in support of her tale of woe that highlight the similarity between renouncers and libertines:

> This is just like those men who have achieved their desire [*arthalabdhā*].[128] When a woman arouses their passion, then they talk about her hundreds of virtues. But when their passion is spent, we are made out to be *piśācanī*s and *rākṣasī*s and censured on account of a hundred blemishes.[129]

The renouncer never marries because he knows that feminine charms are nothing but intoxicating dissimulations. The sensually intoxicated libertine never marries because he has a propensity to wake up stone cold sober in the night and find in his lover only the mere semblance of beauty. Where the renouncer's solution is to remain chaste, the libertine's solution is to seek new and hopefully more enticing lovers, to play the game of love but always remain a bachelor.

Poetic evocations of the spell of love and beauty like the harem scene in Aśvaghoṣa's *Buddhacarita* were probably intended as much for worldly people whose tastes tend toward the erotic end of the *rasa* spectrum as for renouncers who tend to savor the repulsive. The *Buddhacarita* is, after all, widely recognized as a literary masterpiece that set the standards for generations of erotic court poetry; refined, courtly audiences would perhaps derive pleasure from the frisson created by forbidden combinations of antithetical *rasas.* But ultimately, Aśvaghoṣa insists, it is peace and not pleasure that is the goal of his poetry. Aśvaghoṣa explains at the end of one of his works that he has dealt with subjects other than salvation in order to capture audiences who are not particularly devoted to the pursuit of salvation; such is the way of poetry (*kāvya-dharma*): one makes bitter medicine palatable by adding honey to it.[130] If the story of Gotama's "waking" in the night that Aśvaghoṣa describes in the *Buddhacarita* can be appreciated by libertines as well as renouncers, then Aśvaghoṣa has mixed his medicine well.

The scene of awakening in the harem is not only a watershed moment in the story of the Buddha; it also appears as a central turning point in post-Aśokan hagiography. In the lives of prominent members of the Buddha's *sangha*, the erotic space of the women's apartments is often shown to be a funereal place of death and decay. In the following chapter, I explore the role of horrific figurations of the feminine in Pāli hagiographies of the post-Aśokan period, noting the frequency with which the achievements of male saints are linked to the sight of dead and dying women.

CHAPTER THREE

False Advertising Exposed: Horrific Figurations of the Feminine in Pāli Hagiography

If her bowels and flesh were cut open, you would see what filth is covered by her white skin. If a fine crimson cloth covered a pile of foul dung, would anyone be foolish enough to love the dung because of it? . . . There is no plague which monks should dread more than women: the soul's death.

Roger de Caen, *Carmen de Mundi Contemptu*

I desire the body when it is covered (with skin),
So why this distaste for it when uncovered?
Since I have no need for it then,
Why copulate with it when it is covered?

Śāntideva, *Bodhisattvacaryāvatāra*

A woman, infatuated, came to a *bhikkhu* [monk] and stripped off her clothes. The *bhikkhu,* without battling an eyelid, said: "Now take off your skin."

Bhikkhu Khantipālo, *Bag of Bones*

Horrific Transformations in Bedroom Settings

One of the first men to join the Buddha's *sangha* was an affluent youth named Yasa.[1] Yasa, like the Buddha himself, was "delicately brought up,"[2] the pampered son of a wealthy man.[3] Before becoming a monk, he lived in three different mansions: one for the cold season, one for the hot season, and one for the rainy season. Like the youthful Gotama, Yasa was also captivated by the sensual pleasures offered by a harem filled with dancing girls—so captivated that he did not descend from his rainy season mansion for four months.[4]

But one evening Yasa nodded off in the midst of the revelry. Soon all of the women of his harem fell asleep too, clutching their musical instruments to their bodies. With the oil lights blazing, everyone slept soundly until Yasa suddenly woke up in the middle of the night and looked around. The commentary to the *Theragāthā* states that Yasa saw the change in his sleeping retinue and, filled with agitation (*saṃvega*), put on his golden shoes and departed. Exiting through the gates of the city that the gods had opened for him, Yasa left town.[5] In its account of this watershed moment in Yasa's life, the Pāli *Vinaya* describes Yasa observing a scene much like what the *bodhisattva* saw in his harem. One woman has disheveled hair; one is drooling; and one is muttering in her sleep. The women look so different, their appearance so altered by sleep that "one would think a cremation ground was before the eyes."[6] Seeing this, "his mind was established in aversion" and he went forth from home to homelessness with no obstacle, all doors swinging open at his approach thanks to the power of divine supporters of the Dharma.

Making his escape with the assistance of sympathetic deities just as Gotama did, Yasa headed toward the Deer Park at Benares, where the Buddha and the five members of his newly established *sangha* were staying.[7] Beside himself with agitation, Yasa was walking around muttering in a state of gloom and doom when he met the Buddha, who was out walking in the predawn air. The Buddha called Yasa over, comforted him, and explained the basic principles of generosity, moral conduct, the obtaining of heavenly births, and the path that leads beyond birth and death. While the Buddha was attending to Yasa, however, Yasa's father showed up at Deer Park looking for his son. The Buddha took the opportunity to explain the Dharma to Yasa's father, and as he did so, Yasa himself became an Arhat. At this point even if Yasa's father had insisted that his son come home, it would not have been possible for Yasa to do so. Once a layperson becomes an Arhat, there are only two possibilities. He or she must either go forth (*pabbajjā*) from home as a renouncer or go out (*parinibbāna*) by dying.[8] Yasa's father was in no position to argue with the Blessed One; he himself was so convinced by the Buddha's words that he became the first lay supporter (*upāsaka*) of the *sangha.* Far from opposing the ordination of his son, Yasa's father invited the Blessed One and Yasa, as the Buddha's personal attendant, to take a meal at the family home.[9] According to the commentary to the *Theragāthā,* the Buddha then ordained Yasa with the usual formula, "Come, monk" (*ehi, bhikkhu*). The moment he said these two words, Yasa's beard and hair miraculously shrank to a length appropriate to a monk and he was instantly equipped with the eight requisites (such as robes, bowl, etc.) of a monk.[10]

Yasa, like the Buddha himself, renounced the sumptuous lifestyle of a wealthy householder and took on the austere emblems of the monk. In spite of the enchanting luxury of his surroundings, he saw the absurdity of living like a god, the folly of enjoying the best of what *saṃsāra* has to offer. Just like the *bodhisattva,* Yasa abruptly abandoned a harem filled with beautiful women because he was able to see through the semblance of beauty and discern there the squalor of the cremation ground. This is no mean achievement. Yasa could easily have gone the way of the libertine and sought more glamorous women for his harem. Instead he fled from the harem in a state of shock and, in that highly receptive state, listened to the words of the Buddha and become an Arhat that very day.

One may well ask, as certain members of the *sangha* are reported to have asked the Buddha, what accounts for Yasa's perspicacity. It was Yasa's karma, the Buddha explains in a Pāli commentary to the *Dhammapada* (*Dhammapadāṭṭhakathā*), which led him to wake in the middle of the night and discern the speciousness of feminine charms. In a past life, Yasa had perceived the foulness of the body while cremating a pregnant female corpse; this grisly experience (combined with Yasa's determination to become an Arhat in the future) made Yasa so sensitive to the transience of feminine beauty that he was able to see a cremation ground in the luxury of the harem. The *Dhammapadāṭṭhakathā*'s account occurs as part of a series of flashbacks explaining how those who came to hold positions of precedence in the *sangha* laid the karmic foundations for their achievements:

> The Teacher was asked, "Blessed One, what deeds did the fifty-five people headed by the noble youth Yasa do?"
>
> "They also resolved to become Arhats in the presence of a Buddha. Doing many meritorious deeds after that, they became companions before the birth of the [present] Buddha. By banding together in a group, they earned merit going about tending to the corpses of the poor."
>
> "One day they saw a pregnant woman who had died. [Saying] 'Let's cremate her,' they took her to the cremation ground. Five peo-

> ple were selected to cremate her, and the rest went back to the village. The young Yasa reached an awareness of the foul [*asubhasaññaṃ*] while cremating that body, turning it over and over and piercing it with stakes. To the other four men he said: 'Brothers, look at this impure, foul-smelling, loathsome body. Here and there the skin has broken open, resembling [the hide of] a spotted cow.' The others also reached an awareness of the foul right there. These five men then went to the village and told the rest of their friends. And young Yasa went home and told his mother, father, and wife. They all developed awareness of the foul too."
>
> "This is their previous *kamma* [Sanskrit, *karma*]. For Yasa, awareness of the cremation ground [*susānasaññā*] arose in the harem. For all of them, their distinctive attainments arose from that [previous] foundation for achievement."[11]

Another monk who sees a cremation ground in his bedroom is Cittahattha. For those of us who doubt that we have what it takes to follow the Buddha's Dharma, Cittahattha's story is a great inspiration. Except for the omniscient Buddha himself, no one thought this man would manage to stay in the *sangha,* much less become an Arhat. But he was able to achieve that lofty goal thanks to the shock that he received from seeing his wife asleep. The Buddha of the *Dhammapadāṭṭhakathā* paints a delightfully satirical picture of this monk who is ironically dubbed Thera Cittahattha ("Elder Thought-Controlled") because he is as indecisive as the day is long. Cittahattha is a married man of limited means who initially joins the *sangha* to ensure for himself a comfortable life and a plentiful supply of food. But, put to work as an assistant to more senior monks, Cittahattha resents the imposition and returns home to his wife. After a few days of tending the forest-fields at home, however, Cittahattha misses the relative ease of the monastic life. Putting his ploughing implements away and donning his robes, he leaves home and is again received into the *sangha.* The same pattern recurs six times in succession, until on his seventh return to the householder's life, Cittahattha's wife appears visibly pregnant:

> From his going back and forth, his wife became pregnant. On the seventh time, he returned from the forest with his ploughing implements, went to the house to put his yoke away, and entered the bedroom, saying to himself, "I'll put on my yellow robe again." Now his wife had lain down for a nap and was asleep at that moment. Her

> outer garment had fallen off, saliva was flowing from her mouth, snores resonated in her nasal passages, and her mouth was wide open. She looked like a bloated corpse. Thinking, "This is transient [*aniccaṃ*] and dis-eased [*duḥkhaṃ*]" he said to himself: "To think that because of this [*imaṃ nissāya*], all the time I've been a monk, I've been unable to stick to the monastic life!" Grabbing his yellow robe by the hem, he ran out of the house, tying the robe about his belly as he ran.[12]

Attributing the wayward monk's failure to the siren song of the wife is a commonplace in such stories. Apparently, the redactors responsible for framing Cittahattha's story saw no incongruity in blaming the wife of this lazy, indecisive monk for her husband's own flightiness. Indeed, the unsteadiness of his mind must be attributed to her powers of attraction so that the revolting sight of her swollen, cadaverous body can serve as a remedy to Cittahattha's indecisiveness. Here, as in so many cases of feminine transformation for the edification of a wayward monk, the sight of a hideously altered woman has a salutary effect on the male spectator. Cittahattha's lethargy disappears the moment he perceives his wife as a swollen corpse.

In narratives that feature horrifically transformed female bodies, the alteration of the woman is the key to eradicating the man's desire. Although it is technically not the woman but the man's deluded ideas *about her* that are responsible for his desire, the destruction of her beauty often suffices to destroy his desire. Thus Cittahattha's delusions dissolve when his wife's appearance is so radically altered by sleep that he cannot continue to view her as desirable.[13] That a woman's altered appearance can extinguish a man's desire once and for all is suggested not only by Cittahattha but also by his mother-in-law. As Cittahattha runs pell-mell from his home, he attracts the attention of his mother-in-law, who goes inside to see what has happened: "Entering the house and seeing her sleeping daughter, she realized that he saw her, was filled with remorse, and left. She smacked her daughter, saying, 'Get up, you wench! Your husband saw you asleep, became remorseful, and left. He will never be your husband again.'"[14]

Her daughter is considerably more sanguine about Cittahattha's behavior: "Go away, mother! So what if he's left? In a few days, he'll return." But Cittahattha's mother-in-law was right; her son-in-law would never return again. As Cittahattha walked along, muttering about how quickly beauty fades, he reached the stage of path progress known as entering the stream. When he got to the monastery and asked to be ordained again, his fellow monks were justifiably outraged, given the man's track record. They tell him, "We can't ordain you, you blockhead" (literally, "Your head is like a whetstone!").[15] But Cittahattha insists that he be given one more chance and so he is again received into the *sangha.* Within just a few days, Cittahattha becomes an Arhat.[16] When the other monks taunt him with suggestions that it is about time for him to go back to his wife now that a few days have passed, Cittahattha reveals that he is no longer plagued by such thoughts. The monks go to the Buddha to report that Cittahattha is telling a lie.[17] But the Buddha explains that Cittahattha is telling the truth: "Yes, monks, my son [*mama putto*] came and went when he was ignorant of the Dharma and had an unsteady mind; but now his merit and demerit are abandoned."[18]

Thanks to Cittahattha's perception of his wife as a bloated corpse, this indecisive ne'er-do-well saw the Dharma manifest in the world and achieved the mental stability necessary for becoming an Arhat. Cittahattha's wife became a living display board for him, an instantiation of the abstract truth of the Dharma; seeing this truth set him free from his chronic preoccupation with creature comforts, his inability to see the world as a house on fire. In serving this liberative function for her husband, Cittahattha's wife is by no means unique. There are a number of women who, according to Pāli hagiographic tradition, became object lessons for members of the *sangha* after death, when their once alluring bodies had become swollen with putrefaction.

Horrific Transformations Set in Cremation Grounds

Stories featuring grotesquely altered women whose somatic transformations lead to the edification of a wayward monk typically describe a particular named monk who encounters the dead body of an unnamed woman. The story of Sirimā, however, reverses that pattern. In this narrative, appearing in the *Dhammapadāṭṭhakathā* under the title "Sirimā's story" (*Sirimāvatthu*) and in a Pāli commentary to the *Vimānavatthu* under the title *Sirimāvimāna* ("Sirimā's paradise"), we are told quite a bit about Sirimā but very little about the unnamed young monk who encounters her dead body.[19]

Sirimā's story is intertwined with that of a woman named Uttarā, whose equanimity in the face of Sirimā's bellicosity prompted Sirimā to renounce her profitable career as a courtesan and become a lay follower of the Buddha; all accounts begin by referring to this conversion experience.[20] But although the story begins with Sirimā's life history and thus with Sirimā as the subject, by the end of the tale Sirimā no longer occupies the subject position. Her convenient death makes her body an ideal object of meditation for a monk who has fallen madly in love with her. Nevertheless, I would say that Sirimā is an exceptionally well developed character, given the conventions of the genre; no other horrific "heroine" whom I have encountered in post-Aśokan literature has anything like the subjectivity that distinguishes Sirimā from a mere object of sight.

The tale of Sirimā is atypical in another respect. Where other narratives set in the cremation ground describe private encounters involving a single monk or a small group of monks, Sirimā is put on public display at the request of the Buddha. The moral opportunity afforded by Sirimā's dead body is deemed so salutary to the general populace that all citizens are made to contemplate her flyblown corpse.

Sirimā's story goes like this. After her conversion, she becomes a generous patron of the *sangha.* She spends sixteen *kahāpaṇa*s (copper coins) per day on food donations to the *sangha,* providing lavish meals for up to eight monks in her home every morning.[21] With monks from many different monasteries enjoying meals at Sirimā's home, Sirimā's generosity and beauty soon become subjects of idle conversation among members of the *sangha.* A certain young monk hears about Sirimā from another monk who has just eaten at Sirimā's home. As he raves about how Sirimā's beauty is even more pleasing than the delicious foods she serves, the young monk falls in love with this woman whom he has never seen.[22] As a former courtesan of incomparable beauty and grace, Sirimā possesses charms that pose a distinct threat to the equanimity of those monks who are deluded as to the body's true nature (see fig. 4). For them, Sirimā is (in the language of the *Aṅguttara Nikāya*) a snare of Māra, a deadly dissimulation. This particular monk succumbs to the spell of Sirimā's reputed charms[23] and immediately sets off on an all-night journey in order to take alms at her home in the morning.

But, as luck would have it, just as the young monk sets off to see her, Sirimā falls ill. In the morning she has a high fever and is unable to wait on the monks personally. Nevertheless, Sirimā instructs her servants to carry her into the presence of the monks so that she can

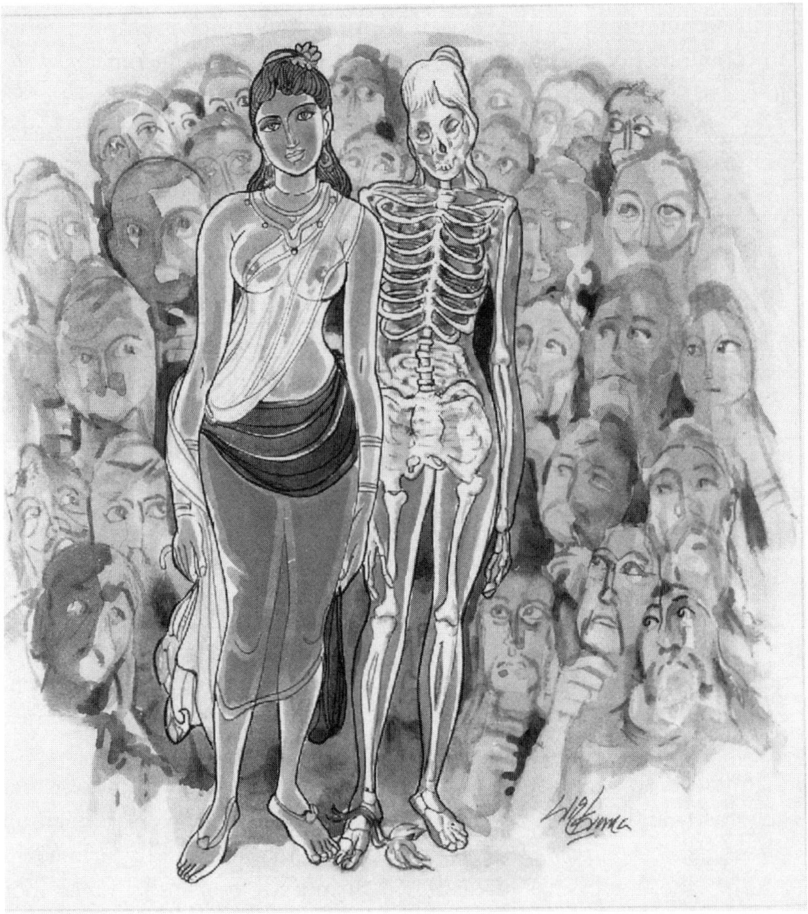

Figure 4. This contemporary image from an illustrated edition of the *Dhammapada* printed in Taiwan shows the beautiful Sirimā (as seen by the deluded) and the skeletal Sirimā (as seen by the wise). In the accompanying stanza from the *Dhammapada*, the Buddha exhorts the viewer not to be fooled by the semblance of beauty that obscures the true nature of Sirimā's body.

pay her respects. The lovelorn monk sees her and, instead of receiving the Dharmic message transmitted by the diseased body of Sirimā, decides that if she is this lovely when ill, she must be even more beautiful when well. "Then passion, accumulated during many millions of years, attacked him. He fell into a stupor and lost all interest in food."[24]

That evening, Sirimā died. When the teacher hears of her death, he sends the king the following message:

"There's to be no cremation for Sirimā. Have her body laid in the charnel field and post a guard, so that crows and dogs will not devour it." The king did so. Three days passed, one after another. One the fourth day the body began to bloat, and from the nine openings of her body, the nine gaping wounds, maggots poured out. Her whole body had burst open like a cracked vessel of rice.[25] The king caused a drum to go through the city and the following proclamation to be made, "Let everyone come see Sirimā. Except for youngsters guarding houses, all who refuse to come will be fined eight *kahāpaṇa*s."[26]

Now that young monk had lain for four days without touching food, hearing nothing anyone said to him. The rice in his bowl had gone putrid and moldy. Then the other monks who were his companions came and told him that the Teacher was on his way to see Sirimā. When the young monk, lying there, heard the word "Sirimā," he jumped to his feet. Someone said to him, "The Teacher is going to see Sirimā. Are you coming too?" "I'm coming," he answered. And tossing the food out of his bowl, he washed the bowl and put it in his bag and then set out with the company of monks.[27]

Not knowing that Sirimā is dead, the young monk eagerly rushes along with the others to the burning ground, where all the citizens have assembled, monks and the Buddha on one side of the body, nuns, laypeople, and king on the other.[28] Once the audience has assembled, the Buddha establishes that this corpse is indeed the lovely Sirimā and then instructs the king as follows: "'Send a drum through the city and let it be known that whoever will pay a thousand *kahāpaṇa*s for Sirimā may have her.' No one said 'ah' or 'hmm.' The king informed the Teacher, 'They won't have her, Blessed One.' 'Well then, great king, lower the price.'"[29]

By dropping the price in gradual increments, the fact that no man will have Sirimā at any price is made evident to all spectators, especially the lovelorn monk. The teacher concludes:

Monks, look at this available woman adored by so many people. In this very city men used to pay a thousand *kahāpaṇa*s for the sake of spending one night with this woman. Now there is no one who will take her even for free. Her beauty has perished and decayed. Saying, "Monks, look at this diseased body," he spoke the following stanza [*Dhammapada* 147]:

> "Look at this decorated image, an elevated mass of wounds. This diseased thing is highly fancied, [although] it's neither permanent nor stable."[30]

The love-smitten monk is cured of his dangerous condition by an elaborate spectacle orchestrated by the Buddha for his edification as well as the edification of the entire populace. With his passion aroused by the thought of seeing Sirimā in all her glory, the hapless monk ends up instead contemplating Sirimā as a flyblown corpse.

The therapeutic conflation of lust and aversion in this story is strikingly similar to aversion therapy. Given that lust, in the Buddhist scheme of things, is a physically and mentally enervating condition,[31] and knowing that the Great Physician was not given to wasting time over elaborate etiological speculation when an effective cure lay readily at hand, I think that the analogy of aversion therapy is not inappropriate.[32] The charming but ultimately cadaverous female forms that serve as object lessons for lovelorn monks beckon one moment and repulse the next. As in aversion therapy, the lust of the male spectator is initially engaged but ultimately subverted as an alluring spectacle is transformed into a repulsive one. Using this technique, the Buddha is reported to have succeeded in curing quite a few of his lust-ridden monks; among the Buddha's success stories are some truly pernicious cases of necrophilia.

A number of sources indicate that necrophilia posed a serious threat to the celibate life of the *sangha* in India. The Pāli *Vinaya* contains lurid passages describing sexual offenses committed by members of the *sangha* with dead bodies, passages that I. B. Horner left largely untranslated.[33] The practice of cremation-ground meditation brought members of the *sangha* into close proximity with dead bodies of both sexes. While the practice of *asubhabhāvanā* calls for decayed or otherwise disfigured bodies, the meditator seeking the signs of foulness must find an appropriate object of meditation among an array of corpses, some less decayed than others. The bodies of paupers and criminals that were abandoned in the charnel fields of ancient India were not likely to have been hidden behind thick funereal shrouds, and thus the meditator would be privy to parts of the body not normally revealed for all to see. If the cremation ground in ancient India was a place where breasts and genitals were clearly displayed, it was also a fine and private place where people probably *did* embrace. Prostitutes on the lower end of the occupational hierarchy sold their bodies near burning grounds, and all manner of illicit activities went on in cremation grounds due to their relative privacy.[34] With the cremation ground a *demi-monde* where prostitutes met their customers, spies met their employers, and criminals divided their booty, it is not surprising that the thoughts of Buddhist monks practicing *asubhabhāvanā* there would occasionally have wandered from the signs of foulness displayed in dead bodies and turned to thoughts of illicit pleasure.

In the *Theragāthā,* a collection of verses ascribed to elder monks of the early *sangha,* several monks tell of having succumbed to the necrophilic charms of relatively undecayed female corpses while practicing meditation in the cremation ground. Their stories, detailed in the commentary to the *Theragāthā,* show that Buddhaghosa had every reason to be concerned about those monks who select female bodies as supports for *asubhabhāvanā.* Those who failed to heed admonishments such as Buddhaghosa's ran the risk of being overcome by sexual urges that could easily defeat the whole purpose of *asubhabhāvanā.* One man, named Kulla, is described in the commentary to the *Theragāthā* as a man of "lustful behavior, benighted by lust."[35] Knowing the ways of Kulla's mind, the Buddha tells him to practice *asubhabhāvanā* unceasingly. But the hapless *bhikkhu* continued to have lustful thoughts, even in the cremation ground. Seeing various kinds of foul corpses, Kulla was able to perceive the sign of foulness momentarily. But as soon as he left the cremation ground, Kulla was overcome by sensual passion. Knowing Kulla's tendencies, the Buddha accompanied the monk to the cremation ground one day. There, through the exercise of his psychic powers, the Teacher created an illusory display designed to modify Kulla's lustful thoughts. First, the Buddha conjured up an undecayed body for Kulla to observe—the form of a young woman who had died quite recently.[36] As soon as he perceived that Kulla was aroused, the Buddha caused this appealing body to become extremely disagreeable in smell and appearance, with maggots pouring from every opening. The Buddha then emitted rays of light and sparked Kulla's mindfulness with the following exhortation:

> See, Kulla, the abject, foul, putrid body,
> Oozing, dripping, cherished by fools.[37]

Hearing these words and observing the condition of the hideous corpse that had only moments ago been the alluring body of a young woman, Kulla finally understood the foul nature of the body. The illusory body's rapid transformation from an object of desire to an object of loathing had afforded Kulla an insight into the foulness of all bodies that he obviously lacked, prior to this lesson, when seeing the bodies of living women that showed no signs of decay. Following this insight, Kulla then achieved several significant stages of path progress in rather short order, culminating in Arhatship.[38]

Where Kulla was too prone to sexual arousal to achieve a breakthrough on his own, the monk Rājadatta was able to discern the sign of foulness in the cremation ground without the assistance of the Buddha. Indeed, this monk even managed to see the sign of the foul in the midst of lust so acute that it became necessary for him to interrupt his meditation. Rājadatta, as the commentary to the *Theragāthā* explains, was a young man belonging to a wealthy merchant family.[39] On coming of age, he led a caravan with 500 carts of merchandise to Rājagaha. There he met a glamourous and beautiful high-class courtesan (*gaṇikā*) who, like Sirimā, charged 1,000 *kahāpaṇa*s per day.[40] Rājadatta fell in love with this courtesan and quickly ran through all his money buying her affection. Having squandered his entire fortune, Rājadatta could no longer afford to pay the courtesan's fee. Barely able to keep himself fed and clothed, the wretched young man wandered around aimlessly in a state of shock (*saṃvegappatto*).[41] One day, however, Rājadatta heard the Buddha teaching and was impressed by what he heard. So Rājadatta joined the *sangha* and, undertaking the *dhutanga*s, began to spend time in a cremation ground practicing *asubhabhāvanā.*

The courtesan, in the meantime, had found herself another caravan leader with a wealth of *kahāpaṇa*s to spend. This merchant wore a precious jewel that the courtesan admired. One day she arranged to have the merchant killed in order to acquire his jewel. However, some of the merchant's servants heard what transpired. Investigators were sent out. They entered the home of the courtesan during the night and killed her, disfiguring her skin and other parts of her body. Her body was then abandoned in the cremation ground where Rājadatta was staying.[42]

When Rājadatta saw the body he approached it in order to study its loathsomeness. But the monk was overcome by sensual passion for this relatively fresh female body, portions of which had not been spoiled by dogs and jackals. With an agitated mind (*saṃviggataramānaso*), Rājadatta stepped away from the courtesan's body for a few moments and then returned, resuming the meditation with his mind intent on grasping only the sign of foulness (*asubhanimittaṃ*).[43] Like Kulla, Rājadatta quickly moved through several levels of attainment of the Buddhist path and became an Arhat there in the cremation ground.

The venal, moneygrubbing courtesan is a stock character in Sanskrit drama.[44] Here, the stereotypically heartless courtesan takes advantage of Rājadatta's desire for her and leaves him without a *kahāpaṇa,* only to reappear later in his life as an object of meditation, a source of equanimity and insight. There is great irony in this. Rājadatta sees a woman whose beauty had exercised an uncanny power over him turned into an abject, charmless thing. The act of contemplating the courtesan's dead body makes Rājadatta the master of his emotions, liberating him from the spell of her feminine charms. Thus the woman that had deprived Rājadatta of his autonomy now helps to restore it.[45]

The experiences of Kulla and Rājadatta suggest that even if monks courted disaster by ignoring the warnings of Buddhaghosa about viewing bodies of the opposite sex, encounters with attractive female bodies in the cremation ground could lead to new insights. The path to wisdom is not always the path of prudence; sometimes the path of prudence is quicker and more efficacious. In the case of Kulla, the Buddha takes the calculated risk of encouraging the prurient interest of the *bhikkhu* in order to subvert that lust in the end. Likewise, in an explanatory narrative in the *Dhammapadāṭṭhakathā,* the Buddha orchestrates an arousing encounter in the charnel field in order to chasten a group of forest-dwelling monks who believe that they have mastered their desires (see fig. 5):

> Five hundred monks, having been in the presence of the Teacher and gotten their meditation subjects, went to the forest. After great exertion and struggle, they achieved success in meditation. [Saying] "We've accomplished our duty as renouncers by overcoming the afflictions [*kilesānaṃ*]; let's notify the Teacher of the virtues we've attained by ourselves," they left the forest. At the moment they reached the gateway, the Teacher told the Elder Ānanda: "There's no reason, Ānanda, for these monks to come in and see me. Let them return to see me after they go off to a charnel ground." The Elder went and told them what the Buddha had said. They didn't ask why they were to go to the charnel ground. They just assumed that the omniscient Buddha must have a good reason for doing this. Going to the charnel ground, they saw corpses that had fallen one or two days ago. They experienced aversion for those bodies, but at the same time found

Figure 5. An illustrated edition of the *Dhammapada* printed in Taiwan depicts one of the overconfident monks chastened after succumbing to temptation in the charnel field.

that they felt desire for the newly fallen bodies. At that moment, they knew that afflictions existed in them.

The Teacher, seated in the Perfumed Chamber, suffused them with radiance and, as if they were face to face, said: "Is it really appropriate, monks, for you to experience passionate attraction on seeing such a collection of bones?"[46]

Cremation as Horrific Transformation

Desire, as Peter Brown has shown with regard to the Desert Fathers tradition, can serve as an accurate seismograph of the soul, an indispensable method of gauging inner states.[47] In the case of these overconfident and somewhat conceited monks, necrophilic arousal provides a clue to the need for further effort. Yet, however useful necrophilic arousal may be in helping the meditator to gauge the purity of his mind, such forms of desire can obviously defeat the purpose of contemplating dead bodies.

One way to overcome necrophilia is to subject the charming cadaver to further transformation through burning. Thus the dead body that should be repulsive but instead arouses desire can be made into a thing of horror by cremation. In the first book of the *Dhammapadāṭṭhakathā,* in a section devoted to the past and present lives of the chief disciples, there are two notable instances of insight achieved through the cremation of a female body. One has already been mentioned—the young man Yasa (who fled from the harem in the middle of the night and became an Arhat in the morning) laid the foundation for his insights in the harem when, in a past life, he perceived the foulness of a pregnant female corpse that he and his companions were cremating. In another narrative found in the first section of the *Dhammapadāṭṭhakathā,* an ascetic older monk named Mahākāla (the Older Kāla) watches as the flames transform a still alluring female corpse into a charmless—and harmless—tangle of limbs.[48]

When Mahākāla joins the *sangha,* he declares himself too old for scriptural study and so adopts the ascetic practice of spending each night in the cremation ground. Kālī, the groundskeeper, sees Mahākāla haunting the grounds late at night and instructs him to report to the proper authorities, lest he be taken for a thief seeking refuge from the law.[49] She then indicates that if he becomes an Arhat in her burning ground, she will cremate the next abandoned body with honors; but if he fails to achieve this goal, she will drag, desecrate, and mutilate the next body to come her way.[50] The elder answered her: "All right, ma'am. But if you see a suitable object for meditation on material form, would you please let me know?"[51] Conveniently, a remarkably good subject dies that day:

> Now a certain young woman of social standing was attacked by a disease which overtook her quite suddenly. She died that evening, without a sign of withering or weariness. During the night, her family and servants brought her body to the burning ground along with some wood and oil. Giving the keeper of the burning ground a fee, they left the body with her and departed. When Kālī removed the cloth

> that covered this one who had died so suddenly and saw her delightfully pleasing, golden-colored body, she thought to herself, "This corpse is a suitable object of meditation for him."[52]

Kālī informs Mahākāla, who "examined the body from the soles of the feet to the tips of the hair," then said: "Throw this extremely attractive, golden-colored form into the fire, and as soon as the tongues of fire have laid hold of it, please tell me."[53] The keeper of the burning ground prepared the pyre and called the monk as instructed:

> When the flames had attacked the flesh, the color of the body was like that of a mottled cow; the feet were curled up and dangled curiously; the hands were bent back; the forehead was without skin. The Elder thought to himself, "This body, which only moments ago caused those who looked at it to forget the precepts, has now attained destruction, has now attained decay."[54]

As a result of seeing this enticing feminine form transformed into a thing of horror before his eyes, Mahākāla develops insight into impermanence and, that evening, becomes an Arhat.

This description of Mahākāla's attainments is set within a larger narrative about Mahākāla and his younger brother, Cūlakāla. The point of the story is to contrast the spiritual success of the older brother with the failure of the younger. The younger brother requests ordination only to be with Mahākāla, whom he hopes to lure back to the householder's life. But his wives are unhappy with Cūlakāla's decision to follow his brother into the *sangha.* Saying "*Now* we'll get our husband," they invite the Buddha and his monks to take a meal at their home.[55] When the Buddha sends Cūlakāla ahead to see that the seating arrangements are done properly, his spurned wives see to it that Cūlakāla's authority is undermined. They put the highest, most important seats out for the novice monks and arrange for the venerable elders to sit on low seats fit only for novices. When Cūlakāla protests that they are doing everything wrong, his wives at first ignore him and then begin to taunt him: "What are you doing wandering around? By what right do you designate seats? With whose permission did you renounce? Who ordained you? Why did you come here?"[56] After rebuking Cūlakāla for failing to consult them about his decision to take ordination, his angry wives then tear off Cūlakāla's robes and dress him in the white clothing of a layman. Being literally defrocked, Cūlakāla is thus made into the householder that his wives wish him to be. Finally, in a brilliant coup de grâce that shows their affinities to such flower-wielding enemies of the renouncer as Kāma and Māra, Cūlakāla's wives adorn their husband with a flower garland. Now there is absolutely no mistaking this man for a monk. For members of the *sangha,* such garlands—along with the application of jewelry, perfumes, and other ways of enhancing the beauty of the body—are expressly forbidden. In adorning their husband with a flower garland, Cūlakāla's wives show themselves to be true daughters of Māra.[57] As we will see in chapter 4, one of Māra's favorite ways of humiliating members of the *sangha* is to bind them with garlands of flowers.

In contrast to Cūlakāla, shamed at the hands of temptresses, the older monk achieves insight with the help of two very impure but ultimately redemptive figures: a female cremation-ground keeper and a female corpse. It is unusual to find two sets of women opposed in this way. In most other post-Aśokan tales of insight achieved through aversion, the same woman plays both the role of temptress and the role of redemptress. Casting one woman in the dual role of temptress and redemptress neatly short-circuits desire by collapsing the opposed forces of attraction and repulsion into one body.

The Duplicity of the Female Body

That what attracts is easily resolved into what repels is due to the widespread Indic idea of the duplicity of the female body. If one can only see through the cosmetics and ornaments a woman wears, Hindu and Buddhist texts of the post-Aśokan period declare, one will discern a walking cadaver, a vessel of filth. Karen Lang notes this emphasis on the artificiality of female beauty in her article "Lord Death's Snare: Gender-Related Imagery in the 'Theragāthā' and 'Therīgāthā.'"[58] In the verses ascribed to the elder monks of the primitive *sangha,* the ornamented exterior of the female body is often depicted as a false facade, an artificial construct fashioned to deceive unsuspecting men. The monk Nāgasamāla, for example, describes a woman he saw dancing in the street as a trap set by Māra:

> Ornamented, nicely dressed, garlanded, and anointed with sandalwood paste, a female dancer swayed to music in the middle of the boulevard.

> I had gone into town for alms and was going along when I saw her—ornamented, nicely dressed, laid out like a snare of Māra.[59]

Using the X-ray vision of a man practiced in seeing through the facade of female beauty, Nāgasamāla reminded himself of what he was really seeing in looking at the dancer: "This is a collection of bones, bound up with sinews, plastered with flesh, covered with skin, foul, smelly, loathsome, disgusting, and subject to impermanence, erosion, abrasion, dissolution, and disintegration."[60] Not only did Nāgasamāla in this way avoid falling into Māra's trap, but he attained insight and became an Arhat then and there.[61]

The monk Raṭṭhapāla, in begging alms at his father's house one day, nearly falls into a trap set by his parents and his former wives—they conspire to lock him in the house and (like the wives of Cūlakāla) dress him in the white clothing of a layman.[62] Raṭṭhapāla extricates himself from this situation by rising into the air and levitating to another location. But before he departs from the locked house, Raṭṭhapāla congratulates himself on having seen through the artifice of feminine beauty and thus escaped the cluthes of Māra's snare:

> See this form decorated with jeweled earrings—it's just bones bound up with skin looking beautiful because of its outer garments.
>
> Feet decorated with red lac and powdered face are fit to delude a fool, but not someone seeking to go beyond.
>
> Hair decorated in a checkerboard style, eyes outlined with kohl are fit to delude a fool, but not someone seeking to go beyond.
>
> The putrid body so adorned, like a clean new jar of ointment that's decorated on the outside, is fit to delude a fool, but not someone seeking to go beyond.
>
> The hunter set down the snare, but the deer did not rub against the net; having eaten the bait, [the deer say] "Let's go," while the deer trappers groan.[63]

A number of analogies found in post-Aśokan texts suggest the duplicity of the hunter's trap that is the female body. As we have seen, the *Lalitavistara* compares women to vases filled with filth and to razor blades smeared with honey. According to the first analogy, the body is a container that is nicely decorated on the outside but excrementally impure on the inside. In the second case, the body is a dangerous instrument of destruction that is covered with a false but inviting facade. A woman's outer appearance is thus a sweet, delectable bait intended to trap some unsuspecting man. The *Brahmavaivarta Purāṇa*, a medieval *Vaiṣṇavite* text, uses another container metaphor to develop this idea of the duplicity of the female body. In this text, the female body is compared to a jar of poison with honey smeared at the mouth.[64]

The import of such metaphors is abundantly clear. Her charms intact, a woman is a deceptive mantrap for those men who lack the insight needed to see her as she truly is. Her beauty is the honey that draws flies and fools onto the razor's edge of destruction. As long as what is inside her remains invisible to a man's gaze, she masters him by wielding the power of attraction. In this way, women lure men "down the garden path" that leads to domestic entanglement and further entrapment within *saṃsāra*. But because the duplicitous female form has two components, an inner and an outer, the power that a woman can exercise over a man is limited by what he sees of her. If he sees the beauty that she constructs through the application of cosmetics, clothing, perfumes, and ornaments, he becomes her captive. But should he get a glimpse of her inner bodily condition, the spell of her specious beauty is broken. A woman whose charms are temporarily disfigured by sleep or permanently destroyed by death leads a man down the path of liberation by disabusing him of his misapprehensions about the female form, teaching him that what appears attractive is not always what it seems.

Punishment as Horrific Transformation

The story of Upagupta and Vāsavadattā is a classic case of the temptress turned redemptress by means of a gruesome transformation of her body.[65] The *Divyāvadāna* presents Upagupta's encounter with Vāsavadattā as a significant episode in the premonastic life of this "Buddha without the marks" (*alakṣaṇako buddho*) who later in life would become an important leader of the *sangha* and adviser to King Aśoka.[66] It was Upagupta's visit with the dying courtesan that put him on the Buddhist path and laid the foundation for his considerable achievements as a teacher of the Dharma.

Vāsavadattā, we are told, is the most celebrated courtesan in the city of Mathurā. She first hears of a young perfume merchant named Upagupta when her servant returns from his perfume shop laden with all kinds of perfumes—much more than one could normally purchase for the money that the servant had been given to spend. When questioned, the servant girl explains that the young merchant Upagupta is kind and generous, doing business "according to Dharma."[67] Hearing that he is also very handsome, Vāsavadattā develops "passionate intentions towards him."[68] She sends her servant back to Upagupta's shop in order to arrange a tryst. But Upagupta refuses Vāsavadattā's offer to "experience pleasure" with her. He tells her very politely that it is the wrong time, that his *darśana,* his occasion of seeing/being seen, has not yet come.[69] Upagupta's enigmatic statement puzzles Vāsavadattā. But for the reader or listener familiar with the story or narratives of its type, Upagupta's statement is a dramatic foreshadowing of the funereal occasion when the two finally do meet face to face. Vāsavadattā decides that Upagupta must have turned her down for lack of funds. Being so resolutely honest in a profession not known for its ethical practices, she reasons, Upagupta must certainly be poor. So Vāsavadattā sends her servant back again to make sure that Upagupta understands the situation: what would cost another man many *kahāpaṇa*s, Upagupta can have for free. Once again, Upagupta refuses, saying that it is not yet time for them to meet.

One day, a handsome young caravan leader from the north arrives in Mathurā with 500 horses for sale. Making a tidy profit on the sale of his horses, this merchant wants to know who is the best of all the women of pleasure in town. When he hears of the famous Vāsavadattā, he is eager to become her lover, and she is more than happy to have him. But Vāsavadattā already has a man cohabiting with her and he refuses to be displaced by the new man in Vāsavadattā's life. After much heart-searching and consultation with her mother (according to Kṣemendra, author of the *Avadānakalpalatā*), Vāsavadattā decides to eliminate her current lover. She has the old lover killed and his body thrown onto a dung heap.[70]

Her crime, however, is discovered by the family of the slain man and reported to the king. The king establishes Vāsavadattā's guilt and then orders his men to cut off the courtesan's hands and feet as well as her nose and ears. Thus disfigured, Vāsavadattā and her dismembered parts are deposited in the cremation ground:

> When Upagupta heard that Vāsavadattā had been left in the cremation ground with her hands, feet, ears, and nose cut off, this thought

> occurred to him: "Before, she desired my seeing/being seen [*darśana*] with the marks of sensuality. But now, with her hands, feet, ears, and nose cut off, this is just the time for seeing her."[71] And he said: "When her body was covered with fine clothing and decorated with various ornaments, the sight of her at that time would not have been good for one set on liberation, having turned from birth and death. But now, because she has lost her conceitedness, passion, and excitement, because she has been wounded with sharp swords, this is the time to see her form that has been restricted to its intrinsic nature [*svabhāvaniyatasya rūpasya*]."[72]

There, in the place where members of the *sangha* contemplate the foulness of decaying bodies, Upagupta finally goes to see the woman he had not wished to visit before. Vāsavadattā is still alive, despite the considerable trauma to her body. Her servant girl, who has stayed with her mistress out of appreciation for past kindnesses, is busy shielding Vāsavadattā's body from crows and vultures when she sees Upagupta enter the cremation ground. She tells her mistress that Upagupta is approaching and surmises that he has come to take advantage of Vāsavadattā's offer before she (and it) expires. "That Upagupta to whom you sent me again and again has arrived; he's come afflicted by passion and desire, no doubt."[73] These are, perhaps, the thoughts of "one who has served too long in a house of prostitution and seen too many skewed forms of sexuality," John Strong hypothesizes. But Strong also notes that Kṣemendra, in an editorial aside, echoes the thinking of the servant girl in suggesting that Upagupta has finally come to enjoy the sexual favors Vāsavadattā had promised him.[74] "Who enters the interior simply because of its covering? Under no circumstances are embodied beings free of passion."[75] If the servant girl's thoughts are jaded by the grim facts of life she has seen in the whorehouse, then Kṣemendra—and by extension other compilers of Buddhist hagiographic tradition—is no less schooled in the perverse ways of the cremation ground that is the world.

Sitting in bloodstained mud with her entire body in terrible pain, Vāsavadattā is by no means eager to expose her body to Upagupta's gaze. According to the *Avadānakalpalatā*, Vāsavadattā modestly asks the servant girl to cover her exposed body using a rag as a makeshift loincloth, while she herself folds the stumps of her arms over her chest.[76] It is a vain gesture—vain in both the archaic sense of bootlessness (e.g., Ecclesiastes 1.2: "All is vanity, the preacher sayeth") and in the modern sense of pride in one's appearance. Vāsavadattā does not want to be seen at her worst because her self-esteem rides on how she looks. Thus in a pathetically vain gesture, she attempts to "pull herself together" in preparation for Upagupta's visit.

The *Divyāvadāna* suggests the possibility that it is not simply modesty that impels Vāsavadattā to cover her body and make herself presentable for Upagupta.[77] Wondering "How could he have desire and passion seeing me on the ground, dyed with blood, my radiance destroyed, afflicted by suffering?," she tells her maid to gather the amputated body parts together and hide them under a cloth.[78] Although presumably in no mood for pursuing pleasure with Upagupta, Vāsavadattā nevertheless wants Upagupta to desire her. Being desirable is everything to a woman who lives off the proceeds of her beauty. To earn her daily wages, Vāsavadattā knows she must always look her very best. It vexes her that Upagupta chose *this* moment to visit her—there were so many occasions when she was ready to be seen but Upagupta was uncooperative:

> When my body was fit to be seen [*darṣanakṣamam̩*], soft like the calyx of a lotus, and adorned with valuable garments and jewels, then I, the unlucky one, did not meet you. Why have you come here to see me now that my body, having lost its grace, pleasure, excitement, and wonder, is a terrible sight, unfit to be looked at [*darṣanākṣamam̩*], plastered with mud and blood?[79]

Vāsavadattā's dismay is perfectly reasonable. When her body was fit to be seen and enjoyed, her sexual overtures were met with enigmatic, sphinxlike responses that did not rule out the possibility of a tryst so much as delay it. Now that she is in no position to make good on her promises, Vāsavadattā is put in the curious position of having to keep up appearances in order not to lose face. Lest she be accused of false advertising, Vāsavadattā vainly attempts to conceal the evidence of her abject suffering and put her best foot forward.

But it is not the foot that is "fit to be seen" that Upagupta wants to look at—the object of Vāsavadattā's visit is the bloody appendages that Vāsavadattā is hiding from him, tucked away under a cloth. One of the ten types of bodies that Buddhaghosa lists in the *Visuddhimagga* as appropriate supports for the contemplation of foulness is the "hacked and scattered" or "cut and dismembered" corpse that has lost its appendages in battle or in retribution for crimes. Buddhaghosa instructs the meditator to gather the dismembered parts together into a facsimile of what the body would have looked like when alive using a stick in order to avoid titillation through tactile contact with the dismembered appendages (see fig. 6).[80] It is not the alluring Vāsavadattā that Upagupta came to see but the Vāsavadattā who is a *revenant,* a reanimated corpse.[81] To Upagupta, the human body is a living corpse in a continual state of putrefaction: "Those who take pleasure in this vile body," he tells Vāsavadattā, "are ignorant and reprehensible":

> Who could desire a body that is bound up with skin, dependent on blood, covered with hide, smeared with a mass of flesh, and entirely enveloped by a thousand veins? How could this be? Though a fool, sister, feels desire when seeing forms that are lovely on the outside, a wise man feels no desire, knowing them to be defiled on the inside.[82]

Upagupta is uncompromisingly candid about the reasons for his visit. It is the body that Vāsavadattā conceals from him—the naked, bleeding, grotesque Vāsavadattā—that he has come to see:

> Sister, I have not come to be with you on account of desire, but have come to see the true nature of foul desires.[83] Formerly, you were disguised by clothes, decorations, and various outer things that lead to passion, such that even those taking great pains to observe you as you really are could not do so. But now, your form is visible resting here in its true nature, free from artifice [*idaṃ tu rūpaṃ tava dṛśyam etat sthitaṃ svabhāve racanād viyuktam*].[84]

It is Vāsavadattā in her true, intrinsic nature—the festering boil with pus oozing out in various places—that Upagupta has been waiting all this time to see. He did not visit Vāsavadattā before now because he knew that she would not show it to him. All of her training as a courtesan would militate against showing Upagupta the phlegm and feces that lurk within her scented, sari-clad form. Even now, lying in a pool of blood without nose, ears, hands, and feet, she does not want Upagupta to see the grotesquerie she has become. Scrambling to cover up the unsightly mess, Vāsavadattā succeeds only in underscoring the ridiculousness of her situation. The pathetic gesture captured in Tibetan woodcut images of this episode conveys the irony of Vāsavadattā's actions; using the stumps of her arms to cover her nakedness, she is as profoundly naked as a human being can be.[85]

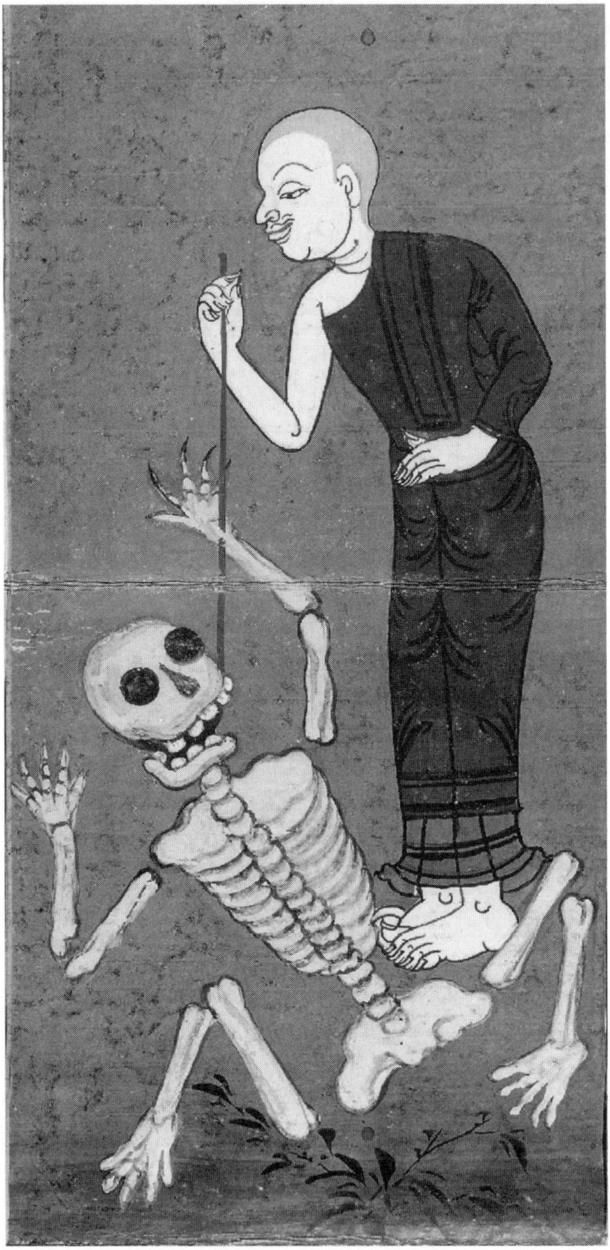

Figure 6. This illustration from a Thai meditation manual shows a monk using a stick to reconstitute a corpse for the purpose of meditation. Reproduced by permission of the British Library.

Laid out before Upagupta's gaze "like a patient etherised upon a table", Vāsavadattā is without outer trappings in a number of different senses.[86] She is not only seminude and unornamented, but she is also devoid of the very appendages that young, eligible women of post-Aśokan India were wont to decorate with cosmetics and ornaments. The palms of the hands and the soles of the feet were regularly embellished with red cosmetic paste (lac). Nostrils and earlobes were pierced and decorated with glittering jewelry. Without her outer covering of clothing, cosmetics, and ornaments—and without her decorated hands and feet, nostrils and ears—Vāsavadattā is wholly naked, entirely free of externals. And, from Upagupta's perspective, this is the appropriate moment for them to meet face to face. Now that she has been pared down to her essential nature, Vāsavadattā is finally fit for him to see.

Being deprived of both adornments and appendages to adorn, Vāsavadattā is as anonymous as a person can be, a true nobody. Like the anonymous cadaver used for dissection, she is a generic body that bears no distinguishing marks (Sanskrit, *lakṣana,* cognate with the English "lac") that declare her identity. In many cultures, ornamental additions to the body's surface have a discursive as well as a decorative function. Through piercing, scarifying, and painting the skin, subtle gradations of social status are inscribed on the surface of the body for all to see and know. Personal adornment silently explains who an individual is, as a social being, in those cultures and subcultures that have well-codified sartorial and cosmetic codes.[87]

It is often the case that adornment also tells how much a person is worth, how much wealth they have at their disposal.[88] This is especially true of women in Middle Eastern and Asian cultures (and also the Gypsies of Europe) who wear their personal wealth on the surface of their bodies in the form of rings, necklaces, anklets, and other ornaments made of precious metals and gems. Wearing one's wealth on the body as personal adornment makes it easy to liquefy one's assets; women who wear their worth in gold do not have to go to the bank when they require money. Since her beauty is her livelihood, Vāsavadattā's personal appearance is not just an index and receptacle of her wealth—it is also the means of production whereby more wealth is generated. Looking "like a million bucks" earned Vāsavadattā 1,000 *kahāpaṇa*s a day. Being shorn of her beauty, Vāsavadattā is thus prevented from turning her good looks into a commodity valued at 1,000 *kahāpaṇa*s. Were she by some miracle able to survive her punishment,

Vāsavadattā would in all likelihood have to find another way to make a living. She would certainly never be able to command such a high fee for her services again.

It is important to bear in mind that Vāsavadattā has been punished, and to understand what that punishment entails. Michel Foucault has written eloquently on the symbolic logic of corporal punishment.[89] In the forms of punishment practiced in Europe before the birth of the prison, the nature of the crime was graphically inscribed on the body of the criminal. Raised up on a scaffolding for all to see, the criminal's anatomy was manipulated so as to reveal the nature of the crime. By whipping, amputating, piercing, or branding the offending body part, the crime was re-presented, and the criminal was made to symbolically confess his or her crimes in receiving his or her punishment. Corporal punishment has its own grammar, and sometimes that grammar can be quite complex. Take, for example, the debate that occurred in the House of Commons concerning the proper punishment of Mr. Edward Floyde, a Roman Catholic condemned for making scandalous comments about an English princess:

> Sir Robert Phillips was of the opinion that since his offense had been without limitation, his punishment might likewise be without proportion. "He would have him ride with his face to a horse's tail from Westminister to the Tower, with a paper on his hat, wherein should be written, 'A Popish wretch that hath maliciously scandalized his majesty's children'". . . . Sir Francis Darcy "would have a hole burnt through his tongue, since that was the member that offended." Sir Jeremy Horsey thought the tongue should be cut out altogether. Sir George Goring agreed with none of the merciful gentlemen who had preceded him. "He would have his nose, ears, and tongue cut off; to be whipped at as many stages as he hath [rosary] beads, and to ride to every stage with his face to the horse's tail, and the tail in his hand, and at every stage to swallow a bead; and thus to be whipped to the Tower, and there to be hanged."[90]

In ancient India, too, the grammar of corporal punishment was complex enough to inscribe complicated messages on the body of the condemned. Books of religious law (*Dharma Sūtra*s and *Dharma Śāstra*s such as the well-known *Mānava Dharma Śāstra*) as well as more narrowly juridical lawbooks (such as the *Daṇḍaviveka of Vardhamāna Upādhyāya*) go far toward systematizing a grammar of penal torture by which the bodies of offenders were to be inscribed with the particular sign or stamp (*cihna*) that would indicate their crimes. The messages that may be written on the body of the condemned are as diverse as the actions that earn such marks. The *Mānava Dharma Śāstra,* for example, describes a variety of ways that the body of a low-caste man who presumes familiarity with or otherwise humiliates a Brahmin should be markedly to specify the offense:

> Should a low-status man try to sit down on the same seat as a high-status man, he should be branded on the buttocks and banished, or have his buttocks cut off. If out of arrogance he spits on a Brahmin, the king should have his lips cut off; if he urinates on him, the penis; if he farts at him, the anus. If he grasps him by the hair or feet, the beard, the throat, or the scrotum, [the king] should without hesitation have his hands cut off.[91]

Vāsavadattā's punishment, too, is an accurate mirror of her crimes. Just as he who pees on his superiors will lose his penis, so she who fleeces her customers will lose the basis of her livelihood. To say that Vāsavadattā has been deprived of the good looks that were her means of production and will henceforth no longer entice men to squander their fortunes on her is just a more complicated Marxian restatement of the old biblical dictum, "an eye for an eye, a tooth for a tooth." Because Vāsavadattā behaved like the stereotypically avaricious courtesan, using her charms to steal the gold of hapless men, the appendages that she painted with lac and embellished with golden ornaments (and, by extension, her good looks) are lawfully taken away from her. The mutilation of Vāsavadattā's face is particularly laden with significance. A mutilated face is much more conspicuous than a branded buttock. It is a fitting punishment for someone who stands accused of concealing her inner nature that she is marked in a way that is impossible to hide. Using gold, silver, and the radiant colors of the sun and moon that are the aesthetic equivalents of precious metals, Vāsavadattā inscribes her body as erotic and auspicious. She makes her hands, feet, ears, and nostrils sparkle to declare that she is conspicuously beautiful, radiantly fair, a luminous site for sore eyes (the Sanskrit noun *śubha*; Pāli, *subha,* connotes all this). But when her transgressions catch up with her and she is made to reenact and atone for them, these self-made marks are erased. Her punishment makes Vāsavadattā a palimpsest in which the marks she had inscribed on herself—and the places she tended to embellish—are removed and replaced by their opposites. When the king punishes Vāsavadattā, he removes the eroticized, fetishized appendages that marked her as fair and in so doing flags her as foul (Sanskrit, *aśubha*; Pāli, *asubha*). He turns her sparkling good looks into a horrible punitive spectacle that exposes her self-advertising as a fraudulent practice. No longer fair, she has become a living corpse—and a hacked and scattered one at that.

In Foucault's view, the salutary educational effect of punishment on the spectators is even more important than punishing the perpetrator. "Punishment is directed above all at others, at all the potentially guilty. . . . The aim was to make an example, not only by making people aware that the slightest offence was likely to be punished, but by arousing feelings of terror by the spectacle of power letting its anger fall upon the guilty person."[92] In a section entitled the "Spectacle of the Scaffold," Foucault argues that the punitive spectacles staged by the monarchical rulers of premodern states were intended to impress upon all citizens the absolute power of the king to uphold the moral order. In the Buddhist context, the spectacle of the mutilated woman serves to display the power of the Buddha, the King of Dharma, over Māra, the Lord of the Realm of Desire. The Buddha reigns supreme by virtue of his superior insight into the link between desire, impermanence, and suffering. When the sexual messages conveyed by the bodies of attractive women are annulled through the gruesome spectacle of mutilation, the superior power of the King of Dharma is made manifest to all citizens of the realm of desire. Spectacularly beautiful women become broadsides in which the speciousness of feminine beauty is exposed and the moral order of the Buddhist Dharma is revealed. The symbolic, educative aspects of Vāsavadattā's punishment are certainly not lost on Upagupta.[93] He attains the status of a nonreturner as a result of his encounter with the mutilated courtesan, and was ordained and became an Arhat shortly thereafter.[94] Later in life, as a teacher with many disciples, Upagupta is reported to have used grotesque figurations of the feminine to help his disciples practice *brahmacarya.* A Chinese version of the *Aśokāvadāna* describes one occasion in which when a disciple tells Upagupta that he is thinking of leaving the *sangha,* Upagupta causes him to dream of his wife's death and the foul odor of her decomposing body being carried out of the home. When the monk reports his dream to Upagupta, he is told to visit his former wife and finds that indeed she has died; her parents are carrying her foul-smelling corpse out of the home. When the monk returns to the monastery, Upagupta asks him if he has seen his wife. "I saw her in her true aspect," he said.[95]

Horrific Figurations of the Masculine?

I know of no comparable scene in post-Aśokan Buddhist literature that presents a horrifically transformed male body to the female gaze as a source of edification. While it is true that self-mutilation in the service of hungry beings plays a role in the *bodhisattva* career, the removal of portions of flesh from the *bodhisattva*'s body is a voluntary act of sacrifice with no discernible punitive dimension. Furthermore, depictions of this heroic act do not underscore the impurity of the *bodhisattva*'s body. To the contrary, the *bodhisattva*'s self-mutilation serves to reveal his adamantine body, since the cutting off of his flesh is compared to the cutting of gems. The *bodhisattva* in the form of King Sibi, for example, willingly sacrifices his body, cutting off flesh from his thighs and other limbs in order to ransom a pigeon from a hungry hawk. The hawk is Indra in disguise, who describes this test of the *bodhisattva* as analogous to the process of testing a jewel to ensure that it is not artificial.[96]

If there is no shortage of disfigured male bodies in post-Aśokan literature, it is nevertheless the case that there are (at least to my knowledge) no male Vāsavadattās among them. Male bodies are undoubtedly disfigured in edifying ways, but the heroically sacrificed body of the *bodhisattva* is hardly comparable to the punitively disfigured body of a homicidal courtesan. It is also important to note the gender of the observer or observers when considering occasions in which the human body is featured as a liberative spectacle. I have yet to encounter any post-Aśokan narratives about women who contemplate dead or disfigured male bodies—or even women who observe male bodies that appear to be dead but are only asleep (like the women's bodies seen by Gotama and Yasa in the harem). Katherine Rennie Blackstone has carefully analyzed those passages in the *Theragāthā* and *Therīgāthā* that involve horrific representations of the human body. She finds that "none of the descriptions of postmortem decay, bodily secretions or internal substances refer explicitly to male bodies or bodily functions. Additionally, with only one exception (Kappa, *Theragāthā* 567), those bodies that are of an unspecified sex are designated female by the commentary."[97]

Other commentarial traditions composed around the same time as the texts Blackstone examined show a similar tendency to gloss as female those bodies that in the text being commented upon are of an undesignated gender. Such is the case, for example, with many of the narratives included in the *Dhammapadāṭṭhakathā*, the Pāli commentary on the *Dhammapada* that is attributed to Buddhaghosa but was probably composed shortly after Buddhaghosa's death.[98] This tendency to gloss gender-neutral language as female is especially evident in the commentator's treatment of a chapter entitled "Jara," or "decay" (*Dhammapada*, chap. 11). This chapter contains verses the Buddha is said to have spoken on the old age, disease, and decay (the term *jara* connotes all three) that reveal the body's transient nature and demonstrate the folly of regarding the corruptible flesh of the human body as intrinsically valuable.[99] The commentary is often gendered where the verses being commented upon are not; the commentator tends to gloss the grammatically neuter terms for the body (such as *rūpaṃ* and *sarīraṃ*) found in the *Dhammapada*'s verses with female nouns, pronouns, and adjectives. But the *Dhammapada* commentator does more than just utilize grammatically feminine terms to interpret the gender-neutral language of the text. The commentator bodies forth a highly gendered interpretation of the text by telling tales intended to shock, tales of seductive female bodies that are revealed to be riddled with corruption. Narratives such as the story of how the Buddha arranged for a monk to see his beloved Sirimā as a flyblown corpse being auctioned off in the cremation ground are offered to explain the original context in which the Buddha uttered the pithy verses of the *Dhammapada* that point out the ills to which all flesh (and not merely female flesh) is heir. These narratives show the Buddha reconfiguring the gaze of lovesick and lustful monks by directing these men to look at women. In two instances—the story of Sirimā and that of the 500 forest-dwelling monks (both of which were discussed earlier in this chapter)—the Buddha arranges for men to visit the cremation ground in order to look at decaying female bodies. Such tales present the original, gender-neutral verses of the *Dhammapada* as verses of admonishment urging these men to overcome their delusion by contemplating the decaying bodies of women. Of the nine verses unpacked by the commentator, there are four instances in which men are asked to look at women, focusing on the ravages to which their flesh is heir. There are also two instances in which the Buddha directs women to look at women. In one case (several versions of which will be discussed at length in chap. 5) the Buddha directs his vain half sister, newly ordained as a nun, to look at a beautiful female phantasm he has created for her benefit; he causes this spectral paragon of loveliness to age rapidly and die before his sister's eyes. In another case, the admonishment is directed to a group of laywomen. In no case does the Buddha direct a woman to look at a male body and observe its abject condition.

In a monograph on the place of women in Buddhism, the Sri Lankan monk Piyadassi Thera recounts an incident involving Ānanda, the Buddha's favorite disciple, that could with certain qualifications be construed as a gruesome figuration of the male body for the edification of a woman.[100] In this author's rendition of a story found in the *Divyāvadāna,* the Buddha describes the loathsomeness of Ānanda's inner anatomy to a young low-caste (Caṇḍāla) woman named Prakṛti who had fallen in love with the renouncer.[101] Prakṛti, in her determination to have Ānanda as her mate, had enlisted the aid of her mother in bewitching the monk with a magical spell. Prakṛti's mother chanted *mantra*s or incantations and made offerings at an altar she constructed in the courtyard of the house. Ānanda, compelled by her magic to leave his monastic cell, found himself approaching the modest home of the Caṇḍāla family. Entering the house, Ānanda walked right up to the altar by which Prakṛti's mother had bewitched him. Seeing this altar and understanding the power of the magic that had compelled him to enter the Caṇḍāla home, Ānanda burst into tears. The omniscient Buddha, however, knew of Ānanda's plight and uttered "Buddha *mantra*s" that broke the spell of the "Caṇḍāla *mantra*s" uttered by Prakṛti's mother, allowing Ānanda to leave of his own volition.[102]

Prakṛti, however, did not give up on Ānanda. As smitten with the handsome monk as ever, the young woman got up bright and early the next morning after Ānanda's visit and, putting on her very best outfit, followed the monk on his begging round. Ānanda was so disconcerted by the embarrassing spectacle he presented while begging for alms with a young woman in tow that he went back to the monastery and asked the Blessed One for his help. Capitalizing on Prakṛti's desire to be near her beloved Ānanda, the Buddha induced Prakṛti to put on monastic robes and have her head shaved. He told her that if she wanted Ānanda as her "lord and master" (*svāmin,* a term used for spiritual preceptors as well as husbands) she must dress the way he dresses. According to

Piyadassi Thera's version of this story, the Buddha then explained the Dharma to Prakṛti, exhorting her to recognize the foulness of Ānanda's body:

> What you see as enrapturous in a person, Prakṛti, is the outer skin. Beauty is only skin deep, superficial and transitory. Our body is not made of gold, pearls or diamonds or of any other precious stones. There are in this body: hair, nails, teeth, flesh, skin, sinews, pus, blood, sweat, fat, tears, grease, saliva, nasal mucus, urine, feces, and so on. Behind this painted image, the superficial beauty, is a body full of wounds; here there is neither permanence nor stability.[103]

This anatomy lesson filled the young woman with determination and she joined the *sangha* as a nun.

In analyzing this story, it is important to recognize that Prakṛti had fallen in love with a man who was off limits to her. As a member of the *sangha,* Ānanda was in no position to reciprocate Prakṛti's love for him. Indeed, not only was Ānanda formally prohibited as a monk from spending time alone with a woman, but it was Ānanda whom the dying Buddha advised not even to look at or talk with women.[104] In falling for Ānanda, Prakṛti was in love with one of the least eligible bachelors in town. And yet this same Ānanda was evidently the darling of many women. The Buddha's personal attendant was, in the words of Piyadassa Thera, "the monk most adored and admired by the members of the fair sex. . . . Queens and princesses, nuns and women of any kind, whether of high or low social position, or without good manners and refinement, took intense delight in seeing him and listening to his sermons."[105] It was Ānanda who felt such compassion on seeing the Buddha's foster mother in tears at being refused entrance into the *sangha* that he convinced the Buddha to relent and establish the *bhikkhunī sangha.* Long after his death, Ānanda continued to be remembered for his role in the establishment of the Buddhist order of nuns. The funerary monument (*stūpa*) of Ānanda, for example, was the object of a special cult celebrated by the nuns of the Mathurā region many centuries after Ānanda's death.[106]

Ānanda is reported to have maintained close friendships with many nuns. In fact, at least one of these nuns was evidently so close to Ānanda that she could not hold her tongue when Ānanda was harshly upbraided by Mahākassapa (Sanskrit, Mahākāśyapa), causing her to violate the special rule (pertaining to nuns only) that prohibits nuns from criticizing monks directly.[107] According to one account, Ānanda apologizes to Mahākāśyapa after his woman friend has lashed out on his behalf, calling himself a "foolish, womanish [*mātṛgrāma*], witless" man.[108] Although one could hardly say that Ānanda is proud of his feminine qualities, nevertheless it is significant that Ānanda, friend of womankind that he is, identifies himself as a womanly man. In my view, Ānanda's identification with the feminine helps explain why the foulness of his body was underscored in the incident with Prakṛti. As a woman-identified male, Ānanda is more likely to be represented as a locus of impermanence and impurity than men of few womanly qualities.

Womanly Wiles and the Cunning of the Buddha

In the story of Prakṛti's conversion, the battle between the ephemeral realm of *saṃsāra* and the eternal truth that is the Buddha's Dharma is played out on two fronts: that of words and that of appearances. Prakṛti's mother makes the first charge, calling down the powers of various deities with her Caṇḍāla *mantra*s. But these *saṃsāri*c words (and the deities thereby invoked) are rendered harmless when the Buddha calls forth the power of the Dharma with his Buddha *mantra.* When the words of her mother are overpowered by those of the Buddha, Prakṛti then takes matters into her own hands and attempts to achieve her aims through presenting the right appearance to her beloved's eyes. She washes and anoints her hair with oil, puts on her finest clothes, and presents herself to Ānanda looking her very best. But the Buddha, appearing to concede to her wish to marry Ānanda, counteracts the young woman's personal charms by skillfully manipulating appearances. He lets Prakṛti believe that he has no objection to her marrying Ānanda and by this pretense induces Prakṛti to transform her appearance into that of a bareheaded nun cloaked in a shapeless robe. Just as the Buddha met the spells of Prakṛti's mother with his own incantations, so too in dealing with Prakṛti he meets guile with guile. He uses the ambiguous term *svāmin* so that Prakṛti will think she is getting a husband when in fact what she gets is a religious father figure, a spiritual preceptor. In meeting womanly wiles with subterfuge of his own, the Buddha shows himself to be adroit at manipulating appearances. Like a talented magician who fools the crowds by concealing certain movements while highlighting others, the Buddha leads Prakṛti to see what he wants her to see and ignore the rest.

It is ironic that the Buddha uses subterfuge to help people achieve insight into what is really real. In a pithy teaching recorded in the *Aṅguttara Nikāya,* the Buddha is said to have contrasted the concealment that makes the *mantras* of Brahmins (traditionally transmitted in secrecy only to the initiated) and the wiles of women efficacious with the openness of the teaching of the Buddhas.[109] The Dharma is accessible to all where the clandestine operations of Brahmins and women require secrecy and concealment. But in his dealings with Prakṛti, the Buddha of the *Divyāvadāna* (and also Piyadassi Thera's text) conceals his real intentions in appearing to acquiesce to Prakṛti's wishes. His speech may be interpreted one way, but he intends it in another way. The Buddha of the *Aṅguttara Nikāya* is clearly right about the *consequences* of the speech of the Buddhas. Unlike the building up of a desirable exterior through dress and ornamentation by Prakṛti, the speech of the Buddhas has the effect of shedding light on what is obscure and helping people see beyond false appearances. I would suggest, however, that there is something equivocal in the choice of words that the Buddhas sometimes use to accomplish their intent. When they conceal another meaning that is not evident to the listener, such utterances resemble the artifice by which women like Prakṛti make themselves desirable. This willingness on the part of the Buddhas to meet the minions of Māra with dissimulations of their own is explored in the following chapter.

CHAPTER FOUR

Lead Us Now Into Temptation: Countering *Saṃsār*ic Duplicity with Dharmic Deceptions

If one's thoughts toward the Dharma
Were of the same intensity as those toward love,
One would become a Buddha,
In this very body, in this very life.
Tsanyang Gyatso, the Sixth Dalai Lama of Tibet

Tell all the Truth but tell it slant—
Success in Circuit lies
Too bright for our infirm Delight
The Truth's superb surprise

As Lightening to the Children eased
With explanation kind
The Truth must dazzle gradually
Or every man be blind—
Emily Dickinson

Salvation for Sick Minds

In this chapter, I reflect on the Buddha's use of trickery and dissimulation to teach the Dharma—the truth/reality that can relieve the suffering of all deluded beings. Slanting the truth that is the Dharma for the sake of meeting his audience at their own level of understanding, the Buddha often mimics his archenemy Māra in catering to the "lower" instincts of those he wishes to save from Māra's snares. In their struggle for dominion over the minds and hearts of human beings, the Buddha and Māra are more closely allied than much of the literature on either figure would suggest.[1]

Māra is the Grim Reaper in the guise of Cupid. As the god of death who lords over the realm of desire (*kāmadhātu*), Māra lures his victims near with enticing displays of beauty that make what is essentially undesirable appear to be desirable. He makes the cremation ground that is the world resemble a pleasure garden. Locked in competition with Māra, the Buddha fights fire with fire by setting traps that are, like those of Māra, often baited with female flesh. He makes the truths of the Dharma that are repugnant to the benighted seem desirable. In this way he entices those who are intoxicated with sensual pleasures to taste of the Dharma that will make them free.

In his zest for saving his lovesick half brother Nanda, for example, the Buddha uses a number of crafty stratagems. The story of Nanda is a very popular, much-repeated example of how the Buddha on occasion uses the power of untoward desires to lure a wayward monk back to the path.[2] Nanda, the natural son of Gotama's foster mother Gotamī Mahāpajāpatī, did not freely choose to become a monk. On the morning Nanda was to be doubly initiated into the social world by being consecrated as king and married to a beautiful princess, the Buddha visits his half brother under the pretense of taking alms.[3] Giving Nanda his alms bowl, the Buddha immediately turns around and leaves Nanda's house. Out of respect for the Buddha, Nanda restrains himself from calling out, "Here, take your bowl." He instead follows the Buddha with the hope that he will turn and ask for his bowl on reaching the courtyard or some other spot. But the Buddha never stops. He leads Nanda all the way to the monastery, where he asks the young man if he would like to renounce. Having been able to shanghai his half brother thus far because of Nanda's reticence, the Buddha succeeds in making a monk of him using the same strategy. Out of respect for Gotama, Nanda indicates that he will renounce. The Buddha has him ordained immediately.[4]

Soon, however, Nanda begins to long for Janapāda-Kalyāṇī, his fiancée. She had seen Nanda as he was on his way to the monastery the day of their wedding and, with tears in her eyes, had begged him to come back soon. Those words "remained in his heart like a hanging creeper."[5] With thoughts of his sweetheart nagging at him night and day, Nanda became dissatisfied and announced to his fellow monks: "I am not very happy [*anabhirato*] practicing *brahmacariya*, venerable ones. I cannot continue *brahmacariya.* Giving up the training, I'll return to the inferior [way of the householder]."[6]

When the Buddha hears of this, he arranges a visit with Nanda. We learn from the *Saṅgāmāvacara Jātaka*'s version of Nanda's story that the Buddha has been waiting for an opportunity to establish his foster brother as an Arhat and regards this as an opportune moment. "Thinking, 'let me now cause Nanda to be established as an Arhat,' he went to Nanda's cell." Hearing Nanda's complaint, the Buddha responds with a seeming non sequitur:

> "Have you ever been on a journey to the Himalayas, Nanda?"
> "No, Blessed One, I haven't."
> "Then we'll go."
> "But I have no psychic powers [*iddhi*]—how can I go?"
> "I'll lead you there with mine."[7]

In order to prevent the unhappy Nanda from leaving the *sangha,* the Buddha takes him by the arm and, using his psychic powers, transports him to the celestial realm of the thirty-three gods (*tāvatiṃsadevaloka*). The Buddha directs Nanda's attention to the 500 pink-footed *apsaras*es who entertain the king of the gods with music and dance. After ascertaining that his half brother finds these women enticing, the Buddha promises to help Nanda acquire these 500 nymphs:

> "Enjoy yourself [*abhirama*], Nanda. I'm your sponsor [*ahaṃ te pāṭibhogo*] for the acquisition of the 500 pink-footed nymphs."
> "Blessed One, if you are my sponsor for the acquisition of the 500 pink-footed nymphs, I will enjoy myself in the blessed state of *brahmacariya.*"[8]

In the *Jātaka* version of this story, the Buddha's promise is quite explicit:

> [Nanda asks] "How, Blessed One, is it possible to get these nymphs?"
> "Doing the duty of an ascetic, you will get these nymphs."[9]
> "If the Blessed One is my sponsor for getting them, I will do the duty of an ascetic."
> "Agreed, Nanda, I'm your sponsor."[10]

Along the way to the heaven of Indra, however, Nanda sees a very unappealing sight which foreshadows the subversion of desire that is the final outcome of the story: "On the way there, the Blessed One pointed out to Venerable Nanda in a certain burned field, seated on a burned stump, a greedy female monkey whose ears and nose and tail had been cut off."[11]

This female monkey has had her ears and nose cut off like Vāsavadattā (the courtesan whose punishment afforded Upagupta an opportunity for insight). Sitting on a burned stump in a burned field with blood streaming down her face, she is a study in degradation. But the Buddha does not explicate the meaning of this sight; he merely calls Nanda's attention to the monkey as they are on their way to the realm of the thirty-three gods. Once they have reached their celestial destination, the Buddha asks Nanda whether these nymphs are as beautiful as his sweetheart, Janapāda-Kalyāṇī. Nanda confesses that his fiancée suddenly seems to him as ugly as the mutilated female monkey he has just seen: "Put beside these 500 nymphs, she doesn't count for much. She doesn't approach a fraction of their beauty, or even a minuscule part of a fraction of their beauty. Next to them, she's a greedy female monkey whose ears and nose and tail have been cut off."[12]

The fact that Nanda uses the monkey's grotesque body as an analogy for all that is lacking in Janapāda-Kalyāṇī suggests that he was not oblivious to the sight of this mutilated monkey. But the unsettling sight does not have the same effect on Nanda as the sight of Vāsavadattā had on Upagupta. His willingness to forget about Janapāda-Kalyāṇī and pursue the nymphs would indicate that Nanda has by no means achieved the renouncer's view of the world as a cosmic cremation ground. He sounds more like the libertine who coldly tosses one paramour aside when a more beautiful woman looks his way. But since the Buddha wishes to establish this libertine as an Arhat, he (at least apparently) accedes to Nanda's desire and guarantees his foster brother that sexual gratification will be his reward for the sexual deprivation of *brahmacariya.*

However, what the Buddha does next indicates that his concession to Nanda's lust was only a means of enticing him to practice *brahmacariya* zealously. Having promised Nanda the gratification of his desires, the Buddha immediately goes about undermining those desires. The Blessed One says nothing to Nanda himself but sees to it that others show Nanda the error of his ways. According to the Pāli *Jātaka* version of the story, the Buddha reports the incident to each member of the *sangha* individually, and one by one they all approach Nanda and express their disapproval. They call him a "hireling" (*bhatako*) and a "dealer" (*upakkitako*) for practicing *brahmacariya* because of celestial nymphs.[13] Thanks to the ridicule that is heaped upon the wayward monk, the Buddha's stratagem works. Feeling ashamed and despicable, Nanda goes off by himself and practices with diligence. One day not long thereafter, he becomes an Arhat. At the end of that night, Nanda goes to visit the Buddha to release him from his promise. But the Buddha explains that Nanda's change in status has already absolved him of the responsibility to make good his promise: "When you became an Arhat, Nanda, I was released from my promise."[14]

Do the Buddhas Lie?

Truthfulness is a virtue expected of all Buddhists. Not only is lying eschewed by those who take lay and monastic precepts, but veracity has a positive, quasi-miraculous effect when one makes a solemn declaration "grounded in truth" (Pāli, *saccādhitthāna;* Sanskrit, *satyādhiṣṭhāna*). Shundo Tachibana has argued that the importance of truthfulness as a moral virtue is underscored by the fact that the Buddhist path is quest for truth.[15] In light of the pragmatic way that the Buddha contrives to lure men like Nanda with promises that he knows he will not have to fulfill, I think it is more useful to see the Buddhist path primarily as a therapeutic of salvation and only secondarily a quest for truth. No one would deny that the Buddhas know and teach the truth. But their goal is to eliminate suffering, not to acquire knowledge for knowledge's sake.[16] Guided by a therapeutic vision of the Dharma as a life-sustaining antidote to the mortal human condition, the Buddhas often teach the truth by circuitous means that allow its significance to dawn gradually in our infirm minds.

This therapeutic vision of the Dharma can be discerned in the unequivocal manner with which the Buddha of the *Nikāya*s refused to discuss certain ontological issues. When the Elder Māluṅkyāputta asked him questions about the duration of the world, the nature of the individual, and the ontological status of the Buddha in *nibbāna,* the Buddha of the *Majjhima Nikāya* responded with a parable about a fool wounded by an arrow whose preoccupation with trivial issues endangers his survival.[17] Rather than take prompt therapeutic action by removing the arrow lodged in his flesh, the Buddha explains, the man delayed the treatment by demanding to know who shot the arrow, what kind of reed the shaft of the arrow was made of, and so forth. The Buddha concludes this parable with a clear statement of his teaching principles:

> And why, Mālunkyāputta, have I not explained this? Because, Mālunkyāputta, it's not advantageous, it's not fundamental to *brahmacariya,* and it doesn't lead to aversion, dispassion, cessation, tranquillity, special knowledge, awakening, or nirvana; therefore I haven't explained it.[18]

It is difficult to maintain *tout court* that the Buddhist path is a quest for truth when speculative questions like those of Mālunkyāputta are deemed fruitless and counterproductive to the task of healing at hand.

In the *Lotus Sūtra* (Sanskrit, *Saddharmapuṇḍarīka*), which is an important composite Mahāyāna *Sūtra* with a mixture of early and late passages, the veracity of the Buddhas is persistently questioned. Although the text stops short of charging the Buddhas with duplicity, it clearly emphasizes the cunning with which the Buddhas slant the truth in order to relieve the suffering of sentient beings.[19] There are a number of parables that illustrate how the Buddha saves by speaking the only language our infirm minds can comprehend. In one, a father with many young sons devises a way of compelling his children to leave their burning house. (Entrapment in a burning house being a common metaphor for *saṃsāra*, the parabolic meaning of this scenario needs no explication.) When the fire broke out, the father instinctively called out to his sons, "Come, boys, get out now! This house is blazing with fire."[20] But the children, too young to understand the situation, continued to play their games unperturbed. They did not know the meaning of "house," much less "fire." So the father lures his boys out of the burning house by promising that each of them will find that toy that he most desires waiting for him just outside the door. The boys understand this utterance clearly; they run out of the house in a mad rush.

Although the father had promised his sons tiny toy carts, what he delivers is a great vehicle that is not precisely what the boys thought they were getting from him. After telling this parable, the Buddha asks Śāriputra, his most philosophically acute disciple, whether or not the father was guilty of falsehood. Śāriputra is quick to defend the father's action on the basis of its expedience: "There's no reason to consider this man a liar [*mṛṣā-vādī*] since these boys got out of the burning house with their lives thanks to the skillful use of expedients [*upāyakauśalyena*] by this man. . . . Even if this man did not even give the children a single cart, he would still be no liar."[21]

When Buddhists ascertain the moral status of an action, the intention of the agent is a central consideration. Thus Śāriputra suggests that the father's intention to save his sons excuses him from charges of wrongdoing. With the best interests of his sons at heart, the father cannot go wrong. He did not deliver exactly what he promised, but he cannot be accused of falsehood. Likewise, the Buddhas' intention in all that they do is to alleviate the suffering of dis-eased beings by whatever means are available to them. Because the awakened ones know they can induce their phlegmatic children to flee the burning house by promising them the trifles they desire, they are exempt from charges of misconduct.

Salvific Stratagems

In Mahāyāna texts redacted during the first several centuries of the Common Era, the idea that awakened beings stop at nothing to relieve suffering is articulated as the principle of skill-in-means or skillful means (Sanskrit, *upāyakauśalya*).[22] Before it was adopted by Buddhists as a technical term, the Sanskrit term *upāya* was used in a variety of contexts to refer to the means or methods by which one's aim is achieved. It appears frequently in the epic literature as a term for devious strategies for achieving victory on the field of battle. The conventional list of *upāya* for winning a war includes such strategies as bribing the enemy and sowing dissension among the enemy. In the *Mahābhārata,* Kṛṣṇa is depicted as a guileful master of *upāya* who councils the warriors under his tutelage to deceive whenever it is to their advantage to do so. For example, he persuades Yudhiṣṭhira, a paradigm of honesty, to lie in order to trick the enemy warrior Droṇa into giving up the fight. He also councils Bhīma, who is ever the honorable warrior, to hit below the belt in order to kill Duryodhana. At one point in the epic, Kṛṣṇa cites mythological precedents for his use of *upāya:* "When outnumbered by enemies, then destruction should be brought about by expedients [*upāyaiḥ*]. This path was followed in the past by the deities themselves in order to destroy their opponents. That path followed by the wise may be followed by all beings."[23]

Just as any expedient that leads to the defeat of the enemies of the gods is considered an appropriate method for the gods to use, so, in Mahāyāna Buddhist contexts, any expedient that leads to that summum bonum which is the alleviation of suffering through awakening is condoned. The skillful selection of expedient means to awakening is elevated to a Dharmic principle of the highest order. The *Vimalakīrtinirdeśa Sūtra,* for example, describes skillful means as the paternal principle that, when combined with the maternal principle of the perfection of wisdom (*prajñāpāramitā*), generates *bodhisattvas* and Buddhas.[24] Because beings differ in their capacity for understanding, the awakened ones use whatever means (*upāya*) are necessary to meet unawakened beings at their own level. Even breaking the precepts is admissible if it leads to the alleviation of suffering through awakening. Thus according to the *Upāyakauśalya Sūtra,* in a previous life Gotama abandoned the practice of *brahmacarya* for twelve years in order to live with a young woman who threatened to die of love for him.[25] Likewise, the *bodhisattva* once killed a man so as to prevent him from killing 500 traders (who happened to be *bodhisattvas*) and falling into the lowest hell as a consequence.[26]

With skillful means being identified with such lurid kinds of salvific transgression, it is easy to lose sight of the fact that the soteriologically oriented pragmatism associated with skill-in-means is anticipated in *Nikāyic* passages that clearly predate the Mahāyāna Sūtras. Although the term *upāyakusalo* (Sanskrit, *upāyakauśalya*) does not appear in the *Nikāyas* as a technical term, nevertheless there are a number of *Nikāyic* passages indicating that the truths that the Buddhas teach are provisional truths, practical tools provided for the limited purpose of the eradication of suffering. The parable of the raft found in the *Alagaddūpama Sutta* of the *Majjhima Nikāya* suggests that the Dharma is not to be retained once it has served its limited purpose.[27] Here, the Dharma is compared to a raft that is used to cross over a river. Once one gets to the other side, there is no point in retaining the cumbersome raft. Likewise, "the Dharma is taught for the sake of crossing over, not for the sake of retaining."[28]

The truth that the Buddhas teach is a soteriologically oriented truth. What is not salutary, not conducive to salvation, is withheld, as the Buddha of the *Dīgha Nikāya* suggests in the *Pāsādika Suttanta:* "If the past means what exists, what is true, but what is not advantageous, the Tathāgata doesn't reveal it. If the past means what exists, what is true, and what is advantageous, the Tathāgata knows the proper time to reveal it."[29]

That something is true does not make it worthy of inclusion in the Buddha's discourses to his disciples, as we have seen in the case of the ontological issues raised by Māluṅkyāputta. What the Buddha chooses to tell of what is true depends upon a process of selection whereby he determines what is most advantageous to his interlocutors. But even within the limited sphere of what is both true and advantageous, the Buddha continues to pick and choose. There are auspicious and inauspicious times for revealing salutary truths. Being a sensitive judge of disposition, the Buddha knows when revealing what he knows will be most beneficial to the listener. In the case of Nanda, the opportune moment came just when Nanda seemed least receptive to it. On the verge of leaving the *sangha,* Nanda evidently needed only a skillful contrivance of the truth to change his attitude and hence his fate.

Buddhist texts sometimes compare the Buddha's skill in teaching to the art of training animals.[30] In the frame story of the *Saṅgāmāvacara Jātaka,* some of Nanda's fellow monks comment on how remarkable it was that the wayward Nanda proved so receptive to advice (*ovādakkhamo,* "advisable," "admonishable") on the matter of practicing *brahmacariya* for the sake of celestial nymphs.[31] The Buddha explains that Nanda was once a royal elephant who, thanks to having been brought up by a skillful trainer (none other than the *bodhisattva* himself), was capable of taking the city of Vārānasī by storm. When the elephant was used in a siege, however, it was so unnerved by the noise and chaos of the battle that it turned tail immediately. But just one word of advice (*ekovāda*) caused the elephant to turn back and heroically force his way into the gates of the city. Likewise, it is implied, the present life Nanda needed only a few words of encouragement for his training to manifest itself. Nanda is superior to the untrained monk compared in the *Majjhima Nikāya* to a forest-born elephant; where the elephant of the forest does not immediately respond to the commands of a trainer, the docile royal elephant trained from birth needs little prompting.[32]

Being a member of the Buddha's family, Nanda was no doubt made docile by contact with the Blessed One in this and previous lives. Even so, Nanda needed more than just a word of encouragement in order to drive the wildness out of him. He would no doubt have left the *sangha* and returned to his sweetheart were he not lured with promises of sensual gratification that the trainer had no intention of keeping. What the Buddha did to keep Nanda in the *sangha* resembles the hunter's craft of enticing wild animals with baited traps. It is also akin to the practices of the elephant trainer, who uses tame cow-elephants as decoys in order to trap wild elephants. In enticing Nanda with the promise of celestial nymphs, the Buddha's actions resemble the methods that Māra and his minions use to trap unsuspecting men. In the *Saṃyutta Nikāya,* for example, Māra's use of his voluptuous daughters as a means to dissuade the Buddha from teaching the Dharma is described as an attempt to capture a forest elephant by means of the snare of passion (*rāgapāsena*).[33]

What Māra tried unsuccessfully to do to the Buddha in offering his daughters as bait the Buddha succeeded in doing to Nanda by offering heavenly nymphs. Since according to Brahminical and Hindu myth, the *apsarās*es are Indra's favorite means of inducing erotic lapses in the celibate practice of renouncers, it is clear that there is much in the way of mythological precedent for what the Buddha does in promising Nanda that he would enjoy the favors of these 500 *apsarās*es. But if the Buddha's use of women as a lure has affinities with non-Buddhist tales of ascetic discipline subverted by irresistible nymphs, it is clear that Buddhist literature turns these mythic precedents on their head. The baited hook that Indra and Māra use to lead disciplined ascetics to their downfall the Buddha uses to strengthen the discipline of his monks. In the *Saṃyutta Nikāya,* Māra is compared to a fisherman (*bālisiko*) who casts a flesh-baited hook (*āmisagata balisaṃ*) into a pool of water. Those fish with an eye for flesh (*āmisacakkhumaccho*) swallow the bait and are destroyed by Māra.[34] But in the skillful hands of the Buddhas, the "hook of the Dharma" baited with female flesh becomes a powerful disciplinary tool for keeping monks out of the traps set by Māra and his minions.[35]

In the *Dhammapadāṭṭhakathā,* the monks who witnessed Nanda's transformation from libertine to Arhat marvel at the strange ways of the Buddhas who discipline men like Nanda by offering them the bodies of women as bait: "The monks were talking in the hall of Dharma, saying: 'Brothers, the Buddhas are marvelous! The venerable Nanda who was discontented on account of Janapāda Kalyāṇī is now, having taken the bait of celestial nymphs [*devaccharā āmisaṃ katvā*], disciplined.'"[36] The Buddha who offers such a bait is not a stern disciplinarian but a cunning fisher of men. The Teacher, like a master of martial arts, does not oppose the force of the pupil but deftly redirects it.[37] In overcoming Nanda's resistance to *brahmacariya* by apparent acquiescence to his carnal desires, the Buddha rechannels the proverbial power of love to move mountains and in this way skillfully establishes Nanda as an Arhat.

As we have seen from the Pāli *Jātaka* account of Nanda's previous life as a skittish battle elephant, there is a tendency to account for Nanda's surprisingly rapid attainment of Arhatship by reference to occasions in the past when Nanda was skillfully disciplined by the Teacher. The *Dhammapadāṭṭhakathā* describes a previous incident in which Nanda was, once again, an animal who was coaxed into submission by a human master identified as the *bodhisattva.* Hearing the monks marvel about how he had disciplined Nanda using heavenly nymphs for his bait, the Teacher said: "Monks, this is not the first time that Nanda, having been enticed by women [*mātugāmena palobhetvā*], was disciplined."[38] The Buddha then launches into a boisterous tale of human ingenuity in mastering a recalcitrant animal.

A merchant from Vārānasī who had come to Taxila with goods to sell allows his donkey to roam free while he takes care of business matters. Wandering along a ditch, the donkey encounters a female donkey. From her, the donkey learns that it is normal to have a mate at home to rub one's back and massage one's feet. Thinking about this, the merchant's donkey becomes dissatisfied (*ukkaṇṭhi*) and refuses to haul its load back to Vārānasī.[39] The merchant responds with coercion, threatening the balky animal with a severe whipping. But the donkey refuses to be intimidated. It threatens to kick with its hind legs and knock the merchant's teeth out if beaten. The merchant wonders what has caused his formerly docile animal to talk like this. Then he sees the female donkey and determines that his donkey had been trained (*sikkhāpito*) in these things by her. So the merchant tells his donkey: "'I'll bring you a female donkey just like her.' But as he said this, the merchant was thinking, 'Enticing him with women [*mātugāmena naṃ palobhetvā*], I'll lead him on [*nessāmi*].'"[40]

The donkey takes the bait. Resuming the journey enthusiastically, the animal goes twice the distance he usually travels in one day. After a few days, the donkey wants to know when his master will procure a mate for him. The master's response is quite ingenious:

> "Yes, I did say that, and I won't break my word. I'll procure a mate for you. But I will provide food for you alone. It may or may not suffice for the two of you—only you can be the judge of that. From your cohabitation, offspring will be born. Only you can judge whether the food will suffice for all of you or not."
>
> As the merchant talked on and on, the donkey lost his desire.[41]

Holding what is advantageous to the listener in higher esteem than what is merely true, the Buddha motivates people with contrivances of truth. He makes promises that he knows he will not be asked to keep (like the promise of toy carts for his children, nymphs for Nanda, and a mate for the donkey). The Blessed One is assuredly no liar, as Śāriputra is quick to point out of the father who saves his sons, but he sometimes exploits the ambiguities of spoken communication. Substituting the Great (*Mahā*) Vehicle (*Yāna*) for a trifling toy cart, he contrives to save his ignorant young sons from the burning house. Leading Nanda and the donkey who was once Nanda to believe that their labors would be rewarded, he sees to it that neither Nanda nor the donkey will wish to claim their reward. In these examples of skillful disciplinary action, the Buddha teaches the truth by salvific subterfuge.

Illusions That Bespeak Reality

The Buddha also contrives to teach the truth by visual dissimulation. That the Buddha wields the power of illusion in order to disabuse us of our delusions should come as no surprise to those familiar with accounts of the Buddha's life, since many highlight the role of illusion in the Buddha's own awakening. According to the Sanskrit accounts of the four signs Gotama saw on four excursions from the palace (i.e., an old man, a sick man, a dead man, and a renouncer), all four were visions produced by the psychic powers of divine supporters of the Dharma—deities with the *bodhisattva*'s best interests at heart.[42] Although technically unreal, these psychically created fabrications revealed the impermanence and suffering that the *bodhisattva* (to his horror) learned were intrinsic to the human condition. Likewise, the female bodies that the *bodhisattva* perceived in the harem on the evening of the Great Departure were not literally dead. Thanks to the good offices of the Akaniṣṭha gods, they were made to appear dead. and in so appearing they served as the final sign that it was time for Gotama to seek an end to death and birth.

After his awakening, the Buddha uses his own considerable psychic power (*iddhibala*) to awaken others. What the Akaniṣṭha gods did for him in creating appearances that bespeak reality the Buddha often does for those members of his *sangha* who, lacking insight, have trouble seeing the Dharma they have heard.[43] In post-Aśokan hagiography, the Buddha's verbal teaching is occasionally accompanied by psychically produced visual displays that create the appearance of decaying bodies when no such body is present, as in the flyblown corpse the Buddha conjured up for Kulla. In the case of Kulla, the Buddha uses his psychic powers to fabricate the realia of decaying flesh for the edification of a lustful monk who lacked a proper object for contemplating the foulness of the body.

It is not only monks, however, who merit such magical displays of what is real. Vain nuns who are too intoxicated with their beauty to use their own bodies as objects of contemplation also merit psychic displays of this type. As we will see in the next chapter (from the testimonials attributed to nuns of the primitive *sangha* that are collected in the *Therīgāthā*), the natural object of contemplation for a nun is her own body. But if a nun is extremely proud of her own appearance, she is unlikely to use her own body as a support for contemplating the body's foulness. The Buddha circumvents this problem in the case of his vain foster sister Nandā (who is Nanda's natural sister and whose story parallels his in many respects) by inducing insight in her through the judicious use of illusion. Presenting Nandā with an illusory display in which a magical double of herself succumbs to the effects of impermanence by aging and dying a horrible death before Nandā's eyes, the Buddha establishes his half sister in Arhatship.

Unlike the dreadful and seductive illusions created by Māra and his minions in their attempt to instill fear and desire in renouncers, the Buddha's use of illusion is truly kind because unerringly therapeutic. By correctly diagnosing the various delusions of those he wishes to cure, the Buddha always provides the saving remedy. It may be useful to think of the Buddha as a homeopath who infuses his patients with controlled quantities of the toxins from which they are suffering. In the case of lustful monks and vain nuns, the Great Physician often overcomes their pathological attachments to the specious beauty of the body by administering controlled doses of the pathogenic toxin. With monks like his half brother Nanda, the Buddha encourages sexual desire only to subvert it in the end. Likewise, with nuns like his foster sister Nandā, the Buddha conjures up beautiful female bodies that invite vanity (Nandā, for instance, compares the body she sees with her own in order to ascertain which is the more beautiful). When the illusion has its intended effect, the beautiful phantasm that arouses lust or vanity is made to manifest the reality of impermanence—a reality that lustful monks and vain nuns often need to see to believe.

Catering to the pathologies of his audience in order to teach the Dharma, the Buddha mimics and thereby defeats Māra, Lord of the

Realm of Desire. It is by appealing to people's lower instincts that Māra captures the ignorant in his snares. As the comments of the monks who witnessed Nanda's transformation suggest, the Buddha also baits the hook of Dharma with flesh (*āmisa*). The Buddha adroitly encourages desire for voluptuous bodies so as to steal Māra's thunder and "fish" the men who would otherwise be Māra's catch of the day.

The Womanly Wiles of the Buddhas

If the saving work of the Buddha resembles the trickery of Māra, it also has affinities with the dissembling displays of Māra's daughters. Māra's daughters are the epitome of feminine duplicity. Like the stereotypically avaricious courtesan satirized in Sanskrit comic literature, they will do anything in their considerable power to rob the autonomy of the man who is their intended victim.[44] The courtesan, with her eye on a man's pocketbook, will say or do whatever is necessary to win a man's affection. Once she has secured his affection and his wealth, she does not bother to misrepresent her feelings toward him any more— she slams the door in his face. Likewise, Māra's daughters (and the female ghouls that are their demonic equivalent) manifest enticing forms designed to captivate the hearts and minds of renouncers. Once they have either captured or lost their prey, they drop all pretense and revert to their own forms.

In the *Upāyakauśalya Sūtra,* the teaching of the Dharma by means of skillful expedients is explicitly compared to the methods by which courtesans dupe their customers. A courtesan, it is explained, pretends to love a man only to get what she desires from him: "To obtain wealth and treasures, she may coax a man into generously giving her his valuables by pretending that she is going to marry him, and then she drives him away without regret when she has obtained the precious objects."[45] Likewise the *bodhisattva* "teaches and converts all sentient beings by manifesting himself in forms they like and by freely giving them everything they need, even his body."[46] But once all sentient beings are awakened, "he abandons without the least attachment the five sensuous pleasures which he pretended to enjoy."[47] The use of skillful means is thus a feminine wile, a dharmic seduction that resembles the *saṃsār*ic overtures of *filles de joie.*

The coincidence of opposites that makes strange bedfellows out of austere renouncers and prostitutes is recognized in secular contexts as well. The secret kinship of courtesans and renouncers is a favorite theme of Sanskrit satirists; by conflating the harlot and the holy man, the comic poet makes fun of the pretensions of both. The *Bhagavad-ajjukīya,* for example, is a comedy about a practitioner of yoga (*yogin*) who psychically enters and reanimates the dead body of a courtesan. Yama, the god of the dead, sees to it that the *yogin*'s unanimated body is inhabited by the soul of the courtesan whose body the *yogin* has already occupied. With the holy man in the body of the hooker and the hooker in the body of the holy man, the possibilities for comedy are endless. Hilarious asides as well as the actions of the characters themselves announce the affinities between the courtesan's venal dispassion and the holy man's spiritual dispassion: "Courtesans are like renouncers; they hardly feel any love."[48]

One of the most characteristic of womanly wiles is the ability to alter one's appearance. Like their father, one of whose epithets is *mahāṛddhika* ("of great psychic power"), Māra's daughters are consummate shape-shifters.[49] They (and the female ghouls that are their demonic equivalent) are skilled at manifesting enticing forms designed to captivate the hearts and minds of renunciant men. Once they have captured their prey, Māra's daughters drop all pretense and revert to their own forms (all the better, in the case of fanged demonesses like *rākṣasīs*, to eat their victims with). Like Māra and his daughters, the Buddha is a master of illusion. Just as Māra is a deity with a mind-made body, so the Buddha has the psychic power (Pāli, *iddhibala;* Sanskrit, *ṛddhibala*) to project mind-made bodies (*manomayakāya*).

Māra's body takes any shape he wishes it to have, manifesting forms that inspire fear and desire in renouncers. The *Saṃyutta Nikāya* describes a number of guises that Māra took for the purpose of dissuading the Buddha from teaching after his awakening. Hoping to make the Buddha experience fear, stupefaction, and excitement, Māra comes to the Buddha as an elephant, then as a cobra, and then in various fair and foul shapes.[50] Māra's form is so labile that, on several occasions, he takes on the guise of the Buddha himself. In his commentary to the *Aṅguttara Nikāya,* Buddhaghosa tells of how Māra came to the door of the lay disciple Sūra Ambaṭṭha in the form of the Buddha.[51] Sūra Ambaṭṭha had just received a visit from the Buddha, who had given him a Dharma-talk after taking a meal. Being somewhat perplexed at seeing the Buddha on his doorstep again so soon, Sūra Ambaṭṭha inquired as to the reason for the second visit and was told:

"When I told you about the Dharma, I made one thoughtless statement. I said that all five constituents of the human being are impermanent, marked by suffering, and without self. But they are not all like that; some of them are really permanent, stable, and eternal."

"This statement," Sūra Ambaṭṭha thought, "is very significant. . . . Since the Buddhas never say anything thoughtlessly, and Māra is the antithesis of the Buddha, this must surely be Māra," Sūra Ambaṭṭha reflected. "You are Māra," he declared, and as soon as the worthy disciple had said this, it was as if an ax blow had fallen on Māra. Being unable to keep up his disguise, he therefore said, "Yes, Ambaṭṭha, I am Māra."[52]

"If a hundred or even a thousand Māras like you came here," he replied, "my faith would not be shaken."[53] "When the great Gotama Buddha taught me the Dharma, he informed me that everything constructed by karma is impermanent. Get away from the door of my house," he said, snapping his fingers. When Māra heard his words, he balked but was unable to say anything in response.[54]

On another occasion, Māra unwillingly takes on the guise of the Buddha for the benefit of Upagupta, the man who entered the Buddhist path while contemplating Vāsavadattā's mutilated body. As the *Divyāvadāna* presents this encounter, Upagupta forces Māra to use his shape-shifting skills to create the appearance of a living Buddha as penance for attempting to undermine the teaching of the Dharma.

Outfoxing the Great Deceiver: The Binding of Māra with Magic

One day when Upagupta was preaching in Mathurā in front of a crowd of several hundred thousand people, Māra caused a shower of pearl necklaces to rain down on the assembly so that the audience would be distracted. Agitated with greed, no one heard a word of what Upagupta was saying that day. Likewise, the next day, Māra distracted Upagupta's audience with a shower of gold. On the third day:

Māra staged a show nearby.[55] Heavenly instruments harmonized and divine *apsarās*es began to dance. The people gathered there were tranquil until, seeing the divine forms and hearing the heavenly sounds, they were enticed by Māra. Because he had enticed Upagupta's as-

> sembly, Māra tied a garland around the elder Upagupta's neck, feeling very pleased with himself.[56]

Hanging a garland of flowers around a monk's neck, as we saw from the incident in which Cūlakāla's wives defrock and garland their husband, is an insultingly inappropriate thing to do to a renouncer. Like the white clothes of a layperson, garlands are emblems of the householder; they are not suitable gifts for a monk. But Upagupta shows no anger. Instead, he seizes upon the gift of the sweet-smelling garland of flowers as an opportunity to teach Māra a thing or two about impermanence:

> Upagupta, seeing that the time for Māra's conversion was at hand, took three carcasses—a snake carcass, a dog carcass, and human carcass—and, by means of magical powers, he made them into a garland of flowers and went up to Māra with them. Māra was so delighted when he saw him; he thought "I've enticed even Upagupta!" Māra bent down in his own bodily form so that he could be garlanded in person. Then the elder Upagupta hung the snake carcass around Māra's head, the dead dog around his neck, and suspended the human corpse from his ears.[57] Taking hold of them, he said: "Just as you, sir, have tied a garland unfit for one who is a monk on me, so I have tied on you these carcasses unfit for desirous people. Show whatever powers you have, but today you have encountered a son of the Buddha."[58]

The transformation of Māra's garland of flowers into Upagupta's "garland" of corpses is fraught with irony, as John Strong demonstrates in his very insightful analysis of this scene.[59] Strong notes that while flowers are not fit to give to monks, they are perfectly acceptable for one who is a Buddha. Indeed, the offering of flowers to a Buddha image is the most fundamental liturgical act performed in the South Asian Buddhist world today, and the liturgical formula that accompanies the act of giving flowers emphasizes the transience of both the flowers and the body of the donor.[60] In turning Māra's garland of flowers into a stinking chain of corpses, Upagupta shows that he has overcome Māra by virtue of his understanding of the transience of those phenomena that Māra used to bind his victims to *saṃsāra.* Transforming the flowers that (like Kāma's flower-tipped arrows) are Māra's weapon of choice against renouncers, Upagupta vanquishes Māra with them.

Now the tables are turned on Māra, the hunter who entraps human beings. The Evil One is astounded to discover that, try as he might, he cannot remove the corpses with which he has been garlanded.[61] So Māra is now like an animal caught in Upagupta's trap. Although he seeks help from various other gods, Māra finds that none of them can help him out of the bondage that Upagupta has imposed on him. So Māra is forced to submit to Upagupta in order to secure his freedom. Upagupta agrees to release Māra from his fetters on the condition that Māra, using his psychic powers, manifests the form of the Buddha.[62] Explaining that this would be a great favor to one born too late to see the Blessed One, Upagupta agrees to release Māra in exchange for this service.

Upagupta is reported to have bound Māra with corpses on another occasion. A Mongolian rendering of the *Damamūkhanidāna Sūtra* describes how once, in the distant past, Upagupta and some other monks were visited each day by a dog who showed a marked appreciation for the teaching of the Dharma. Every day the dog would come and sit with its ears cocked as the Dharma was being taught. One day, however, the faithful canine auditor died. The dog was then reborn in Māra's divine realm (the *Parinirmitavaśavartin* realm) where—to Māra's great consternation—it presumed to sit on the same seat as Māra himself. Upon investigating the matter, Māra discovers that this presumptuous being was a dog in its last life, and he suspects that the monks have done this to humiliate him.[63]

Seeing that Upagupta is absorbed in meditation, Māra seizes the opportunity to exact his revenge, placing a jeweled diadem on Upagupta's head. When Upagupta ends his meditation and discovers the diadem, he knows that this is Māra's doing. So, using his psychic powers, Upagupta puts a headdress consisting of the dead dog's body on Māra's head. As in other accounts of Upagupta binding the Evil One with corpses, Māra goes to various gods but finds that none can help him remove the dead dog. Forced to submit to Upagupta in the end, Māra is surprisingly unrepentant. He complains to Upagupta:

> The Buddha was endowed with great virtue and compassion, but you *śrāvaka*s are terrible people.[64] It is true, I did surround the *bodhisattva* with eighty thousand hosts of Māra and tried to confuse him, but he never held it against me and was always compassionate. Why do

> you do something so terrible to me in return for a little joke I wanted to play?[65]

Māra implies that Upagupta has let his temper carry him away in a manner that is unbecoming to members of the *sangha.* The Buddha, Māra insists, never lost his temper and was always compassionate toward his adversary, taking Māra's tricks gently in stride. But other accounts suggest that the Buddha was not always so compassionate when vexed by Māra. On one occasion, as we will see shortly, the Buddha is alleged to have bound Māra with corpses just as Upagupta did.

Although Upagupta is still remembered today throughout Southeast Asia for his legendary binding of Māra with corpses, there are also Buddhist legends of how Māra was hoist by his own petard when trying to humiliate Dharma-masters other than Upagupta.[66] In the *Damamūkanidāna Sūtra,* Upagupta's contemporary Yaśas likewise vanquishes Māra with symbols of impermanence. Here, a different sort of magical transformation takes the place of Upagupta's binding Māra with a chain of corpses. After sending a shower of gold coins and a shower of flowers down to distract an assembly of people listening to the Dharma, Māra:

> Took on the form of a blue elephant with six tusks from which flowed sparkling water. Out of each stream of water emerged an enchanting singing maiden made of crystal. As the elephant walked softly back and forth, the assembly was amazed; everyone stopped listening to the teaching and watched the elephant. The next day Māra returned and transformed himself into a beautiful woman. Just as before, when the people saw her they forgot to listen to the Dharma.
>
> Thereupon Yaśas transformed the woman into a skeleton of dry, white bones. When the assembly saw this, they were horrified and listened to the Dharma with concentrated minds, and there were many who attained to the first fruits.[67]

Once again, the psychic powers of a prominent member of the *sangha* are pitted against Māra's shape-shifting craft. Only here Māra's spellbinding overtures to the audience are more shameless. Moving from pecuniary to erotic enticement, Māra finally turns into a voluptuous woman who distracts the entire audience. But like the garland of corpses with which Upagupta binds his victim, the skeleton that Yaśas makes of Māra succeeds in breaking the spell of Māra's magic. Like the stinking carcasses that Upagupta uses to bind Māra, it is a sign that Yaśas has slipped out of Māra's stranglehold by virtue of his insight into the Dharma. Knowing the ills to which all flesh is heir, Yaśas made that knowledge visible for all to see using Māra's assumed form as a medium of instruction.

"He Who Feeds on Death That Feeds on Men Possesses Life"[68]

With these examples before us of Māra's weapons being ingeniously turned against him, we are in a position to appreciate the irony of Māra's lamentations after being bested by the Buddha after seven years of struggling with him:

> "Oh my—that an ascetic should defeat the likes of me with my great magic power . . . that Gotama the ascetic should defeat the likes of me with my great prominence . . . that Gotama the ascetic should defeat the likes of me with the great extent of my majesty . . . that Gotama the ascetic, who is a mere human being, should defeat the likes of me—a divine being!" So Māra the Evil One lamented in a melancholy state, burning with the pain of an inner dart, extremely miserable. "The body of Gotama was born of mother and father; it depends on his stomach; it's a heap of boiled rice and sour gruel, and is subject to being covered [by clothing], being rubbed, sleep, dissolution, disintegration and destruction, while my body is made of mind. Oh my—that an ascetic should defeat the likes of me!"[69]

Māra laments that a god of such magical potency as himself should be overcome by a mere human being, a being conceived in the "boiled rice" and "sour gruel" issuing from his parents' genitals. But it is precisely the gross mortal condition of the human body that defeats this Māra who is death personified. Death has no dominion over the Buddha and his Arhats because, unlike those caught in Māra's snares, they are not blind to the disturbing signs of the body's mortality. Rather than running from death and the drips and leaks that bespeak our mortal condition, the worthy (Sanskrit, *arhat,* Pāli, *arahant*) sons and daughters of the Buddha seek out signs of the foulness of the body in every setting in which bodies are found.

Although he does not know it, Māra is also subject to death. Because he is ignorant of his own mortality, because he does not understand that even his splendid mind-made body is subject to dissolution, Māra himself is an animal caught in the snare of Death (*mṛtyupāśa*). Māra is continually vanquished by the Buddha because he does not understand that he is one of a series of Māras, beings who win the exalted position that Māra occupies in the cosmos through their actions and enjoy the celestial body of a Māra until their karma runs out and they die.[70] Māra's body, for all its splendor, is still a *saṃsāri*c body, a body born to die. With an immortal body of saving knowledge at their disposal (Pāli, *dhammakāya;* Sanskrit, *dharmakāya*), the sons and daughters of the Buddha find Māra no threat. They have only to consult their state-of-the-art anatomical knowledge of what a gross mortal thing the *saṃsāri*c body is to break the spell of Māra's magic.

When Upagupta and Yaśas defeat Māra by transforming his psychic productions into anatomy lessons, they are using their psychic powers to make visible what would happen to Māra and his minions in any case, given the passage of time. The Buddha, it will be remembered, pulled a similarly real rabbit out of his psychic hat when he froze Māra's daughters into the decrepit forms of old women they had assumed in order to arouse his pity. That such transformations are only dharmic subversions of the spell of Māra's magic and not really magical deeds at all is suggested by an episode recounted in a fifth-century Chinese translation of the *Sūtrālaṃkāra* in which a courtesan who disrupts a Dharma-assembly becomes a walking, talking corpse.[71] She is told that her cadaverous appearance is not due to magic—it is simply the outward manifestation of her true inner nature.

There was once a famous master of the Dharma whose teaching drew huge audiences. All the people of the city and surrounding area flocked to the monastery each day to hear him speak. And everyone who heard the man preach, even the little children, "lost their indifference." With so much zealous support for the Dharma, the courtesans of the town could no longer find lovers to support them. They were women of advanced age, unfit for manual labor. They had already exhausted the wealth their paramours had given them, and had no idea how to support themselves. Seeing how desperate the situation was becoming, the beautiful young daughter of one courtesan came up with a plan. At the next Dharma-talk, she promised her mother and the other courtesans, she would appear decked out in her finery and "make all the men of the assembly follow me here."[72]

On that day, the young woman bathes, rubs her body with perfumes and lac, and puts on her finest clothes and most precious jewels. Brilliantly outfitted and accompanied by a splendidly dressed retinue, she sets out for the monastery in a riotous procession. "Her bearing was bewitching: she strutted; she boasted her charms; she displayed her good looks in every way."[73] Strutting their stuff along with her are colorfully dressed dancers who from time to time raise their right hand and point the way to the bordello. As the procession approaches the monastery, people begin to hear music and laughter and notice the smell of flowers and perfumes.

The courtesan and her party stop short of entering the monastery. She instead leads the way to an empty house nearby where she waits for the Dharma-teaching to begin. Thousands of people are gathering to hear the Dharma, and the courtesan waits for the most opportune moment to reveal her presence to the massive numbers of potential customers assembled there. As the white-haired, bushy-eyebrowed Dharma-master mounts the high seat and begins to speak, the courtesan appears at the door of the house in full view of the crowd. The attendants disperse themselves among those assembled to hear the Dharma and say to the men: "This woman is perfect—a ravishing beauty. Just look at her! Why listen to the Dharma?"[74]

The Dharma-master, noticing that he has suddenly lost the attention of his audience, asks: "Why are your eyes fixed so strangely? Why are your hearts troubled? Don't you know that death comes like a galloping horse and thus it's necessary to practice zealously?" For a moment, the men of the assembly recover their interest in the Dharma, but then the courtesan redoubles her efforts at attracting their attention. When the men lose all sense of decency in their lascivious agitation, the Dharma-master warns the courtesan that Māra attempted this kind of thing with the Buddha and was soundly rebuffed:

> Then the master of the law, although free of taint, showed signs of rage. Crying out with a loud voice, he spoke to the courtesan:
>
> "You are like an anthill that would measure itself against Mount Meru, the king of mountains. Don't you understand that in the past, when the Buddha still lived in this world, Māra with his infinite forces dared to pester the Buddha with his artifices? But the Blessed one bound him with a corpse around the neck and thus, covered with shame and humiliation, he became the laughing stock of gods and

> men. Do you believe that the teaching of the Dharma is dead? That these *śrāvakas* whose energy is directed toward a single goal are no more? That the heroes of the law are all gone?"

Then, without waiting for her answer, the master of the Dharma concludes:

> "If this is what you think, I must show strength and resolve toward you." Accordingly, the master of the law transformed the courtesan through the use of his psychic powers. Her skin and flesh fell away and nothing remained of her but white bones; the five types of intestines were laid bare.[75]

As improbable as it may sound, the courtesan is still alive after the Dharma-master transforms her in this way. Thanks to the teacher's psychic powers, she has become the living corpse that Buddhist discourse holds her to be at all times. "Reduced to a skeleton standing up in front of the assembly," the young woman resembles the perpetually active *danse macabre* woodcut figures made famous by Hans Holbein. She is an animated study in the ravages of death, her flesh fallen away to expose the snarl of intestines underneath. When she responds to questioning at one point in the narrative, the assembly is shocked to learn that "this mass of bones can speak." But the Dharma-master knows that she is as alive as ever, and he addresses her with a variety of questions and arguments. Chastising her for having "dared to enter into battle with the Dharma of the Buddha," the master of the Dharma explains to the young woman what she looks like now:

> Before, you were a marvelous beauty;
> you attracted the gaze of everyone.
> Now, your skin and flesh are missing,
> and you are nothing but these bones.
> Before, you delighted the foolish;
> now they are beginning to see the truth.
> Your frontal bones resemble a white shell,
> and you look like the root of the water lily.
> The bones that shelter your eyes are standing out,
> and your cheeks have become two gaping holes.
> Your joints have come apart;
> your nerves and veins are all mixed up together;

your intestines hang exposed to the eye in the chasm [of the pelvic bones].
Your own followers are disgusted with your appearance.
How much less is this vast crowd
able to derive pleasure from your appearance?[76]

At this point the skeletal courtesan joins her fleshless hands together and faces the Dharma-master while he offers her the chance of acquiring a more sublime body by understanding the foulness of her own bag of bones:

> If you are ready to stop your vain gestures and renounce your finery, I will show you where the sublime body of nirvana exists and how to acquire it on the market of the knowledge of the foul. For the body, covered with a thin layer of flesh, is full of impurities. Covered on the outside with a deceptive disguise, it agitates the eyes of fools. Common men are beguiled; blinded by their desire, they are filled with impure passion. But where is the wise man who, having taken complete account of it, could find pleasure in it?[77]

In a notable example of skillful means, the Dharma-master uses the commercial terms most likely to appeal to a woman who attends to her own business affairs, offering to help her acquire the sublime body of nirvana "on the market" of the knowledge of the foul.

But the courtesan does not admit defeat until the assembled people begin to point their fingers at her and marvel at the disgusting sight she has become. Humiliated by their derision, she prostrates herself on the ground, acknowledges the man's power, and begs the Dharma-master to remove the spell that has turned her voluptuous body into a hideous scaffolding of bones. Alluding to mythological precedents for her behavior, she suggests that the punishment inflicted is excessively harsh: "When Viśvāmitra transformed the *apsarās* Rambhā, he changed her into a mare for twelve years. But you, by your curse, have transformed me into a cremation-ground dweller. I've never seen a curse like this. Please have pity on me, kind sir, and deliver me from this." But the Dharma-master, "smiling a thin smile," denies that he has cast any sort of spell on her:

> Stand up, young lady. There isn't a trace of animosity in my heart, and those who have shaved their hair and wear ocher robes do not

> resort to curses. Those who are full of desire and attachment are capable of hurting and causing suffering; they are always quick to feel anger. And, dominated by ill will, they pronounce curses. I have liberated myself from the bonds of ill will. I have removed my ignorance; my mind and body are liberated. I wish to save all beings—how could I pronounce a curse on those who are afflicted by birth, old age, and death? How could an intelligent man pronounce a curse on beings who are in misery? This would be like putting burning embers on a nasty wound.

The courtesan's present condition is not due to a curse, the Buddhist teacher insists, since no one who understands the suffering of sentient beings would impose more suffering by pronouncing a curse. Her present appearance merely makes visible the true body that women are wont to hide beneath their jewels and makeup: "With a thin skin covering the machinery of your joints, foolish men were seized with love for you. By my psychic power I have exposed the casket of your impurities."[78] Protesting that he has not harmed her through a magical curse but simply revealed her true nature through powers akin to X-ray technology, the Dharma-teacher restores the courtesan's youthful form and exhorts the crowd to practice zealously. Many people entered the stream that day, and others entered the path at even higher levels.

Although the Dharma-master admits that he used his psychic powers to transform the courtesan, he wants it to be understood that he did not use black magic. Indeed, it would behoove him not to admit to using magic at all, since it is a punishable offense (*dukkaṭa*, "misdeed") for a member of the *sangha* to display psychic powers in the presence of the laity. In the Pāli *Vinaya*, Piṇḍola Bhāradvāga is sharply dressed down by the Buddha for using his psychic powers in a competition sponsored by a wealthy merchant.[79] He and Mahā Moggallāna, along with a number of non-Buddhist ascetics, were invited to recover a costly sandalwood bowl from the top of a bamboo pole using their psychic powers.[80] Piṇḍola Bhāradvāga rose up in the air, took the bowl, and circled the city of Rājagaha three times. He was rewarded the precious bowl for his efforts and, after this amazing display, became something of a celebrity with the laity. When the Buddha hears of this, he rebukes Piṇḍola Bhāradvāga for displaying the superhuman quality of his psychic powers before householders for the sake of a miserable wooden bowl.[81] The Buddha has the bowl ground down into a fine powder to be used medicinally (as an additive to eye ointments) and tells the monks not to work wonders in the presence of householders.

One reason why the display of psychic powers is prohibited is that too often such displays are a frivolous use of powers that Buddhas use to help sentient beings (like knowing the mental disposition and karmic condition of other beings).[82] Members of the *sangha* who use their psychic powers merely to show off or curry favor with householders thereby trivialize the powers that Buddhas use for the benefit of suffering beings. Thus the Buddha compares what Piṇḍola Bhāradvāga did to a cheap prostituting of his superhuman power: "Just like a woman who displays her loincloth for the sake of a miserable penny [*māsaka*], so you have displayed the superhuman quality of your psychic powers before householders for a miserable wooden bowl."[83]

In exposing the inside of the courtesan's body to the gaze of the crowd, the Dharma-master has not used his psychic powers in a frivolous manner that trivializes those powers. Where Piṇḍola Bhāradvāga could be said to degrade himself and the Dharma by rising up in the air for a worthless bowl, this teacher used magical transformation to achieve a clear soteriological goal. Exposing the woman's fleshless skeleton to the eyes of the crowd, he made available to men in a state of erotic agitation the insights of one who has understood the body's foulness and he thereby taught an unforgettable lesson on the folly of lust.

Not a Magician but an X-Ray Technician

Buddhist discourse on the body constitutes the skeleton as the body's mainstay. It is the foundation of the house that is the body. But this foundational structure that keeps the body upright is scarcely visible to the naked eye while the body is alive. Plastered over with flesh, sealed with skin, painted with cosmetics, and rubbed with perfumed oils and pomades, the scaffolding of bones that supports the flesh is profoundly obscured from view. Members of the *sangha* who select skeletons as their objects of meditation, however, learn a way of viewing the body that penetrates the many-layered facade that obscures the body's ossiferous foundation. What the meditator gains from contemplating skeletons is a penetrating vision that is not impeded by dress, ornaments, skin, and flesh. Cutting through the many layers that obscure the skeleton within, this X-ray vision reveals the grimacing skull that lurks behind every bright smile (see fig. 7).

Figure 7. The body as a shed plastered with flesh and skin. From a contemporary illustrated edition of the *Dhammapada,* printed in Taiwan.

In the *Visuddhimagga,* Buddhaghosa reports that this way of viewing the body helped the Sri Lankan monk Mahātissa to preserve his equanimity when he was out seeking alms one day.[84] On the road to Anurādhapura he saw a beautiful woman. "Dressed up like a celestial nymph," she was on her way to her parents' home, having just broken off relations with her husband. No longer under the guardianship of her husband and not yet under her father's watchful eye, she was the renouncer's worst nightmare—a woman as beautiful as a divine *apsarās* and, like the celestial nymph, a free agent readily available for sexual pleasure. When she saw the elder, she was filled with "perverted thoughts" and laughed aloud.[85] Mahātissa looked at her laughing mouth with its gleaming teeth and, perceiving a grinning skeleton instead of a laughing woman, became an Arhat. When the woman's husband passed by moments later in pursuit of his wayward spouse, he asked Mahātissa if he had seen a woman pass by recently. The elder replied: "I don't know if a man or woman went by here, but there was a collection of bones going by on the road."[86]

In his commentary to the *Theragāthā*, Dhammapāla tells a similar story about a dwarf named Bhaddiya.[87] Bhaddiya saw a certain courtesan (*gaṇikā*) riding in a chariot with a Brahmin on a festival day.[88] When she saw Bhaddiya, she laughed and showed her teeth. Bhaddiya took her teeth as a basis for meditation and entered into a state of concentration. He then began to engage in meditation on mindfulness of the body and, through these practices, became an Arhat.

In *The Legend and Cult of Upagupta*, John Strong relates a similar tale of what he calls "visionary ossification" found in a Chinese collection of legends about Upagupta.[89] A disciple of Upagupta began to practice cremation-ground meditation and, thinking that he had attained enlightenment, grew overconfident. Like the conceited monks that the Buddha sent to the cremation ground for a chastening experience of lust (see above, chap. 3), this monk was bound for a fall. One day while seeking alms he visited the house of a ravishing beauty. She smiled at him while offering him food, and he became so flustered that he failed to remove his bowl from its sling. She then perceived his excitement, became aroused herself, and commented on how excited he had become without even so much as touching her or hearing her voice. At this point, the monk realized that he must regain control of himself. So he, like Mahātissa, proceeded from the sight of her ossiferous teeth to ossify her entire body. When the beautiful woman standing before him had become a skeleton of dry white bones, the monk became an Arhat.

Through visionary ossification and through dharmic displays that expose Māra's duplicity, the Buddha and his *sangha* steal Māra's thunder and secure liberation for themselves and others. In private contemplative transformations of seductive bodies and in great public wars of wizardry, the forces of delusion and *saṃsāra* are pitted against the forces of insight and nirvana. Very often, those forces converge on the contested ground of women's bodies. Exposing feminine beauty as false advertising, the Buddha and his *sangha* tear away the outer facade, the bait that covers Māra's deadly hook, and reveal the horror that lurks within. But sometimes the Buddha and his *sangha* subvert Māra and his minions by joining forces with them. Fighting fire with fire, the Buddha dangles the carrot of female flesh in front of wayward monks like Nanda in order to extricate them from Māra's deadly clutches.

With the female body serving so readily to instantiate the truths of the Dharma that emerge out of the lies of *saṃsāra*, it is rather surprising that the dying Buddha advised members of his *sangha* to avoid seeing women (see chap. 1). It would have been more sensible to advise them to keep their eyes fixed on the female body whenever possible. Sooner or later, the false facade of a woman's beauty crumbles, and even the smile of a young woman in the full flower of youth contains a grimacing skull.

Buddhist discourse endows the female body with extraordinary powers—powers of *saṃsāri*c persuasion as well as dharmic dissuasion. Having seen ample evidence of the ambivalent power that the renunciant psyche of the post-Aśokan age attributed to the bodies of women, one wonders what effect this discourse might have had on women who joined the post-Aśokan *sangha.* Were these women prone to view themselves as female or as beings who had, through ordination, transcended the gender of their birth? If post-Aśokan nuns continued to regard themselves as female after their ordination, how did they understand their femininity? Were they influenced by the constructions of the feminine typical of the male hagiographic tradition that we have seen in the last two chapters? Did they, for example, view themselves as duplicitous mantraps standing in the way of male equanimity? In the next chapter, I explore these questions through the lens provided by post-Aśokan hagiographies that depict nuns using their own bodies as objects of contemplation.

CHAPTER FIVE

Seeing Through the Gendered "I": The Nun's Story

I met the Bishop on the road
And much said he and I.
"Those breasts are flat and fallen now
Those veins must soon be dry;
Live in a heavenly mansion,
Not in some foul sty."

William Butler Yeats,
"Crazy Jane Talks with the Bishop"

Separate but Equal Paths?

Early Buddhist scholars like Caroline Foley (more widely known by her married name: C. A. F. Rhys Davids), Mabel Bode, and Isabelle Horner viewed Buddhism as liberative for women because it allowed them to leave their domestically subordinated, feminine social roles as wives and mothers and join with other men and women in a spiritual path that rendered gender largely insignificant. According to Foley, the Buddha offered women a gender-free refuge whereby a woman could become "an asexual, rational being walking with wise men in recognized intellectual equality on higher levels of thought."[1] Contemporary students of Buddhist women's history such as Diana Paul and Karen Lang have challenged this view of Buddhism as egalitarian and gender-neutral. In their studies of misogynistic characterizations of women in Buddhist scripture, Lang and Paul argue that women are frequently subordinated to men and villainized by men in texts that privilege the androcentric perspective of the male renouncer.[2]

Jonathan Walters has attempted to forge a middle path between what he regards as overly optimistic early characterizations of Buddhism as liberative for women and overly bleak contemporary characterizations of Buddhism as androcentric and oppressive to women. Drawing attention to the importance of the Buddha's foster mother, the Great Pajāpatī Gotamī, as an exemplary figure for women, Walters suggests that a distinctively feminine model for women's spiritual achievement was articulated in post-Aśokan Pāli texts through the singling out of the Buddha's foster mother Gotamī as an exemplary figure equivalent to the Buddha on many levels.[3] She is called Gotamī to highlight the fact that she shares her son Gotama's worldly name and lineage. She is the founder of the women's monastic order (*bhikkhunī sangha*), as the Buddha is founder of the men's (*bhikkhu sangha*). What Gotama as founder of the men's order is by way of example for men, Gotamī as founder of the women's order is for women. As head of the order of nuns, she is the exemplary female renunciant. As founder and sustainer of that order, she is the female counterpart to her foster son, the Buddha. On the basis of such analogies, Walters argues that Gotamī occupies an important place in post-Aśokan Buddhism as an exemplar for women. Gotamī is the female double of Gotama; she is thus symbolically (if not theologically) a female Buddha.

On one level, Walters is absolutely correct. The shared lineages (both worldly and spiritual) and reciprocal nurturing that relates Gotamī, the foster mother of Gotama, to her adopted son does constitute her as the female counterpart to him. However, I would hardly characterize these male and female roles as "precisely parallel."[4] As I argued in chapter 1, comparisons between the Buddha and his stepmother as nurturers are frequently offered only to highlight the contrast: Gotamī lactates; Gotama preaches. Gotamī's milk will never quench the thirst of desire; Gotama's will. What Gotamī has to give is an extension of her transient physical body, the milk produced by her breasts; what Gotama has to give is an extension of his unchanging textual body. He gives the milk of Dharma which flows from the eternal body of the teaching or *dhammakāya.*

Further contrasts become evident when we examine the lives of Gotamī and Gotama from a biographical perspective. Her story is in many ways the inverse of his. When Gotama renounces the world, he abandons his wife, making Yaśodharā a virtual widow (in the sense that her husband has become symbolically dead to the world). Gotamī renounces the world after her husband Suddhodana makes her an actual widow by his physical death.[5] Gotamī's decision to renounce after the death of her husband makes sense given the culturally pervasive Brahminical view that a woman needs no independent spiritual life while her husband exists, for marriage is to her what initiation and spiritual learning are to him. A woman's spirituality consists entirely in serving her husband. The timing of Gotamī's renunciation also makes sense as a pragmatic move to avoid the hardships of the widow's life by seeking refuge in the Buddhist *sangha.* But in either case the decision is the result of a crisis over which Gotamī has no control: the death of a loved one.

Using the psychological distinction between internal and external loci of control, one may attribute Gotama's decision to renounce the world when still young to his possession of a highly developed internal locus of control. The future Buddha goes forth from the palace at the worst possible time, domestically speaking, since it was reportedly at the birth of his son Rāhula that Gotama decided to depart.[6] He goes forth from the palace despite the opposition of his family, leaving his wife husbandless and his parents without heir. If, in the language of Carol Gilligan, Gotamī operates out of an "ethic of responsibility" in delaying her pursuit of the path until after her husband's death, Gotama by contrast may be said to operate out of an ethic of priority.[7] When the universe is a house on fire, the first priority is to find an escape route so that all who are trapped within may be released. According to Gotama's ethic, nirvana (escape from the burning house of *saṃsāra*) is the supreme good from which all others are derived. Worldly concerns like marital responsibility and filial obligation must take a back seat as less urgent priorities.

Gotama is the renouncer par excellence: he renounces a harem full of female consorts who offer pleasures, a chief queen who offers him a son, and a father who offers him a kingdom. Gotamī is a former consort promoted, at the death of the Buddha's natural mother, to the position of chief queen of Suddhodana. By marrying the Buddha's father, she becomes the Buddha's foster mother. Thus Gotamī encompasses in her life all that Gotama rejects in his. She represents the social locations of consort, wife, and parent—in short, everything that Gotama must renounce in order to become the Buddha.

Ordination as Subordination: The Status of Women in the *Sangha*

If Gotamī is a female Buddha, or at least the exemplary female Arhat that all women should emulate in pursuing their separate path, Gotamī's deference to and dependence on her kinsmen in religious matters is also exemplary for those who tread the women's path. Gotamī renounced the world at the death of her husband and became a disciple of her son. In her immediate transition from being Suddhodana's chief queen to being Gotama's chief female disciple, we see a pattern of female subservience like that idealized in Brahminical culture. Brahminical texts such as *The Laws of Manu* state that a woman should always be under the care of a male guardian, whether her father (as a maiden), her husband (as a matron), or her son (as a widow).[8] When a woman immolates herself at the death of her husband, her son (as the double of the father in this world) presides over the ceremony; it is he who lights the cremation pyre. If a widow's son should die before his mother dies, another paternal kinsman succeeds the son as the woman's guardian. Since a woman should never be without a male guardian, the worst tragedy that can befall a woman is for her to survive after her husband, sons, and other male guardians have died.

That Gotamī is not the self-guarded (*sarakkhasī*) independent agent early scholars like Foley, Bode, and Horner considered her to be is amply attested in her biography. When her husband dies, she places herself in the care of her son. The 500 women of the Sakya clan who accompany her into the *sangha* are also reacting to a loss of male authority in their lives: their husbands have all renounced the world and left them virtual widows. Another biographical detail that provides evidence for my thesis is the fact that according to the *Gotamī Apadāna*, Gotamī passes out of the world of conditioned existence well before the Buddha. Walters views Gotamī's final passing (*parinirvāna*) as evidence of her implicit Buddhahood since she, like her son, attains not just the nirvana of the Arhats but the *parinirvāna* of the Buddhas. But where the Buddha dies at a ripe old age after a long teaching career, leaving a thriving monastic community as heirs of his Dharma and his person, Gotamī achieves *parinirvāna* in anticipation of the possibility that her otherworldly kinsmen might die and leave her spiritually bereft. Because she fears the death of her stepson, the Buddha, her natural son, Nanda, and her stepgrandson, Rāhula, as well as other key male figures, Gotamī chooses to end her life:

> I can't bear to see the Buddha's final passing, nor that of the two foremost disciples,
> nor that of Rāhula, Ānanda, and Nanda.

> Destroying and dismissing life's constituents,
> I should go out with the permission of the world's lord, the great sage.[9]

Gotama, in effect, lights the pyre of his mother Gotamī by granting her permission to pass from the world before his own final passing.

Women were admitted to the *sangha* under one decisive condition: that they submit to male authority. That is the gist of the eight special rules that Gotama imposed upon Gotamī and her followers in granting them entry into the *sangha*:

> 1. Any nun, no matter how long she had been in the order, must treat any monk, even the rudest novice, as if he were her senior. 2. Nuns should not take up residence during the annual rainy season retreat in any place where monks were not available to supervise them. 3. Monks would set the dates for the biweekly assemblies. 4. During the ceremony at the end of the rainy-season retreat, when monks and nuns invited criticisms from their own communities, the nuns must also invite criticism from the monks. 5. Monks must share in setting and supervising penances for the nuns. 6. Monks must share in the ordination of nuns. 7. Nuns must never revile or abuse monks. 8. Nuns must not reprimand monks directly (although they could and did report one monk's offensive behavior to another, who might then take the appropriate actions to correct it).[10]

According to Nancy Falk, the eight special conditions that Gotamī agreed to accept at the establishment of the *bhikkhunī sangha* meant that women would always be subordinate to men in the life of the *sangha* and would therefore always enjoy less respect and support from the lay community: "The discriminatory provisions meant that women would never be leaders in the life of the whole community or have any decisive voice in shaping its direction. They meant that the men would never be beholden to any of the nuns, in the way that students are beholden to teachers whose efforts have helped them find meaning and direction."[11] The structure of the primitive *sangha,* in Falk's view, reflects the subservient position of women vis-à-vis men in Brahminical culture. Nuns and monks could not be equals because equality presupposes a symmetry between the rules and statuses of the two *sangha*s. Where the *bhikkhu sangha* operates independently of the *bhikkhunī sangha* in matters of ordination, penance, and so forth, the special rules for the *bhikkhunī sangha* prohibit its operation as an independent body.[12]

Submission to male authority is also indicated in the process of obtaining consent to join the *sangha.* Where men are accepted into the *sangha* without consulting their wives, women cannot be ordained without the permission of their husbands. Once permitted by their husbands and fathers to enter the *bhikkhunī sangha,* women do not thereby achieve self-guardianship. Rebirth in the lineage of the Buddha may indeed bestow autonomy on women with respect to the social world left behind. The Pāli *Vinaya* reports several cases in which the former husbands of recently ordained nuns were thwarted in their efforts to recover their wives. But the autonomy gained through renunciation is limited for women. The pseudofamilial structure of the *sangha* subordinates the daughters of the Buddha to male authority figures, namely the Buddha as father and, in his post-*parinirvāṇ*ic absence, the sons of the Buddha as the father's doubles on earth.[13]

It is crucial to understand that rules limiting the independence of a female renouncer contain "buried tributes to her disruptive power," to use the language of Nina Auerbach.[14] This power is amply attested to—not only in occasional scriptural references to women as agents of Māra, but also in accounts of the founding of the *bhikkhunī sangha.* All versions of the story depict the Buddha conceding to his stepmother's wishes against his better judgment. But many end with this dire prediction: allowing women access to the homeless life, the Buddha predicts, will hasten the decline of the Dharma.

> If womankind had not been allowed to go forth from home to the homeless life into the discipline of Dharma made known by the Buddha, then, Ānanda, the celibate life [*brahmacariya*] would have lasted long; the true Dharma would have stood for a thousand years. But now, Ānanda, since women have gone forth from home to the homeless life into the discipline of Dharma, the celibate life will not last long; now, Ānanda, the true Dharma will stand just 500 years.
>
> Just as those communities that have many women and but few men are easily destroyed by robbers and thieves; even so, Ānanda, in whatever discipline of Dharma women are allowed to go forth from home to the homeless life, that celibate life will not last long.
>
> Just as when the disease known as "white-as-bones" falls upon a perfect field of rice, that field does not last long; even so, Ānanda,

> in whatever discipline of Dharma women are allowed to go forth from home to the homeless life, that celibate life will not last long.
>
> Just as when the disease known as "red-rust" falls upon a perfect field of sugarcane, that field does not last long; even so, Ānanda, in whatever discipline of Dharma women are allowed to go forth from home to the homeless life, that celibate life will not last long.
>
> And now, Ānanda, just as a man might build a dike to a great reservoir, with a view to the future, so that no water could pass beyond it; so I, Ānanda, with a view to the future, have laid down for nuns these eight cardinal rules which are not to be transgressed as long as they live.[15]

What better image of the disruptive power of women than that of a vast body of water capable of carrying off entire towns in its wake? The eight special rules keep the flood tide of feminine misconduct at bay, a least for a time. But even circumscribed by rules that contain their destructive energy, the mere presence of women renouncers still hastens the dystopian doomsday when the Dharma will cease to prevail.

On behalf of the 500 Sakyan women, Gotamī accepts the special rules most graciously, as if she, too, understood them as necessary fortifications against the flood tide of female transgression. The subordination of nuns to monks is clearly precedented by the deference with which Gotamī submits to the authority of Gotama. Gotamī may on one level be the female counterpart of Gotama, but there is no denying that she is Gotama's disciple. And Gotama, clearly, is not the disciple of his mother; he relates to her as a teacher or mentor behaves toward a student or disciple. Within the *sangha,* this subordination of Gotamī to Gotama is reduplicated pedagogically. Where nuns are frequently depicted going to monks for instruction in the Dharma, no monks are seen to take instruction from nuns. Post-Aśokan accounts describe many celebrated teachers in the *bhikkhunī sangha.* Gotamī Mahāpajāpatī, Dhammadinā, and Khemā are all depicted as masterful teachers of the Dharma. But although some nuns may have taught men while addressing lay audiences, within the *sangha* their teaching was strictly segregated, with no monks in attendance.[16] Thus those daughters of the Buddha who had a flair for teaching had no opportunity to teach the sons of the Buddha; they gave instruction in the Dharma to the *bhikkhunī sangha* only. In accepting the special rules dictating that nuns should treat monks with deference, and in setting a pedagogical precedent by taking her *sangha* to monks for instruction, Gotamī makes the asymmetry of her relationship with Gotama the norm for the *bhikkhunī sangha*'s relationship with the *bhikkhu sangha.*

Indeed, not only the asymmetry of Gotamī's relationship to Gotama but also the very apposition of mother and son is reduplicated in the post-Aśokan hagiographic tradition. Post-Aśokan reconstructions of life in the primitive *sangha* (such as Dhammapāla's commentary on the *Therīgāthā and Theragāthā*, which are collections of verses attributed to early nuns and monks, respectively) include several stories of mothers who follow their renouncer-sons into the *sangha.* In each case, the mother was formerly self-guarded (*sarakkhasī*) as a courtesan, a woman without a husband to serve as her guardian. After renouncing her profession and taking ordination in the *bhikkhunī sangha,* the mother turns to her son for religious instruction. In each case, the son leads the mother to liberative insight by urging her to appreciate the impermanence and inherent impurity of her body. Since recognizing the repugnant inner nature of the female body is a dominant theme in hagiographies of prominent monks redacted during the post-Aśokan period, it appears that the instruction that these mothers receive from their sons is far from gender-neutral in content.

Women's Ordination as a Process of Mortification

Dhammapāla's commentary on *Therīgāthā* 26 tells such a story of a mother instructed by her son. Where other verses of the *Therīgāthā* and *Theragāthā* are ascribed to named nuns and monks, the verses upon which Dhammapāla comments are ascribed to "Abhaya's mother," underscoring the fact of her subordination to her son. Dhammapāla explains that in the past, Abhaya's mother acquired merit by giving alms to former Buddhas. Due to this merit, she was born as a courtesan named Padumavātī ("Lotus-like"). Padumavātī became a consort of King Bimbisāra of Magadha and had a son named Abhaya by him. Abhaya became a monk and eventually achieved Arhatship. One day, Padumavātī heard her son giving religious instruction. Moved by what Abhaya said, she renounced the world and entered the monastic order, becoming an Arhat in due course, like her son. In explaining the verses she spoke upon becoming an Arhat, Dhammapāla indicates that the insight which enabled Padumavātī to become an Arhat stemmed from an anatomy lesson she received from her son. "She spoke the stanza whereby her own son Abhaya the Elder had admonished her, and with the power of inspiration responded with her own":

> "Upward from the sole of the foot, mother, downward from the crown of the head
> Consider this body, this impure, foul-smelling thing."
>
> "With this mode of thought, all passion is abolished.
> My fever is broken; I'm cool and calm."[17]

Why did Abhaya find it necessary to explain the foulness of the body to his mother? One might suppose that as a former courtesan who made her living through her sexuality, she was thought to be in need of such instruction. But it seems that Abhaya himself had trouble suppressing his sexual urges and that he meditated on the inner repulsiveness of the female body as a means of overcoming sexual desire. There is a telling stanza attributed to an Abhaya in the *Theragāthā*, and although this Abhaya was not the son of Bimbisāra but a Brahmin's son, it is reasonable to assume that post-Aśokan tradition has conflated the two Abhayas. According to Dhammapāla's commentary on *Theragāthā* 98, Abhaya saw an attractively dressed woman one day while making an alms round in a village. His composure shaken, he returned to the monastery thinking about how the sight of this woman had disrupted his mindfulness. "Censuring his own mind, insight developed and he became an Arhat right then and there."[18] In the stanza he spoke upon attaining Arhatship, Abhaya reviewed what happens if one allows the mind to fix on the beauty of a woman:

> With the mind fixed on what is pleasing, one sees beauty and suddenly mindfulness is destroyed.[19] One experiences passion in the mind and heart, and becomes addicted to this. In such a person grow the afflictions [*āsavā*] that bring new existence in their wake.[20]

Abhaya achieved insight into the conditions that bind one to the cycle of birth and death (*saṃsāra*) by falling prey to and then overcoming the beguiling sight of an attractive woman. Because the verses Abhaya's mother quotes suggests the standard procedure for meditating on the foulness of the body's component parts, we can safely assume that Abhaya suppressed the desire arising in him by reflection on the impure constituents of the alluring body he had seen. This meditation on the foulness of the body, in turn, formed the basis for the instruction he imparted to his mother.

The nun Ambapālī became an Arhat under circumstances very similar to those of Abhaya's mother.[21] Like Abhaya's mother, Ambapālī was a courtesan. She, too, had a son by King Bimbisāra. That son, named Vimala Kondañña, preceded his mother in renouncing the world. After hearing her son teach the Dharma, Ambapālī, like Abhaya's mother, joined the order and became an Arhat. Presumably, Vimala Kondañña taught Ambapālī to meditate on the foulness of her body just as Abhaya taught his mother, for Ambapālī began to use her own body as an object of meditation after taking instruction from her son. "Having heard the Dharma from her own son, Vimala Kondañña, she worked for insight, and became agitated about the existence of old age and decay in her own body."[22] Ambapālī became an Arhat by gaining insight into the law of impermanence as illustrated by her own aging body; the verses she speaks upon attaining Arhatship reveal the decayed condition of her aged body in a point by point contrast with the excellence of her youthful body:

> My hair was black, the color of bees, curled at the ends;
> with age it's become like bark or hemp—
> not other than this are the Truth-speaker's words.
>
> My hair was fragrant, full of flowers like a perfume box;
> with age it smells like dog's fur—
> not other than this are the Truth-speaker's words.
>
> Thick as a well-planted grove and pretty gathered up with comb and pin;
> with age it's thin here and there—
> not other than this are the Truth-speaker's words.
>
> Black tresses beautified with gold, resplendent, adorned with a braid;
> with age my head has become quite bald—
> not other than this are the Truth-speaker's words.
>
> Before, my eyebrows were arched as though drawn by artists;
> with age they now hang down with wrinkles—
> not other than this are the Truth-speaker's words.
>
> Flashing and brilliant as jewels, my dark eyes were large;
> overcome with age, they are no longer beautiful—
> not other than this are the Truth-speaker's words.

In youth my nose was long, beautiful, and delicate;
with age it has become pendulous—
not other than this are the Truth-speaker's words.

In the past, my earlobes were beautiful like well-crafted, finely polished bracelets;
with age they hang down with wrinkles—
not other than this are the Truth-speaker's words.

In the past my teeth were beautiful, the color of plantain buds;
with age they have broken and yellowed—
not other than this are the Truth-speaker's words.

My voice was sweet as a wild cuckoo in the forest grove;
with age it falters now and then—
not other than this are the Truth-speaker's words.

Formerly my throat was beautiful like a well-polished conch;
with age it is broken and ruined—
not other than this are the Truth-speaker's words.

My beautiful arms used to be round as door-bars;
with age they are weak as the trumpet creeper—
not other than this are the Truth-speaker's words.

Adorned with gold and delicate rings my hands were once beautiful;
with age they look just like twisted roots—
not other than this are the Truth-speaker's words.

Once my two breasts were full and round, quite beautiful;
they now hang pendulous as water-skins without water—
not other than this are the Truth-speaker's words.

My body was once beautiful as a well-polished tablet of gold;
now it is covered all over with very fine wrinkles—
not other than this are the Truth-speaker's words.

At one time my thighs were as stately as the trunks of elephants;
with age they have become like bamboo-stalks—
not other than this are the Truth-speaker's words.

My legs used to be lovely, adorned with fine golden anklets;
with age they are like little sticks of the sesame plant—
not other than this are the Truth-speaker's words.

My feet were quite shapely, as if stuffed with cotton;
with age they are cracked and wrinkled—
not other than this are the Truth-speaker's words.

Such was this body which is decrepit now, the abode of many sorrows;
an old house with its plaster falling off—
not other than this are the Truth-speaker's words.[23]

Both Ambapālī and Abhaya's mother renounce the world in imitation of their renunciant sons. Both become Arhats by taking their own bodies as objects of meditation. Abhaya's mother chose this meditation topic at the instigation of her son, and Ambapālī may also have been instructed in the foulness of her body by her son. The *Therīgāthā* records the story of another courtesan—named Vimalā—who becomes an Arhat after receiving an anatomy lesson from a member of the *bhikkhu sangha.*[24] But unlike Ambapālī and Abhaya's mother, Vimalā receives her lesson at the hands of an angry monk whom she had attempted to seduce. The daughter of a woman who "earned her living by her beauty," Vimalā was just beginning a career as a courtesan in Vesālī when she saw the monk Mahā Moggallāna going on an alms round.[25] She followed him to his dwelling and tried to seduce him. "Some say," Dhammapāla reports, "she was instigated to do so by heretics." In any case, as the *Theragāthā* reports, she was rebuked in no uncertain terms by the Great Moggallāna:[26]

Oh you skeletal hut of bone plastered over with flesh and tendons—
You should be ashamed of yourself, oh foul-smelling flesh belonging to others which you treat as your own.[27]
Oh bag of dung wrapped in skin; oh demoness [*pisācinī*] with swollen breasts!
There are nine passages in your body that ooze constantly,
Your body with its nine foul-smelling passages
A monk should avoid just as someone who desires purity avoids excrement.
If only people knew you in this way, as I know you,
They would keep their distance from you as they avoid a cesspool in the rains.[28]

Seeing the vanity of her attempt to entice the Great Moggallāna with "a bag of dung wrapped in skin," Vimalā drops her head in shame and self-reproach. In his final words to her, Moggallāna tells her that it would be as difficult to captivate his heart/mind (*citta*) as to paint the sky yellow. Clearly, he knows something she has yet to learn about the body's true nature, and this knowledge steels him against the power of her charms.

Thus censured by the Great Moggallāna, Vimalā becomes a lay supporter of the *sangha* and later enters the order herself. Not long afterward, she becomes an Arhat. In her verses, Vimalā sets up a contrast between her former occupation as a bewitcher of men and her present condition as a renunciant woman indifferent to male attention, content with enjoying the peace of nirvana:

> Intoxicated with my glowing skin, my beauty, my luck, and my fame;
> Utterly confident of my youthful charms, I scorned other women;
> Having decorated myself, that attractive body called out to fools.
> Like a hunter putting out his snare,
> I stood at the gate where prostitutes stand in hopes of wealth;
> Showing myself to be well put together,
> I revealed a great deal of what should be hidden;
> I managed all kinds of deception, and made fun of many people.
>
> Today I wander for alms—bald and wearing a robe;
> Seated at the foot of a tree, I've achieved a state of thoughtless trance;[29]
> I've cut off all the bonds to which deities and humans are subject;
> Having destroyed all the afflictions [*āsave*], I'm cool and tranquil.[30]

With her head shaved, Vimalā has dispensed with one of the most readily discernible markers of gender. It has been argued by more than one theorist that the shaving of the head in Buddhist ordination plays an important symbolic role. In sporting hairless heads, Buddhist renouncers symbolically encode their social identity as celibate renouncers.[31] By virtue of the body's bilateral symmetry, Freud observed, the head often stands in for the genitals in dreams and symbolic discourse. A shaved head, it is argued, connotes a castrated penis, while a head with rampant hair growth indicates virility.[32] Whether it is indeed universally true that shaved heads bespeak celibacy,[33] it is in any case clear that Vimalā regards her present condition as intentionally unalluring. She used to paint her body in order to make it "speak" for her, communicating her availability to potential customers. She used to make heads turn, beguiling men with her self-presentation. And she used to savor her power, heaping scorn on her admirers and mocking them "with insolent laughter." Now she sports a shaved head and begs for alms cloaked in a shapeless robe. She keeps her eyes downcast, avoiding the gaze of others. And she spends her days in meditation, using—in all likelihood—her own body as a support for understanding the anatomy lesson the Great Moggallāna taught her.

Now that Vimalā has donned the robes of a renouncer, her body no longer bespeaks her gender. Indeed, it would seem that Caroline Rhys Davids was correct in viewing the female renouncer as "an asexual, rational being." In outward appearance, Buddhist nuns and monks tend to look quite similar. Gender differences are muted by their baggy robes and hairless heads, not to mention their docile, highly controlled bodies that avoid the exaggerated, stylized motions that encode gender differences.[34] But while the ideal toward which nuns and monks strive may indeed be that of an asexual being, such beings are not born at ordination. They are, to the contrary, painstakingly constructed. Gender plays an all-important role in the *sangha*'s production of asexual beings, and it is women who (as objects of meditation) most readily serve as the means of production whereby such beings are created.

It seems to me that Buddhist nuns who delight in cataloging the imperfections of their bodies have learned to see themselves through the gendered "I" that is presupposed in the tales of male insight and awakening narrated in the four preceding chapters. It should be remembered that Ambapālī, Abhaya's mother, and Vimalā all receive their meditation subjects from male mentors—either from their sons, in the case of Ambapālī and Abhaya's mother, or from a prominent monk, as in the case of Vimalā. It is only natural that Vimala Kondañña, Abhaya, and Moggallāna should recommend that these women use their own bodies as objects of meditation, since female bodies figure so prominently as object lessons and sources of insight for men. In urging these women to use their own bodies as supports for meditation, Vimalā Kondañña, Abhaya, and Moggallāna in effect teach Ambapālī, Abhaya's mother, and Vimalā how to occupy the subject position associated with men of insight.

But unlike the monk who, as observing subject, contemplates with horror a body that is not his own, the loathly nun who performs this meditation is both the observing subject and the observed object. In order to occupy the subject position, she turns her gaze on her own body as object. Surveying her own body as an ideal object of meditation, the loathly nun achieves the enlightened subjectivity made normative by exemplary men of insight. She thus incorporates within herself both the male and female roles characteristic of the monks' stories. This double identification that enables the loathly nun to apprehend herself with a male gaze is reminiscent of the elision of subject and object that feminist art historians and film critics regard as one of the hallmarks of female spectatorship within cultural media that mark the female body as a "site of sight."[35] Art historian John Berger, for example, argues that the gaze of a female subject is self-reflexive; because it incorporates within itself a male "surveyor," the female gaze tends toward self-objectification:

> Men look at women. Women watch themselves being looked at. This determines not only the relations between men and women but also the relation of women to themselves. The surveyor of woman in herself is male: the surveyed, female. Thus she turns herself into an object—and most particularly, an object of vision: a sight.[36]

The German feminist Frigga Haug argues that women are socialized to appreciate themselves as they are seen by others because of the commodification of female beauty.[37] Since a woman's ability to arouse desire through outward appearance has traditionally been regarded as a commodity comparable to a man's strength, aptitude, and wealth, it is in the family's best interest to produce daughters with the self-possessed grace of women who know what kind of figures they cut in the world. This is achieved through self-surveillance. Consider, for example, the ritual of congregating in bathrooms and striking poses before the mirror that adolescent girls in contemporary America engage in so readily. Through such openly self-reflexive activities, young women learn how to evaluate themselves from the perspective of potential admirers, how to accentuate those features that are most likely to turn heads. As long as women are encouraged to capitalize on their looks, such rituals will inevitably continue, making the process of socialization for women one of sexualization.

"Woman, we suspect, lives always before her glass, and makes a mirror of existence," opined Mrs. E. Lynn Linton, a nineteenth-century social critic.[38] If the male gaze is voyeuristic in its relentless focus on the eroticized other, the female gaze is essentially narcissistic; the other serves as an audience or a mirror for exhibitionistic self-display.[39] A kind of seeing that uses the entire objective world as a mirror for self-evaluation, the narcissistic gaze directs itself to others only inasmuch

Figure 8. Lucas Furtenagel, *The Burgkmair Spouses* (1529). Reproduced by permission of the Kunsthistorisches Museum, Vienna.

as others mirror the self. Linton suggests the self-reflexivity of the female gaze in observing that women possess a "self-consciousness of a very peculiar and feminine sort—a consciousness not of themselves in themselves, but of the reflection of themselves in others."[40] When a woman meets a man's gaze, then, it is to see herself as he sees her, to find a reflection of herself in the mirror of his eyes.[41] Iconic statements about female narcissism abound in Western art and literature. Nineteenth-century images of women lost in semiconscious reverie while observing themselves in mirrors or pools of water have their iconographic roots (and precedent for their moral tone) in medieval and Renaissance renderings of the momento mori theme in which the vanity of cherishing the flesh is represented by skulls placed on vanity tables or reflected in ladies' mirrors (see fig. 8).[42] The woman-and-her-mirror theme is also well attested in Indian art, where celestial and earthly courtesans are often depicted holding mirrors in such a way as to view their rounded buttocks ornamented with jeweled girdles.

In post-Aśokan hagiography, the nuns who were once courtesans still view themselves as if in a mirror. But unlike stereotypical courtesans lost in narcissistic self-objectification, however, these former courtesans do not accentuate those aspects of their appearance most readiliy appreciated by admirers. To the contrary, these women abjure cosmetics and ornaments, cloak their feminine forms in a unisex uniform, and reflect at length on those aspects of their appearance most likely to induce revulsion. In the mirror that is their world, they no longer seek a confirmation of their beauty and power. The image they wish to see in the mirror of men's eyes is an unattractive and unassuming form, a body that repels rather than attracts. By celebrating the grotesque nature of their bodies, former courtesans like Ambapālī, Abhaya's mother, and Vimalā render a great service to the *bhikkhu sangha.* They impart a liberative knowledge to monks whose ignorance of the body's true nature makes them susceptible to feminine charms.

Not all nuns, however, were able to serve the *sangha* with such alacrity. Post-Aśokan tradition records many instances of vain nuns who had to be taught a lesson in humility. These are generally women who did not wish to join the *sangha* in the first place. The vain nun is often a woman persuaded to renounce, against her better judgment, after the loss of loved ones through death and renunciation. Unlike the loathly nun who abjures her power to turn heads, the vain nun continues to seek confirmation of her beauty after entering the *sangha.* But in each case where a vain nun is involved, the Buddha makes a true renouncer out of her by creating a magical double of herself and then causing the spectral body to undergo grotesque disfigurations.[43]

Female Phantasms as Aids to Women's Self-Objectification

Rūpa Nandā was the natural daughter of Gotamī, the Buddha's stepmother, and the natural sister of Nanda, the Buddha's stepbrother. Her story, told in the *Dhammapada* commentary, begins with Rūpa Nandā renouncing the world out of loneliness and attachment to her relatives, most of whom had left home for the monastic life. After the ordination of her unnamed husband, her nephew Rāhula, and her mother Gotamī, Rūpa Nandā joined the *bhikkhunī sangha,* thinking "Now that these kinsfolk have renounced, what's the point of a home?" Like her brother

Nanda, who became a monk out of reticence and respect for his half brother Gotama, Rūpa Nandā leaves the world "only out of affection for her kinsfolk, not out of faith."[44]

At the time of ordination, members of the *sangha* receive a name that indicates something of their character. The name that is bestowed upon this nun announces both her appearance and her outlook. Being both very beautiful and very vain, she is a joy to look at and one who enjoys looking at her own beauty. Her name may be translated variously as "Shapely [*rūpa*] Delight [*nanda*]," "Beautiful [*rūpa*] Joy [*nanda*]," or "She Who Enjoys [*nanda*] Physical Form or Beauty [*rūpa*]." When Rūpa Nandā hears that the Buddha teaches that beauty is impermanent, without essence, and intrinsically dissatisfying, she thinks, "Then he might talk about the inadequacy [*dosa*] of my beautiful, delightful form."[45] For this reason, she avoids her brother's presence, even though by this she deprives herself of his religious instruction. One evening she hears nuns and laypeople returning from the monastery where they have heard the Buddha give a discourse. Praising the appearance, the sound, the austerity, and the virtue of the Buddha, the nuns and laypeople inspire in Rūpa Nandā the desire to see her brother's physical form without herself being seen:

> Seeing the Tathāgata [the Buddha] as a physical form, a golden-colored body adorned with the major and minor marks [characteristic of the Buddhas], those who see him are pleased and pacified. . . . Hearing the Tathāgata as sound . . . , those who hear him are pleased and pacified. On account of the Tathāgata's austerity, the austerity of his robes, etc., they are pleased and pacified. . . . Thinking, "The Blessed One has no counterpart in mortality and virtue," they are pleased and pacified. When describing the virtues of the Tathāgata, the mouth does not suffice.
>
> In the midst of the nuns and lay supporters, Rūpa Nandā heard talk of the Tathāgata's virtues and thought, "They tell of my brother's incredible beauty. Declaring the inadequacy of my form, just think how much he could say in only one day![46] What if I go together with the nuns but, not showing myself, just look at the Tathāgata and listen to his Dharma?"[47]

When she announces her intention to hear the Dharma, the nuns rejoice. "At last, Rūpa Nandā has produced the desire to visit the Teacher. On account of this, the Teacher will teach a vivid lesson in

Dharma today."[48] Meanwhile, the omniscient Buddha, aware of his sister's intentions, selects with skill the best means of curing his sister's vanity:

> He thought, "Today Rūpa Nandā will come to honor me. What kind of lesson in Dharma would be most appropriate for her?[49] Holding physical form in esteem, she has a fierce affection for her body." He concluded that her disintoxication from intoxication with form would be best achieved by form itself [*rūpen' ev' assā rūpamadanimmaddanaṃ*]. And so, just as one draws out one thorn using another thorn, he conjured up [*abhinimmi*] a beautiful woman by his psychic power [*iddhibalena*] at the moment Rūpa Nandā entered the monastery. She was the very definition of sweet sixteen [*solasavassuddesikaṃ*], standing there in his presence dressed in red, wearing all her ornaments, holding a fan, and fanning herself.[50]

As she looks at the perfectly shaped, richly adorned phantasm, Rūpa Nandā sees herself "as a crow standing in front of a golden colored royal goose." Her eyes wander up and down the surface of her body, admiring her various features. The Teacher knows that "fierce affection" has arisen in his sister, who is wholly absorbed in the contemplation of this lovely feminine form. He causes the body to age in appearance, so that Rūpa Nandā suddenly sees a twenty-year-old woman. His sister notices the difference instantly, and "her mind was a little displeased."[51] The Buddha then causes the spectral woman to age in a time-lapse sequence. First, he gives her the appearance of a woman who has given birth once, then the appearance of a middle-aged woman, and then the appearance of an "old woman broken with decay." Rūpa Nandā, aware of the changes wrought by each stage of the phantom's aging process, becomes disgusted (*virajji*) upon seeing the last stage: a grey-headed, toothless, hunchbacked, palsied old woman leaning on a walking stick.

On the verge of achieving his goal, the Teacher moves in for the kill:

> Then the Teacher mastered her with disease [*vyādhinā abhibhūtaṃ*]. Screaming loudly, she threw down her stick and fan, fell to the ground, and rolled back and forth, wallowing in her own urine and feces. Seeing her, Rūpa Nandā was extremely disgusted [*ativiya virajji*]. The Teacher then caused her to see the death of this woman.

> Her body immediately assumed a bloated condition; putrid lumps and maggots oozed out through her nine orifices. Crows and the like fell on her and tore into her flesh. Rūpa Nandā, observing this, thought, "This woman has fallen prey to old age, disease, and death right here in front of me; my body will also experience old age, disease, and death." She saw the body from [the perspective of] impermanence [*attabhāvam aniccato passi*]. Because of this seeing from [the perspective of] impermanence, it was seen also from [the perspective of] dissatisfaction [*dukkhato*] and essencelessness [*anattato*]. Then for her the three states of existence appeared like burning houses, like carrion wrapped around [her] neck. Her mind flew toward its object of meditation [*kammaṭṭhāna*].[52]

At this point, Rūpa Nandā's iconic lesson in Dharma is completed. It now remains to be seen whether she will realize the meaning of this lesson without verbal instruction.

> Knowing that she had seen from the perspective of impermanence, the Teacher observed her. "Will she be able to establish a foundation on her own? Probably not; she ought to have some external support." Thus for her benefit he spoke this lesson in Dharma:
>
> See, Nandā, the abject, impure, putrid body,
> Oozing, dripping, cherished by fools.[53]
>
> As this, so that; as that, so this,
> See the elements [*dhātuyo*] from [the perspective of] emptiness
> [*suññato*]; do not return to the world again!
> Discarding delight in existence, you will wander in peace.[54]

Hearing these verses, Rūpa Nandā "organized her knowledge in accordance with the teaching" and attained the fruit of a stream enterer (*sotāpattiphalaṃ*). Wishing to propel his sister even further, Gotama taught her "emptiness as a object of meditation" (*suññatākammaṭṭhānaṃ*):

> "Do not entertain the thought, Rūpa Nandā, that there is any essence [*sāro*] in this body. It is nothing but a city made of bones, constructed with 300 bones." Saying this, he spoke the following stanza [*Dhammapada* 150]:
>
> "A city made of bones plastered with flesh and blood,
> Where decay and death, pride and hypocrisy are stored."[55]

The word-glossing portion of the commentary then unpacks the simile of the body as a city. Just as one erects structures for the storage of food, so the body, in which the fruits of deeds are deposited, is a constructed thing. It is a scaffolding of 300 bones plastered with flesh and blood and covered with skin (see fig. 7 above). The physical afflictions (*kāyika ābādho*) of death and decay, and the mental afflictions (*cetasiko ābādho*) of pride and hypocrisy, are deposited there. Hence there is nothing exalted (*uddhaṃ*) to be found there. Seen from the perspective of emptiness or essencelessness, the body is a hollow shed, a container containing nothing of value (see fig. 7). At the conclusion of this verbal exhortation, "Therī Rūpa Nandā became an Arhat, and for the multitude, also, there was a useful Dharma-lesson."[56]

In the *Therī-apadāna,* Rūpa Nandā (here known as Kalyāṇī Nandā, *kalyāṇi* being a synonym for *rūpa*) tells her own story in an eloquent first-person narrative.[57] This version of the story describes an even more vivid lesson in Dharma than that of the *Dhammapada* commentary with its time-lapsed spectacle of decay. Here the phantom woman is bitten by a poisonous spider as she rests in Nandā's lap, and she dies a horrible death in Nandā's arms. The story begins with Nandā in a past-life encounter with a previous Buddha named Padumuttara. She makes a donation to him and his *sangha* and vows to attain, one day, the rank of chief among the contemplative nuns (*jhāyinīṃ bhikkhunīnaṃ aggaṭṭānaṃ*). The Buddha Padumuttara predicts her future birth as Nandā, declaring that she will be a legitimate heir (*dāyādā orasā*) of Gotama's Dharma. Because of her meritorious actions, she is reborn in a series of exalted celestial locations. Then, in her final existence, she is born in Kapilavastu as the beautiful (*kalyāṇī*) daughter of Suddhodana and Mahāpajāpatī:

> Of all the young women in this very charming city, with the exception of Yaśodharā,
> I was famous as "the Beautiful One" [*kalyāṇī*].
>
> With my oldest brother the chief of the three worlds, and my middle brother an Arhat,
> I, the sole householder, was scolded by my mother:
>
> "You were born in the Sakya lineage, child, and you resemble the Buddha.
> Being without Nanda, why do you remain at home?[58]

Youthful form, when overpowered by old age, is considered impure.
Even healthy life has its end in disease, has death as its terminator.

Look at this, your pleasing, delightful, and captivating form,
That when decorated with ornaments resembles the adorned Sri.[59]

Worshiped as the best in the world, it is an elixir for the eyes,
A generator of fame for the meritorious, the joy of the Okkāka family.

In just a short time, it will be altogether destroyed from decay.
Leaving home while still young, choose the Dharma, blameless one."

Here we see Gotamī in a Buddha-like role, exhorting her daughter to renounce while she is still young rather than postponing renunciation until the later years of life. And in conformity with her mother's wishes, Kalyāṇī Nandā does renounce. But, like her double Rūpa Nandā, she renounces "with the body but not with the heart" (*dehena na tu cittena*). Far from seeing the world as a burning house or a carcass around her neck, Kalyāṇī Nandā is apathetic, "languid with beauty and youth." Meditation and study do not come easily to her: "Mother said to do it, but I wasn't zealous about it."[60] At this point, her elder brother intervenes with a private Dharma-lesson:

Then the greatly compassionate one saw me lingering in lust.
For the sake of aversion to beauty [*nibbindanatthaṃ rūpasmiṃ*], the conqueror, in the range of my vision,

Produced by his own majesty a radiant woman. She was a sight to see—more splendid, even, than I, so shapely was she.

I gazed at her fathomless body and was astonished.
Thinking, "I'm lucky to have attained human eyes,"

I said to her, "Come here, lucky one, and tell me why you've come.
Tell me, if you don't mind, your family, your lineage, and your name.

But, of course, this is no time for questions, lucky one.
Lie down on my lap and rest yourself on my body for a moment."

Then, having put her head on my lap, the lovely eyed one lay down.
An extremely poisonous spider dropped onto her forehead.

Even as it fell, boils rose up, and pus and blood oozed out of her broken corpse.

Then her face became disfigured and her body became putrid-smelling; her entire body was now bloated and discolored.

Trembling all over and sighing repeatedly, she declared her own misery and wept pitifully.

"I'm miserable with misery [*dukkhena dukkhitā*].
I'm drowning in great misery—be my refuge, friend!"

"But what's happened to the splendor of your face, your aquiline nose? What's happened to your mouth, with its fine copper-colored lips?

And your neck as shapely as a conch shell? Your ears, quivering like swings, are now discolored.

Your juglike breasts, resembling the buds of the celestial coral tree, are now burst open.[61] You've become an evil-smelling, putrid corpse.

Your waist like a sacrificial altar [*vedimajjhā*] and your broad buttocks are stained with wounds [*vaṛitakibbisā*] like a slaughterhouse.[62] You're now filled with impurity [*abhejjabharitā*].[63] Beauty clearly doesn't last.

All that arises in the body is putrid-smelling and frightful, like a loathsome cremation ground where only fools find delight."[64]

As in Ambapālī's catalog of her decaying features, here the conventions of feminine beauty are turned on their head. The firm, round breasts of a conventional Indian beauty are normally compared to the shapely buds of the celestial coral tree. Here, the breasts have burst open with putrescence—a horrible subversion of the breast-as-bud motif. A shapely woman's waist would normally remind a poet of the *vedi,* a sacrificial altar that is narrow in the middle and broader at the top. But this spectral woman's wasit reminds Nandā of a slaughterhouse, a benighted place where profane beings are unceremoniously sacrificed.

Kalyāṇī Nandā has clearly seen the foulness that lurks just beneath the surface of a splendid female form. As she observes at close range the grisly transformation of the captivatingly beautiful woman, Nandā is released from the spell of her own specious charms. Beginning with incredulity ("But what's happened to the splendor of your face, your aquiline nose?"), she ends by heaping scorn on those fools who cherish the fetid charnel field that is the body. Her language shifts from dismay to ironic mockery, suggesting that a sea change as momentous as the transformation of the phantom is occurring inside Kalyāṇī Nandā. Her brother observes and encourages in Nandā a state of agitation that signals a cognitive breakthrough:

> Seeing me with agitated heart and mind [*saṃviggacittaṃ*], he said these verses to me:
>
> "See, Nandā, the abject, putrid corpse that is the body.
> By means of what's foul, cultivate a calm, well-composed heart and mind."[65]

As a result of this powerful experience, Kalyāṇī Nandā becomes an Arhat and fulfills her vow to become the chief of the contemplative nuns in the *bhikkhunī sangha.*

Making a Spectacle of Oneself: Self-Denigrating and Self-Disfiguring Practices in the Life of the *Bhikkhunī Sangha*

One of the most eloquent nuns whose insights are preserved in the *Therīgāthā* is Sumedhā. Sumedhā's verses, appearing last in a compilation arranged in ascending order of complexity, constitute an elaborate and moving argument for maintaining chastity in the face of societal pressure to marry and reproduce.[66] Sumedhā had been taking instruction from the nuns as a lay disciple for many years and, as a young woman of marriageable age, had decided not to marry but to join the *bhikkhunī sangha.* When she learned that her parents had promised her in marriage to King Anikaratta, Sumedhā retired to her room and defiantly cut off all her hair in imitation of the tonsure ceremony that heralds entry into the *sangha.* While getting their heads shaved, novice nuns and monks are given a lock of tonsured hair as an aid to meditation on impermanence; Sumedhā, recreating the ordination ritual in her own home, likewise focused her mind on impermanence while contemplating her shorn hair. In doing this meditation, she entered a trance state and was absorbed in contemplation when her parents entered her room to prepare her for marriage.

Sumedhā was no mean orator, and in the end she not only convinced her parents to let her join the *sangha* but she made Buddhists out of her family and household staff as well as her bridegroom and his retinue. Not only does Sumedhā speak most eloquently to her parents and bridegroom about the folly of sensual pleasure—she also shows a certain dramatic flair in using her symbolically laden tresses as a stage prop. Interrupted from her hair-induced meditation, Sumedhā holds her dark tresses in her hands while admonishing her audience with images such as this:

> What is this foul, impure thing smelling of its own emissions, a horrible bag of skin filled with corpses,[67] always flowing, full of impurities?
>
> What do I know it to be like? The body is repulsive, smeared with flesh and blood, food for worms and birds. How can it be given away?[68]
>
> Before too long the insensate body is carried off to the charnel field and disgusted relatives throw it out like a piece of wood.
>
> When they have thrown it out in the charnel field as food for others, even one's own mother and father are disgusted and wash themselves; how much more so people in general?
>
> People are attached to a body that has no essence: an aggregate of bones and sinews that's full of saliva, tears, excrement, and urine—a putrid thing.
>
> If it should be turned inside out while being dissected, even one's own mother would be disgusted, being unable to bear the smell of it.[69]

After thirty such verses, Sumedhā concludes by tossing her hair on the floor in a final dramatic gesture of repudiation. At this point, the suitor rises to his fiancée's defense. King Anikaratta convinces Sumedhā's parents to allow the young woman to pursue her chosen path.

Sumedhā's oratory summarizes the gist of many verbal teachings addressed by the Buddha to worldly nuns. Indeed, Sumedhā's verses crystallize just about everything the Buddha was reported to have said about the foulness of the body and the folly of lust. There was another woman, according to the *Therīgāthā* commentary, who spoke as eloquently as Sumedhā of the transience and foulness of the body.[70] But this nun, named Subhā, went on to use her body as an iconic teaching device when the verbal teaching did not suffice. Subhā not only repeated what the Buddha said but also disfigured her body in illustration, thus reproducing in her own body the gruesome transformation of the female body that so frequently accompanied the Buddha's verbal teaching.

Like Sumedhā, this nun was faced with a situation that threatened her chastity. Subhā, whose name implies radiance, beauty, luck, and pleasure, was a lovely Brahmin girl living in Rājagaha. When the Buddha came to Rājagaha, Subhā became a lay disciple and later joined the *bhikkhunī sangha.* It was Subhā's habit to visit Jīvaka's mango grove in the afternoons, taking advantage of this quiet spot for her midday rest. One day a young rogue (*dhuttapurisa*) followed her to the mango grove and cornered her there, barring Subhā's exit in a manner that suggests his ability to use physical force to overcome her resistance. Hoping to persuade Subhā to renounce her robes and precepts, he tells her: "You're young and flawlessly beautiful; what's the advantage of going forth for someone like you? Toss aside your yellow robe. Come, let's enjoy ourselves in the flowery grove."[71] He promises Subhā fine garments, ornaments, garlands, and scents. "Like wrought gold, like an *apsarās* in a stellar chariot [*cittarathe*]," he suggests, Subhā could live with him in leisure and sensual indulgence.[72] Lingering on a sumptuous couch, waited on by servants, Subhā could remain beautiful even in old age by renouncing her austere life and joining him in the pursuit of pleasure. Subhā then asks the libertine a rhetorical question about the attraction such a foul body as hers could hold for him. But the young man misses the point of her question and confesses that Subhā's eyes are what have bewitched him:

> "What do you consider as valuable in this body
> that is full of corpses [*kuṇapapūramhi*], meant for the burning ground,
>   destined for destruction,
> that seeing it you are beside yourself as you gaze at me?"
>
> "Your eyes are like the eyes of a doe,
> like the eyes of a celestial nymph [*kinnarī*] in a mountain;
> gazing at your eyes, my passion grows greater."[73]

Subhā then explains how ludicrous his proposition is to a renouncer who is beyond temptation:

> You want to go along where there is no path;
> you seek the moon as a plaything;

you want to leap over Mount Meru;
you who pursue a child of the Buddha.

. . . .

My mindfulness is fixed, both in honor and shame,
both in pleasure and pain;
I know that all conditioned things are foul;
therefore my heart and mind cling to nothing at all.[74]

Subhā then uses the analogy of the body as a marionette to instruct the young man in the Buddhist view of the body as a compound entity without essence:

For I've seen lovely wooden figurines, puppets,
put together with cords and pegs,
being made to dance about.[75]
When these cords and pegs are taken away,
tossed aside, defaced, scattered,
not to be found, broken into fragments,
what will you set your mind and heart on there?

Just so these puny bodies do not exist without these things;
since they don't exist without these things,
what will you set your mind and heart on there?[76]

Subhā then switches to images of artistic illusion and magical delusion to describe the common but mistaken perception of the body as an integral and enduring thing of beauty:

Not as I have looked upon a little picture
plastered on the wall with yellow pigment,
not so have you looked upon this body;
mere human judgment is worthless.

You have run after a phantom, as it were,
wrought by a magician before your eyes,
or after a tree of gold that appears in a dream,
Oh, you blind man!
Running after an image made of silver,
a hollow piece of nothing
wrought by a magician in the crowd.[77]

Finally, Subhā gives the libertine an anatomy of the eye:

> [The eye] is like a ball lodged in the hollow of a tree;
> it has a bubble in the center; it has tears; secretion occurs there; and [because it consists of various membranes] it is like various orbs lumped together.[78]

After all this dissuasive verbal effort on Subhā's part, the libertine is still totally smitten with her. Seeing that his passion had not abated in the least, Subhā made a decisive move: she tore out one of her eyes and gave it to him:

> With her mind free from attachment, that beauty
> tore out her eye right then and there and gave it to that man:
> "Here is your eye! Take it!"
>
> His passion disappeared on the spot and he begged her pardon:
> "I wish you well, chaste lady; this sort of thing won't happen again.
>
> Accosting such a person is like embracing a blazing fire! It's as if I'd grasped a poisonous snake! I wish you well; please pardon me!"[79]

It is interesting that the libertine uses the blazing fire and venomous snake as analogies to describe his gruesome encounter with this most ascetic young lady, since these are common scriptural images of the erotic danger women pose for renouncers. They are found, for example, in the harsh rebuke the Buddha gave to Sudinna after he impregnated his ex-wife: "It would have been better, confused man, had you put your male organ inside the mouth of a terrible and poisonous snake than inside the vagina of a woman. It would have been better, confused man, had you put your male organ inside the mouth of a black snake than inside the vagina of a woman. It would have been better, confused man, had you put your male organ inside a blazing hot charcoal pit than inside the vagina of a woman."[80]

Members of the *sangha* are forbidden to flaunt the psychic powers (*iddhibala*) to which progress on the path gives them access, as we saw in the last chapter. Thus in contrast to the Buddha, who uses magical creations to impart iconic teachings on the nature of the body, Subhā chose to make a grisly spectacle of herself in order to provide the obtuse young rake with the iconic teaching he so clearly needed. Extracting her own eye, Subhā transformed the object of his obsession into an object of revulsion. The bloody orb spoke much more persuasively to the young sybarite than all of Subhā's well-crafted arguments, sparking immediate understanding and sincere apologies. The persuasive power of disgust should not be underestimated; the virgin philosopher Hypatia of Alexandria reportedly convinced a pupil who had fallen in love with her that his love was misdirected by showing him a rag that she used as a sanitary napkin and explaining: "You are in love with this, young man, not with [the Platonic ideal of] the Beautiful."[81]

There is great irony in the fact the Subhā must blind herself in order to get the attention of the rogue and make him listen to her. It is only by blinding herself, it seems, that Subhā is at last treated as a woman of insight—a seer and not just a sight to be seen. Perhaps we can also read Subhā's willingness to give up her own organs of sight as an indication that she eschews the female gaze. Having achieved the kind of X-ray vision associated with men of insight, perhaps she no longer has need for her own (female) organs of sight. In any case, at the end of the story Subhā's eye is miraculously restored to her: "And then that nun, released, went before the perfect Buddha. When she saw the one with the marks of perfect merit, her eye was restored to its former condition."[82]

The Heroics of Virginity

In the late antique and medieval Christian hagiographic traditions, there are a number of tales about women who succeed in preserving their virginity by making their bodies into repugnant spectacles. Several cases involve the intentional loss of one or both eyes by a woman who wishes to avert the erotic gaze of an admirer or fiancé. To avoid an unwanted marriage, Saint Brigid of Kildare asks the Lord to "inflict some deformity on her body, so that men would cease to seek after her."[83] Her eye miraculously burst and dissolved in her head, with the desired antierotic effect. Then, just as Subhā's eye was restored in the presence of the Buddha, so Saint Brigid's eye was restored to her when she knelt down to take the veil as a nun. Saint Lucy of Syracuse was plagued by a persistent male admirer who protested that her beautiful eyes made it impossible for him to leave her alone:

> Lucy, considering these things, and calling to mind the words of Christ, "If thine eye offends thee, pluck it out, and cast it from thee," and fearing lest her eyes should be the cause of damnation to the young man, and perhaps also to herself, called for a knife and took

> out her beautiful eyes, and sent them to her lover in a dish, with these words: "Here hast thou what thou hast so much desired; and for the rest, I beseech thee, leave me now in peace." Whereat the young man, being utterly astonished and full of grief and remorse, not only ceased his pursuit, but also became a convert of Christ, and lived ever afterwards an example of virtue and chastity.

Saint Lucy is often represented holding a dish containing her detached eyes (see fig. 9). But like Saint Brigid, the Blessed Lucy did not remain blind. One day, as she knelt in prayer, her eyes were restored to her "more beautiful than before."[84]

Medieval Christian hagiography abounds with stories of young Christian women who suffer miraculous afflictions (such as blindness, madness, the abnormal growth of facial hair, leprosy, and scrofulous tumors) that allow them to avoid unwanted marriages. The stories of Saint Brigid and Saint Lucy represent only a small subset of a much larger body of hagiographic literature explored by Jane Tibbetts Schulenberg in an article entitled "The Heroics of Virginity: Brides of Christ and Sacrificial Mutilation."[85] That these medieval accounts of miraculous affliction reflect social reality and not just hagiographic convention is evidenced by the laws of the period. The *Lombard Code,* for example, states: "If it happens that after a girl or woman has been betrothed she becomes leprous or mad or blind in both eyes, then her betrothed husband shall receive back his property and he shall not be required to take her to wife against his will."[86] Such strategic afflictions appear to give women the means to achieve in an oblique way ends that they could not attain directly without transgressing the norms of feminine behavior. As oblique strategies of self-assertion, these miraculous afflictions may be compared to the possession states that I. M. Lewis has identified as indirect means of self-assertion for women whose aims are in conflict with familial and societal expectations.[87]

Disfiguring afflictions and self-disfiguration appear in medieval Christian hagiography not only as methods for avoiding forced marriages but also as a means of deterring sexual assault. Because the threat of rape broods over Subhā's encounter with the young libertine, her self-mutilation may be fruitfully compared to the self-disfiguring practices that medieval Christian nuns are reported to have utilized in order to deter rape during times of invasion. Schulenberg gives three examples of collective self-mutilation for the purpose of repulsing invading

Figure 9. Carlo Crivelli, The Demidoff Altarpiece. The heavily lidded eyes of Saint Lucy are depicted on the dish with which she offered them to her male admirer. Reproduced by permission of the Trustees of the British National Gallery.

barbarians. In the eighth century, at the monastery of Saint Cyr in the south of France, Saint Eusebia and the nuns in her care cut off their noses just as the invaders were entering the monastery:

> The infidels burst into the monastery, and Eusebia urged the holy virgins, caring more for preserving their purity than their life, to cut off their noses in order to irritate by this bloody spectacle the rage of the barbarians and to extinguish their passions. With incredible zeal, she [Eusebia] and all her companions accomplished this act; the barbarians massacred them in the number of forty, while they confessed Christ with an admirable constancy.[88]

The nuns of Coldingham, cloistered at an isolated site on the coast of Scotland during a ninth-century Danish invasion, resorted to even more extensive facial mutilation in following the example of their abbess, Saint Ebba:

> The whole assembly of virgins having promised implicit compliance with all her maternal commands, the abbess, with an heroic spirit, affording to all the holy sisters an example of chastity profitable only to themselves, but to be embraced by all succeeding virgins forever, took a razor, and with it cut off her nose, together with her upper lip unto the teeth, presenting herself a horrible spectacle to those who stood by. Filled with admiration at this admirable deed, the whole assembly followed her maternal example, and several did the like to themselves. When this was done, together with the morrow's dawn came those most cruel tyrants, to disgrace the holy women devoted to God, and to pillage and burn the monastery; but on beholding the abbess and all the sisters so outrageously mutilated, and stained with their own blood from the sole of the foot unto their head, they retired in haste from the place.[89]

During a Saracen invasion, some 300 nuns at the Spanish monastery of Saint Florentine allegedly lacerated their faces "in their attempts to make themselves ugly and detestable."[90] Schulenberg also cites several accounts of saintly women who successfully avoided forced marriages by cutting off their noses and lips or simply by threatening to do so.[91]

Less permanent but equally repulsive forms of self-presentation were also reportedly used by medieval women to preserve their sexual purity. Two resourceful women of Lombard concocted a simple but effective rape deterrent during the Avar invasion. Tying raw chicken flesh to their cleavage, they left it there to rot. The invading Avars, thinking this stench was natural to all Lombard women, left them alone.[92] Smell also figures prominently as a deterrent to sex in the literature of the Desert Fathers tradition. In his *Lausiac History,* Palladius tells of a virgin of Corinth who, taken to a brothel during a period of persecution by order of a sybaritic judge, kept potential customers at bay by telling them, "I have an ulcer in a hidden place which emits an unpleasant odor and I fear that you will hate me."[93] An incident reported in a collection of anonymous Desert Fathers sayings has a monk dipping his cloak into the putrefying flesh of a dead woman in order to banish sexual fantasies about her from his mind.[94] The same text depicts a woman preventing sexual assault by alleging that no man could tolerate intimacy with her due to her disgusting menstrual odor.[95] In this story, the assailant is a monk who regularly visited a certain household in town while doing errands for the cenobium. He was "assaulted by desire" for the recently widowed daughter of the house. "She, being intelligent, knew this and kept herself from appearing before him." One day the woman's father left her alone in the house. The monk arrived, found her alone, "began to be agitated by the assault, and wanted to fall upon her." The possibility of rape is then suggested by the young lady's response. She parlays her consent in the hope that prayer will defer or prevent the attack:

> She thought quickly and said to him, "Do not be agitated. My father is not coming back for a while; here we are, just the two of us. I know that you monks do nothing without praying. Therefore stir yourself to pray to God, and if something occurs to you, we will do it." He did not want to pray, and was still agitated by the assault.[96]

This strategy proving ineffective, the woman changes her tack to that of self-degradation:

> She said to him, "Have you ever known a woman?" He said to her, "No, but for that reason I want to find out what it is like." She said to him, "That is why you are so agitated, for you are unaware of the odor of suffering women." And, wanting to lessen his agony, she said, "You see, I am in my menses, and no one can come near me because of the odour." When he heard this, he was disgusted, came to his senses, and wept.[97]

The epitome, perhaps, of the heroics of virginity in the Christian West is self-entombment. The *Lausiac History* eulogizes a saintly maidservant named Alexandra who immured herself alive in a tomb for ten years in order to save a man who was smitten by her beauty. Alexandra told the famous Melania, who spoke with her through the window of her tomblike cell, that "a man was distracted in mind because of me, and rather than scandalize a soul made in the image of God, I betook myself alive to a tomb, lest I seem to cause him suffering or reject him."[98] During the medieval period, rules for Christian nuns emphasized the need to protect virginity through claustration so strict it could border on self-annihilation. In the *Regula Monacharum,* for example, life in the convent is represented as living death in a tomb: "On account of this, dearest one, let your convent become your tomb: where you will be dead and buried with Christ, until rising with him you will appear in His glory."[99]

The Heroics of Virginity versus the Heroics of Pedagogy

In terms of strategy, there are clear affinities between the heroics of virginity in the Christian West and the self-denigrating and self-disfiguring practices of Subhā and the other loathly nuns of post-Aśokan Buddhist hagiography. It is of paramount importance, however, to see the ideological differences that would vitiate any claim that Subhā's actions exemplify a Buddhist heroics of virginity. Christian traditions have from an early date placed a premium on sexual purity as exemplified by the bodies of virgins.[100] Indeed, the integrity of an unbroken hymen serves as a virtual root metaphor for patristic eulogies to virginity. Medieval images of the Virgin Mary emphasize the physical closure that makes Mary an example of the *vita perfecta* for women. She is a "closed gate," a "spring shut up," a "fountain sealed."[101] In the *Regula Monacharum*'s depiction of the convent as a tomb, virginity, integrity, and perhaps also bodily incorruptibility at death are equated in the image of cloistered nuns as holy relics or buried treasure that must be guarded from grave robbers:

> Finally, the thing that is most frightening to the one lying in a burial mound is the grave robber who sneaks in at night to steal the precious treasure. Thieves dig this up, to steal with infinite skill the treasure that is inside. Therefore the tomb is watched over by the bishop whom God installed as the primary guardian in His vineyard. It is

> guarded by a resident priest who discharges his duty on the premises: so that no one enters recklessly nor that anyone tries to weaken the tomb.[102]

Although Buddhist monastic codes include special measures for protecting nuns from sexual assault (e.g., strictures against forest dwelling and certain meditation postures deemed sexually inviting), the sexual purity of nuns is not regarded as a precious relic that must be jealousy guarded from thieves. Physical virginity has no such prestigious status in Buddhism.[103] Where some patristic writers suggest that those women who have lost their virginity due to rape can no longer be considered brides of Christ, those portions of Buddhist monastic codes dealing with sexual offenses highlight the importance of intention in maintaining sexual purity; no one can corrupt the purity of a renouncer against her will.[104] Rape victims are never banished from the *sangha,* although all consensual sexual activity constitutes a banishable offense.[105] Unlike the late antique and medieval Christian cult of the virgin, no special admiration is accorded those persons who renounce the world without ever having engaged in sexual intercourse. It is much more important in the Buddhist view that one be able to give up sexual experience after having tasted its pleasures, as the fact that Gotama renounced as a married adult (and one well initiated in the extravagant sexual practices of royalty) would indicate.

If Subhā went to heroic lengths to discourage a potential rapist, it was not to maintain a sexual purity defined as corporeal *integritas.* It would be more accurate to classify Subhā's story under the rubric "the heroics of pedagogy" than "the heroics of virginity." What Subhā did was to make a spectacle of herself for the education of a man too enthralled by her beauty to see the repulsiveness of her form. Like Sumedhā, whose oratory led to the conversion of her family, her bridegroom, and his entire retinue, Subhā reproduces the teachings of the Buddha for the edification of the ignorant. But unlike Sumedhā, Subhā is not content to use verbal exhortation alone. She reproduces in her body the iconic lessons on Dharma that the Buddha so frequently uses to illustrate his verbal teachings, thus imitating the pedagogical style of the Buddha.

But even if Subhā wanted to achieve a state of bodily integrity comparable to that of the Virgin Mary, she could not, according to Buddhist conceptions of the nature of the body, do so. Buddhist texts dwell on the porousness of the human body, on the fact that effluvia leak from all the body's apertures like oil leaking from a cracked clay pot. One can assiduously clean one's bodily orifices daily, but there is no stopping the flow. Because the human body is pocked by orifices, it is not amenable to closure. But since women have an additional aperture that men lack, and since the blood emitted from this vaginal opening is clearly less subject to voluntary control than the flow which issues from male sexual orifices, women's bodies are even less amenable to bodily closure than men's.[106]

Bakhtin's contrast between the "grotesque body" valued in the premodern world and the "classical body" cherished by the modern bourgeoisie offers a convenient shorthand for describing how the bodies of exemplary Buddhist women differ from those of their Christian counterparts.[107] This well-known distinction between the canons of grotesque and classical representation hinges on the contrast between bodily openness and bodily closure. The grotesque body is not sealed off from material exchange with the world; it is an array of orifices through which matter constantly flows. Emphasis is laid on those parts of the body that are open to the outside world, such as the mouth, the nose, the genitals, and the anus, as well as other channels through which matter can enter the body or emerge from it.

Like the Rabelaisian hero Gargantua flooding the world with urine, semen, and excrement, the bodies of the horrific "heroines" of Buddhist literature are not neatly and decorously sealed off from the world.[108] Nuns like Subhā rend their bodies, giving the observer a graphic view of the more hidden aspects of the body's anatomy. Nuns like Abhaya's mother, Ambapālī, and Vimalā proclaim in their enlightened utterances the decaying condition of their bodies, emphasizing the cracks and leaks that make their bodies permeable, sievelike vessels. What Abhaya's mother, Ambapālī, and Vimalā say about their bodies is graphically represented in the bodies of women who serve as objects of contemplation and sources of insight for celebrated monks. The inner recesses of their bodies are grotesquely exposed; blood, pus, and worms flow out through their orifices and ruptured skin. Even the women who are not dead or mutilated but merely sleeping are described in accord with the canons of grotesque realism. Their mouths are wide open; saliva trickles from their parted lips. The integrity of outer form that comes with ornamentation and decorum dissolves in sleep-death.

Such grotesque figurations of the feminine unleash the power of horror for the edification of the spectator by exposing the repulsive inner condition of the female body that is normally hidden from the male gaze. Dead and disfigured women are inversions of the duplicitous female body since their outer forms serve to reveal, not conceal, the grim reality within. Like the Hindu goddess Kālī (see fig. 10) decked out in human entrails, skull necklaces, and fetus earrings, grotesque figurations of the feminine in Buddhist literature display the inside of the body on the outside. The vile substances that the body contains spill out of their ruptured skin. These bodies have become open, permeable forms accessible to the elements and to the life forms that feed on death.

Where the bodies of Buddhist women become sources of insight when they cease to function as clearly bounded, impermeable containers, descriptions of the bodies of exemplary Christian virgins emphasize the boundedness and inviolability that are the hallmarks of Bakhtin's "classical body." Modern etiquette and self-surveillance, Bakhtin suggests, produce the appearance of an impermeable, closed body that does not drip or leak or allow penetration. Whatever protrudes or bulges or opens out to the world is eliminated from representations of the classical body. All apertures of the body are closed, presenting an impermeable facade to the world. While it is true that the bodies of many sainted Christian women of the Middle Ages were reported to have performed miracles of a grotesque nature (such as the miraculous emission of milk and healing oils from their bodies), such miracles were produced by bodies closed to ordinary material flow (e.g., the intake of ordinary food and drink and the excretion of feces and menstrual blood).[109] Such grotesque figurations of the bodies of sainted medieval women did not displace the more classical figurations of the perfected female body developed by Jerome and other Church Fathers associated with the radical wing of fourth-century Christian ascetic thought. On the contrary, adherence to the classical image of the virginal female body as sealed off from ordinary material exchange from the world becomes a precondition for the production of extraordinary effluvia characteristic of medieval figurations of holy women's bodies.

The bodies of exemplary Buddhist nuns and female objects of meditation who appear as sources of insight for monks are unsuitable vehicles for attaining such a state of perfect integrity because they are chronically open and perpetually leaky. Bodily closure is thought to be regularly simulated by women as a seduction strategy, but this bodily

Figure 10. India–Guler, The Goddess Kālī on Śiva/Śava, 1820–30. The Hindu goddess wears a string of decapitated heads as a necklace and a pair of fetuses as ear-rings. She is shown in a cremation ground standing on her consort, Śiva, who is represented in both an animated and an unanimated form. Reproduced by permission of the Philadelphia Museum of Art, Private Collection.

integrity is viewed as a specious dissimulation. Indeed, from the andro-centric perspective of post-Aśokan hagiography, bodily closure is a desideratum for no woman. An integral female body is a threat to the integrity of the *sangha.* When a woman appears to have achieved a modicum of bodily closure, when her inner filth is concealed through the maintenance of an outer facade of cosmetics, jewelry, and clothing, such a woman is considered a mantrap laid by Māra. Her beauty holds men in thrall, and she inevitably disrupts the life of the *sangha,* leading unwary monks down the primrose path to temptation. But women who desist from vain attempts at achieving corporeal closure can enhance the life of the *sangha.* These grotesquely represented women appear as exemplary models of enlightened female behavior in post-Aśokan hagiographic literature.

Far from being considered as asexual, gender-neutral beings "walking with wise men in recognized intellectual equality on higher levels of thought," the stories analyzed here suggest that Buddhist nuns in the post-Aśokan period were most useful to the life of the *sangha* when they gendered themselves as feminine and then deconstructed their feminine charms as specious dissimulations. Exposing in their self-effacing utterances the repulsiveness of their formerly alluring bodies, nuns like Abhaya's mother, Ambapālī, and Vimalā serve the aims of the *sangha* with alacrity. They speak as former courtesans, accomplished at attracting the male gaze, and in obsessively cataloging the undesirable qualities of their bodies they effectively reconfigure the male gaze. Self-disfiguring nuns like Subhā who edify men through heroic displays of their bodily repulsiveness put into action what the loathly nuns indicate with their words. Both the self-effacing and the self-defacing nuns thereby repudiate their role as agents of Māra. In so doing, these potential minions of Māra show themselves to be dutiful servants of their male counterparts within the *sangha.*

Conclusion

By way of conclusion, I return now to a trope I used at the beginning of this work, where I suggested that the eye that is so dramatically gouged out by sainted Buddhist and Christian women can serve as an icon of a distinctly female way of seeing. What kind of "I" is this eye that Subhā tore out, that Lucy holds on her plate? It is, no doubt, a Medusa-like eye that repels the gaze of the observer, but let us arm ourselves with the aegis of Athena and try to meet the gaze of this uncanny eye. To what laws is the movement of this eye subject? Is it alive? Is there a perceiving subject that directs the gaze of this eye? What is that subject thinking as it gazes at us? Of what is the "I" behind that eye conscious at this moment, and what words and actions are likely to follow from that consciousness?

Before we attempt to understand the gaze of this eye by considering what kind of subjectivity may be attributed to it, a disclaimer is needed. Many Buddhists would be uncomfortable with a discussion of the "I" or "self" perceived in the eyes of a person, if by "self" what is meant is an enduring essence that does not dissipate at death. That enduring essence is not the "I" that I am looking for when I try to meet the gaze of Subhā or Lucy or Brigid. I am only interested in what laws (if any) govern the movement of their eyes; I want to know what forces direct the gaze of a Subhā, a Lucy, a Brigid, or a woman who models herself on one of these women as she looks around in the hope of perceiving her essential nature.

Just as painters invite the viewer's imaginative participation in a painting by providing a point of view by which the viewer can see and imaginatively enter the scene depicted on the canvas, so post-Aśokan hagiographers structure their narratives in ways that encourage people to identify with and participate in the process of achieving an enlightened subjectivity that is depicted in the narratives. Hearing hagiographies of celebrated monks, the listener is encouraged to see the world through the eyes of those accomplished monks. The consumer of post-Aśokan hagiographic literature is thus invited to identify with the observing eye that becomes an enlightened "I" by the end of the tale. In a genre of literature in which the visual presence of women as objects of contemplation is an indispensable element, what the observing eye most often sees is a female object of sight who is herself without consciousness, without the capacity to return the gaze of the observer. She is not an "I" or site of consciousness but rather an "it," an object apprehended by another. Such is obviously the case in hagiographies of men who achieve insight while contemplating dead women's bodies: these women have no "I," no sense of themselves as bearers of consciousness. This is also the case when men (such as Gotama, Yasa, and Cittahattha) observe women who are not dead but merely sleeping. The sleeping women are not aware of their surroundings, nor are they conscious of themselves as sleepers. They are clearly in no position to apprehend and return the gaze of the men who observe them. Although alive, the wives of Gotama, Yasa, and Cittahattha are as oblivious to what is happening around them as are the decaying bodies of dead women observed by men meditating in cremation grounds.

Not every woman who appears as an object of contemplation in post-Aśokan literature is dead or asleep. Vasāvadattā is still alive when Upagupta goes to see her. Indeed, he addresses her and engages her in conversation, just as Yaśas addresses the young woman who tried to disrupt his Dharma-teaching. But I would submit that the consciousness that can be ascribed to a Vasāvadattā or others like her is highly circumscribed. To be the object of another's gaze is to have a diminished sense of one's position as a subject. In his meditation on what it is like to be the object of another's gaze, Sartre notes how difficult it is to retain the prerogative of an observing subject when one is the object of another's gaze. "It is never when eyes are looking at you," Sartre suggests, "that you can find them beautiful or ugly, that you remark on their color . . . to apprehend a look is not to apprehend a look-as-object in the world (unless the look is not directed at us); it is to be conscious of being looked at."[1] To observe the most basic features of a person whose gaze is turned on you is no easy task; to analytically break that person down into component parts and contemplate the truth of Dharma displayed therein would seem to be virtually impossible. We surely cannot apprehend the looker as an object of meditation if we are unable even to identify the color of his eyes at the moment his gaze meets ours.

In the gendered system of point of view that post-Aśokan hagiographies set up in linking the insights of male observers to the contemplation of female objects, the female "I" has a highly anomalous position. The observing eye that becomes an enlightened "I" through the contemplation of others is not readily gendered as female, since the female eye is so frequently depicted as an unseeing eye. It is typically a dead or unconscious eye, an eye that cannot observe its surroundings. Those female eyes that do see and gain the insight associated with enlightened subjects tend to operate reflexively, turning their gaze back upon the female body as object (as Abhaya's mother, Ambapālī, and Vimalā were reported to have done). Tutored in meditation practices associated with the enlightened "I" of male hagiographic literature, women like Abhaya's mother, Ambapālī, and Vimalā learned to see themselves as their sons and male teachers saw them. It would seem that for a female eye to see it must become, as it were, a detached observer—literally detached, in the case of Subhā, or figuratively detached in self-contemplation, as with Ambapālī, Abhaya's mother, and Vimalā.

In the drama of salvation as post-Aśokan hagiographies present it, female characters play rather circumscribed roles. They often appear as mere stage props to be looked at and commented on by male protagonists. When women do take center stage as protagonists, when the drama unfolding on stage is *their* story and not that of another, they nonetheless follow gendered scripts and gendered directions that limit the range of actions available to them. They are likely to appear on stage holding mirrors or other devices by which to observe themselves, and in their discourse they are likely to comment on how they appear in the eyes of others. Their own eyes, seeing nothing but reflections of themselves in the world around them, do not engage the eyes of other characters: they may appear to be observing others, but the focus of their gaze is inward.

Following the script for exemplary conduct laid down by Gotamī, head of the women's monastic order, the nun who shares the stage with male characters is likely to be upstaged by them. She never presumes to instruct male members of the *sangha* but recognizes the need to take instruction from them. Thus when sharing the stage with monks, the nun's speech generally takes the form of a soliloquy. Her musings—addressed to no one in particular—often begin with quotations from the lessons her male instructors have taught her. The nun who is cast as a protagonist in the drama of salvation often has quite a lot to say. But she does not so much speak her lines as pantomime them, having somatized the lessons she has learned and thereby made her body into an instrument of instruction.

APPENDIX

The Post-Aśokan Milieu

From the Sanskrit biographies of the Buddha (such as the *Buddhacarita*) to the Pāli commentarial literature that narrates the interpersonal contexts behind canonical accounts of what the Buddha said, post-Aśokan literature abounds with narratives in which human women are transformed in revolting ways for the benefit of the spectator. Such narratives were clearly not the literary product of a single school or sectarian orientation. Scrutiny of the texts in which such stories appear gives access to a remarkably broad cross-section of post-Aśokan Buddhist practice. Since narratives about male edification achieved by means of female mortification can be found in the scriptures of so many post-Aśokan schools, we can safely assume that such narratives belonged to a common stock of Buddhist story literature shared by all schools of the post-Aśokan period.

One cannot assume that such grisly figurations of the feminine were *not* important in the pre-Aśokan era; it may be the case that these stories were already circulating as oral traditions in the pre-Aśokan period. However, it is largely a matter of conjecture to inquire about the content of the literary traditions of the pre-Aśokan period since there is little textual or epigraphical evidence for the existence of codified collections of Buddhist scripture before the reign of Aśoka.[1] What one can say with some certainty is that while the early post-Aśokan editors of the first century B.C.E. who redacted the Pāli *Nikāyas*—generally accepted as some of the oldest sources for the study of Buddhism—may possibly have been aware of these tales, they did not consider them important enough to include them as such in their collections of the discourses of the Buddha. The tales appear in commentaries to the *Nikāya*s redacted approximately six centuries later. I would argue that even though our knowledge of the pre-Aśokan literary legacy is highly conjectural, there is something to be said about the relative lateness of the texts that I draw upon in this study. I suspect that horrific representations of the feminine figure prominently only in texts redacted about one thousand years after the time of the Buddha because in some ways *brahmacariya* was more difficult to practice during this era of Buddhist history. Buddhism grew into a worldly, successful religion during the reign of the Gupta dynasty (from the fourth through the sixth centuries C.E.) in North India. Revolting tales of women ravaged by decay would have helped monks of the Gupta and post-Gupta age to remain celibate and thus maintain an appropriate social distance from a world they were increasingly drawn into as Buddhist institutional power, wealth, and privilege waxed strong in that period.[2]

The story of institutional Buddhism's rise to power during the Gupta age begins earlier with the reign of the Mauryan emperor Aśoka. Aśoka lavished considerable wealth and conferred a great deal of authority upon the Buddhist community of his day after uniting India under the banner of the Dharma in the third century B.C.E.[3] As Buddhists garnered elite patrons from the royal and merchant classes of India and Buddhist texts began to circulate along the silk routes of Central Asia along with the warriors, diplomats, and merchants who traveled there in the centuries immediately before and after the birth of Christ, Buddhist teachings gained a currency wider than that enjoyed by any established religion of the time. Buddhism expanded beyond the confines of its Indian roots to the further reaches of Asia, and thus Buddhist renouncers found a larger market for their teachings. Enjoying more prestige as a result of the expansion of the markets in which their ideas and practices circulated, Buddhist authors became as a consequence authorities to be reckoned with outside the monastery as well as within. As the monastic institutions that supported the production of texts and teachers became centers of power throughout the subcontinent, it is easy to see how the fruits of renunciation could become commodities to be sold to the highest bidder. Chinese pilgrims visiting India in the fifth and seventh centuries of the Common Era wrote of the tremendous social prestige, wealth, and political influence wielded by the Buddhist monks they encountered there:

> [The monastics] proceed to the king's court to lay down before it the sharp weapon (of their abilities); there they present their schemes and show their (political) talent, seeking to be appointed in the practical government. When they are present in the House of Debate, they raise their seat and seek to prove their wonderful cleverness. When they are refuting heretic doctrines all their opponents become tongue-tied and acknowledge themselves undone. Then the sound of their fame makes the five mountains reverberate, and their renown flows, as it were, over the borders. They receive grants of land, and are advanced to a high rank; their famous names are, as a reward, written in white on their lofty gates. After this they can follow whatever occupation they like.[4]

But with the success of Buddhism and its clever monks came problems. Like Christians of the post-Constantinian era, Buddhists of the Gupta and post-Gupta age faced the problem of how to maintain a rhetoric of opposition to the social world at a time when Buddhists were, on the whole, no longer a marginalized, otherworldly group. Adolf von Harnack argued that the Christian spiritual athletes of the fourth and fifth centuries of the Common Era who pursued the celibate life with such grim determination did so in part as a form of protest against the laxity of the post-Constantinian Christian church. Not only were they fleeing from the social world at large, but they were also in flight "from the worldly church" with its lowered standards of discipleship.[5] Given the pronounced interest in techniques for maintaining celibacy that is evident in post-Aśokan Buddhist texts, it would seem that many post-Aśokan Buddhist authors resembled their ascetically minded post-Constantinian Christian counterparts in their concern that renouncers not be dazzled by the prospects of fame and fortune. Redoubling their vigilance with regard to the social disengagement appropriate to the renouncer, post-Aśokan Buddhist authors hoped to counter the motivational problems that can easily follow in the wake of institutional success. In the comments of the Chinese pilgrim Hsuan-tsang, one can see both the considerable rewards Indian society offered clever Buddhist monks and the high premium Buddhists placed on ignoring the possibility of material gain and maintaining an attitude of disengagement appropriate to a homeless, propertyless renouncer:

> There are men who, far seen in antique lore and fond of the refinements of learning, are content in seclusion, leading lives of conti-

> nence. These come and go outside of the world, and promenade through life away from human affairs. Though they are not moved by honor or reproach, their fame is far spread. The rulers treating them with ceremony and respect cannot make them come to court. Now as the state holds men of learning and genius in esteem, and the people respect those who have high intelligence, the honors and praises of such men are conspicuously abundant, and the attentions private and official paid to them very considerable. Hence men can force themselves to a thorough acquisition of knowledge. Forgetting fatigue they "expatiate in the arts and sciences," seeking for wisdom while "relying on perfect virtue" they count not 1,000 *li* a long journey. Though their family be in affluent circumstances, such men make up their minds to be like the vagrants, and get their food by begging as they go about.[6]

If celibacy provides a bulwark against untoward forms of engagement in the social world, it would have been needed more than ever during Buddhism's post-Aśokan heyday. Thus it is not surprising to find a marked concern with techniques for maintaining celibacy in virtually all forms of post-Aśokan Buddhist literature. One might argue, of course, that celibacy is not of great concern in Tantric literature promoting left-handed (*vāmācāra*) practices in which ritualized sexual union serves as an aid on the path to awakening. But there is a strong affinity between the Tantric path of the hero (a person of heroic disposition, or *vīrabhāva,* who engages in sexual contact or *maithuna*) and the path of the practitioner of cremation-ground meditations in non-Tantric Buddhism. Both perform their meditations in cremation grounds rather than in more auspicious settings. Both face the prospect of having to deal with the rapacious animals and demons who haunt cremation grounds in search of food as well as the prospect of being mistaken by civic authorities for criminals in search of refuge from the law. And it is a risky soteriological path that both practitioners embark on, as the cremation-ground meditator who has studied Buddhaghosa's meditation manual well knows. Just as the practitioner of left-handed Tantric meditations must be a hero who is not readily subject to base desires as he engages in rites that activate sublime sexual desire as a means of transcendence, so too the cremation-ground meditator engages his desire with the awareness that the meditation may backfire on him should the female corpse he contemplates prove more appealing than disgusting to him. Instead of liberating himself from all desires through a recognition of the rapacity of the sexual act, he may well find himself behaving like the rapacious vultures with whom he shares the cremation ground.

An Introduction to the Sources

Story literature that links male edification with female mortification found its way into a large portion of the literary output of Buddhists in the Gupta and post-Gupta periods. Cutting across the seemingly rigid sectarian boundaries posited by the received wisdom on the history of Indian Buddhism, these tales problematize some of the most familiar conventions of scholarly writing on Indian Buddhism. Although the Mahāyāna/Hīnayāna distinction has long provided scholars with a handy conceptual tool whereby Buddhism's complex history can be simplified by reference to the transition point provided by the emergence of the Mahāyāna sect, the distinction seems less heuristically useful in the light of a growing body of counterevidence in the form of fairly late post-Aśokan texts and epigraphs that evade precise sectarian classification.[7] The Dharma that can appear deeply divided by sectarian rivalry when seen from the perspective of highly polemical Mahāyāna texts may not have appeared so neatly partitioned to the Gupta age Buddhists who composed, copied, and gave donations to support the production and transmission of the texts that I draw upon in this study.

During the early post-Aśokan period, Northwest India grew into an important center for the propagation of the Buddhist teachings, a site of great intellectual and artistic innovation. The milieu of the Northwest was culturally diverse due to the influence of successive Greco-Bactrian and Central Asian invasions. Buddhists contributed to the exchange of ideas in this cosmopolitan milieu, composing Sanskrit texts accessible to the intellectuals of the highly Sanskritized Northwest. During the post-Aśokan period, various Buddhist schools produced Sanskrit versions of the canon and noted individual authors produced philosophical and literary works in Sanskrit. Aśvaghoṣa's *Buddhacarita,* a poetic reworking of the Buddha's biography dating to the first century of the Common Era, is an example of a Buddhist literary masterpiece composed in Sanskrit for a refined, cosmopolitan audience. It may have been composed at the court of Kaniṣka, a Central Asian conqueror who is reported to have been converted to Buddhism by his celebrated court poet.[8] The *Buddhacarita* exemplifies the spirit of innovation that is characteristic of many Buddhist cultural productions from this period; as one of the earliest examples of classical Sanskrit poetic form (*kāvya*), it is a work of profound literary as well as religious significance.

Writing in the early years of the Common Era, Aśvaghoṣa probably had access to the first full-scale biographies of the Buddha produced in Sanskrit. These biographies were redacted by various schools active in the Northwest Indian Buddhist world during the centuries immediately preceding and succeeding the birth of Christ.[9] The Sanskrit biographies flesh out in rich detail the bare bones of the Pāli accounts. Legendary material which may have been orally transmitted from an early date appears for the first time in these accounts which present details of the *bodhisattva*'s birth and youth that are absent from the pithier Pāli accounts.

Taken as a whole, the Sanskrit biographies represent a broad cross-section of Buddhist thought in the post-Aśokan period. The *Mahāvastu*, the oldest of the autonomous biographies, is a composite work that includes passages dating back to the second century B.C.E. It describes itself in a preface as a text of the Lokottaravāda branch of the Mahāsaṅghika school, an important precursor to the Mahāyāna. The *Lalitavistara*, redacted around the second century C.E. by Sarvāstivādins, is technically the product of a Hīnyāna school. Although the now extinct Sarvāstivāda tradition of Northwest India should be distinguished from the Theravāda tradition prevalent today in Southeast Asia, it would, as a Hīnyāna school, typically be classified by scholars as closer in outlook to the Theravāda than to the emerging Mahāyāna. But the *Lalitavistara*, like the *Mahāvastu*, has the catholic quality of a composite work. There are signs of Mahāyāna thought in the *Lalitavistara* that make it difficult to classify this work with any precision. The text refers to itself, for example, as a developed or *Vaipulya Sūtra*, a common term for the Mahāyāna *Sūtra*s being redacted during the same period.

Like the *Mahāvastu* and the *Lalitavistara*, Aśvaghoṣa's *Buddhacarita* cannot easily be identified with a single sectarian viewpoint. Although it is the product of a single author, it shares the catholicity of these composite biographies of the Buddha.[10] The identity of Aśvaghoṣa is somewhat uncertain due to the number of works attributed to him. Chinese tradition holds that Aśvaghoṣa was a Sarvāstivādin, which would make the *Buddhacarita* a Hīnyānist text, but E. B. Cowell and others have detected traces of Mahāsaṅghika thought in it.[11] Like the *Mahāvastu* and the *Lalitavistara,* then, the *Buddhacarita* appears to cut across sectarian boundaries and is therefore an excellent resource for understanding common themes in post-Aśokan Buddhism.

As the Sanskrit biographies were being redacted in the northern, Sanskritic portion of the Indian Buddhist world, the Sinhalese-speaking Buddhists of Sri Lanka were compiling a voluminous commentarial literature on the Pāli *Nikāya*s. According to the Theravāda tradition, the commentaries (*aṭṭhakathā*) were originally composed in Pāli; they were transmitted to Sri Lanka along with the Pāli texts of the Theravāda canon (*tipiṭaka*) after the first council, translated into Sinhalese by Aśoka's son Mahinda, and then retranslated into Pāli by Buddhaghosa in the fifth century of the Common Era. Whether or not the commentaries were originally transmitted from India in Pāli, it is likely that much of the commentarial literature contains adaptations of material which had long circulated in Indian oral tradition.[12]

Grotesque figurations of the feminine occupy a particularly prominent place in two Pāli commentarial texts: the *Dhammapadāṭṭhakathā* or commentary to the *Dhammapada* and the *Jātakāṭṭhakathā* or commentary to the *Jātaka*. Both are ascribed to Buddhaghosa but probably slightly later in origin than the commentaries for which Buddhaghosa's authorship has been established. These two commentaries are quite similar in literary style and content. They are short on grammatical and lexical explanation and long on storytelling. Many of the stories found in these commentaries are known to world literature. As compilations of common source material available in oral form, Pāli commentaries such as the *Dhammapadāṭṭhakathā* and the *Jātakāṭṭhakathā* elaborate in detail many episodes that are briefly alluded to but not given in toto in the Pāli *Nikāya*s.

Like the Sanskrit biographies, the Pāli commentaries problematize familiar divisions of the Buddhist world into "Northern and Southern," "Hīnayāna and Mahāyāna," or "Theravāda and Mahāyāna" traditions. Buddhaghosa, author of many Pāli commentaries, exemplifies the ecumenical spirit typical of Gupta age Buddhists living in an international, cosmopolitan Buddhist milieu.[13] He is reported to have been born near Bodhgaya and educated in the Hindu scriptural traditions before traveling to Sri Lanka to rework the Sinhalese commentaries into Pāli-language compilations that bear a distinctively catholic flavor. The authentically Buddhaghosan commentaries as well as the spurious ones include many stories found in Sanskrit compilations originating in Northwest India, such as the body of literature known collectively as *Avadāna*. Authentic Buddhaghosan commentaries contain passages apotheosizing the Buddha that would be rather out of place in the *Nikāya*s on which he is commenting but very much at home in the Mahāyāna *Sūtra*s.[14]

The texts upon which this study is based stem from a period of Buddhist history in which practitioners of the religion left little evidence in the nontextual historical record of the sectarian fragmentation that scholars have been led to expect (given their familiarity with Mahāyāna textual polemics directed at Hīnayāna rivals). Sectarian concerns do not hold a prominent place in the epigraphic record of Gupta age Buddhism; in inscriptions identifying the donors who supported the building of monuments and the transmission of texts at prominent Buddhist centers, harmonization is perhaps more evident than fragmentation and schism.[15] While it is something of an exaggeration to claim that the Gupta age saw the emergence of a Buddhist world unified by common practices and common literary legacies, there is nevertheless ample evidence to suggest that Buddhists of this period created cultural productions (monuments and liturgical formulas as well as texts) that were truly pan-Buddhist.

If my reading of the narratives in this book is correct, it problematizes the received wisdom on the gradual disappearance of androcentrism and misogyny from Indian Buddhist texts and institutions. The historical narrative that is generally accepted (as I have detailed in my introduction) sketches a picture of an egalitarian Buddhist faction that emerges from the misogyny and androcentrism of the early (and presumed to be unified) Buddhist tradition in the form of a nonandrocentric, nonmisogynist Mahāyāna majority opinion. Thus the "problem" of early, pan-Buddhist androcentrism is solved by positing the emergence of a nonandrocentric faction. While this faction did not succeed in reunifying the Buddhist tradition under the banner of egalitarianism, it nevertheless proved influential and made it possible for many Asian women to participate as fully enfranchised members of the Asian Buddhist community. One problem with this received history is that it posits a Buddhism that was unified in the early, pre-Aśokan period but splintered into factions during the post-Aśokan period. My reading of the historical record behind my narratives suggests that just the opposite may have been the case: the post-Aśokan period saw the emergence of a pan-Buddhist consensus much broader in scope than that achieved by the handful of communities that produced the influential Mahāyāna texts that Diana Paul identifies as the evidence for a nonandrocentric majority opinion within the emergent Mahāyāna faction. But if my findings are correct, there is an even deeper flaw in the received history of Buddhist attitudes toward women. The historical narrative that I would propose is in many ways precisely the reverse of the received narrative, with its emphasis on the gradual decline of androcentric thinking in the millennium after the death of the Buddha. While I certainly would not dispute the fact that there is strong evidence for the emergence of gender egalitarianism in the post-Aśokan period, I would question the interpretative weight given to a handful of Mahāyāna scriptures. In the light of the fact that a broad cross-section of post-Aśokan literature encourages men to see women (and women to see themselves) through the gendered "I" of a subject position that is clearly marked as masculine (by the fact that it consistently takes women as its object of reference), it is hard to maintain that one can chart in the history of Indian Buddhism a gradual movement from gender-based discrimination to a mode of apprehension in which gender becomes irrelevant.

Notes

Introduction

1. *Buddhacarita* 3.60. See E. J. Johnston, ed. and trans., *The Buddhacarita, or Acts of the Buddha,* 2 vols. (Lahore: University of Punjab, 1936; reprint, New Delhi: Oriental Books Reprint Company, 1972), 1:28, 2:42 (page references are to the 1972 edition, unless otherwise noted).

2. Indeed, an awareness of death may even induce us to gather rosebuds while we may. On the ambivalent fruits of memento mori, see below, ch. 2.

3. See George Bond, "Theravāda Buddhism's Meditations on Death and the Symbolism of Initiatory Death," *History of Religions* 19 (1980): 237–58; Frank Reynolds, "Death as Threat, Death as Achievement: Buddhist Perspectives with Particular Reference to the Theravāda Tradition," in *Death and Afterlife: Perspectives of World Religions,* ed. Hiroshi Obayashi (New York: Praeger, 1992), pp. 157–67; Mathieu Boisvert, "The Use of Death for Meditation Purposes in Theravāda Buddhism," *Buddhist Studies Review* (forthcoming); Winston King, "Practicing Dying: The Samurai-Zen Death Techniques of Suzuki-Shosan," in *Religious Encounters with Death: Insights from the History and Anthropology of Religions,* ed. Frank E. Reynolds and Earle H. Waugh (University Park: Pennsylvania State University Press, 1977), pp. 143–58; Glen Mullin, *Death and Dying: The Tibetan Tradition* (London: Arkana, 1986).

4. On death in Hindu mythology and practice, see Jonathon Parry, "Sacrificial Death and the Necrophagous Ascetic," in *Death and the Regeneration of Life,* ed. M. Bloch and J. Parry (Cambridge: Cambridge University Press, 1982); Wendy Doniger O'Flaherty, *The Origins of Evil in Hindu Mythology* (Berkeley: University of California Press, 1976), pp. 212 ff.; J. Bruce Long, "Death as a Necessity and as a Gift in Hindu Mythology," in *Religious Encounters with Death,* pp. 74 ff; David White, "Ashes to Nectar: Death and Regeneration among the Nāth Siddhas," in *The Living and the Dead: The Social Dimensions of Death in South Asian Religions,* ed. Liz Wilson (in progress).

5. In Buddhist texts, the normal emission of defiling substances from the apertures of the living body is often equated to the emission of putrid matter from the apertures of a rotting corpse. See below, chap. 2.

6. The Pāli compound *āmakasusāna* refers to a particular spot in a cremation ground (*susāna*) where uncremated bodies (*āmaka* means "raw, uncooked") were left to rot. I have translated this compound as "charnel field." Charnel fields are all but nonexistent in today's Buddhist world, so contemporary Buddhist meditators in Thailand and Sri Lanka have turned to the autopsy room as an alternate place for apprehending the

foulness of dead bodies. In "The Use of Death for Meditation Purposes in Theravāda Buddhism," Mathieu Boisvert describes how observing postmortem examinations in hospital settings has come to replace the traditional practice of observing corpses in the cremation ground.

7. On the special conditions laid down by the Buddha, see H. Oldenberg, ed., *Vinaya Pitaka,* 5 vols. (London: Pali Text Society, 1879–83), 2:253.

8. Nancy Auer Falk, "The Case of the Vanishing Nuns: The Fruits of Ambivalence in Ancient Indian Buddhism," in *Unspoken Worlds: Women's Religious Lives and Non-western Cultures,* ed. Nancy Auer Falk and Rita M. Gross (San Francisco: Harper and Row, 1980), p. 215.

9. Jonathon Walters, "A Voice from the Silence: The Buddha's Mother's Story," *History of Religions* 33 (1994): 358–79.

10. Caroline A. Foley, "The Women Leaders of the Buddhist Reformation as Illustrated by Dhammapāla's Commentary on the Therī-gāthā," in *Transactions of the Ninth International Congress of Orientalists,* vol. I (Indian and Aryan Sections, ed. E. Delmar Morgan (London: Committee of the Congress, 1893), p. 348.

11. I. B. Horner, *Women under Primitive Buddhism: Lay Women and Alms Women* (New York: E. P. Dutton, 1930), pp. 3, 113, 117.

12. Edward Said has shown how Orientalist scholars tended to praise the brilliance of past civilizations in North Africa and Asia while characterizing the (potentially and often actively rebellious) cultures of modern North Africa and Asia as having degenerated from their proud pasts to a squalid present in which irrational natives live uncomprehendingly amidst the ruins of a glorious past. See Said's *Orientalism* (New York: Vintage, 1979), pp. 52 ff.

13. Walters, "A Voice from the Silence," p. 360.

14. Diana Paul, *Women in Buddhism: Images of the Feminine in the Mahayana Tradition* (Berkeley: Asian Humanities Press, 1979; 2d ed., Berkeley and Los Angeles: University of California Press, 1985). In her preface to the second edition (pp. ix–x), Paul writes: "All of us are becoming increasingly aware of assumptions made about women and how these assumptions affect women and men. Scholars in Feminist Studies have focused on theories about gender and its relation to power and prestige, resulting in highly innovative and pioneering humanistic and scientific studies of American and European societies. Scholars in other disciplines are beginning to investigate the depth and pervasiveness of gender stereotypes and images in our society. This is part of the legacy that the women's movement has given us."

15. Although Diana Paul regards early Buddhist texts such as the Pāli *Nikāya*s as more misogynistic than Mahāyāna texts, she nevertheless acknowledges many instances of character assassination directed against women in the Mahāyāna canon. In Paul's view, however, "the most popular Mahāyāna texts did not support hostile arguments against women who endeavored to realize their spiritual goals" (*Women in Buddhism,* p. 303). Thus the misogyny of some Mahāyāna texts is not representative of the movement as a whole. The egalitarianism of the more influential, widely transmitted texts (i.e., the *Vimalakīrtinirdeśa Sūtra, Srīmālā Sūtra,* etc.) represents, according to Paul, the majority Mahāyāna view. For other arguments that depict a diminution of misogyny as Buddhism develops from the time of the Buddha through the rise of the Mahāyāna, see Karen C. Lang, "Lord Death's Snare: Gender-Related Imagery in the 'Theragāthā'

and the 'Therīgāthā,'" *Journal of Feminist Studies in Religion* 2 (1986): 78; and Janice Willis, "Nuns and Benefactresses: The Role of Women in the Development of Buddhism," in *Women, Religion, and Social Change,* ed. Yvonne Yazbeck Haddad and Ellison Banks Findly (Albany: State University of New York Press, 1985), p. 77.

16. See Śāntideva's compendium of the Mahāyāna path, the *Sikṣasamuccaya,* ed. C. Bendall (St. Petersburg: Russian Bibliotheca Buddhica, 1897), where various antifeminine fulminations are quoted from a variety of early Mahāyāna texts. For example, "Women are always the root of misfortune and poverty; how can men controlled by women be happy?" (p. 44). To show how men smitten by women make fools of themselves, Śāntideva quotes a series of analogies from the *Udayanavatsarāja-paripṛcchā Sūtra*: "A fly that's seen a wound flies toward it, a donkey that's seen filth trots off to investigate it, a dog that's seen meat pounces on it; so too fools who are aroused by women rush off" (p. 49). The same text declares: "The Buddhas say that women are as foul smelling as excrement; such is the intercourse of a wretch with wretches. The fool who grasps a bag of excrement and enters this abode will experience retribution of the same sort as the deed he's done" (p. 49). All translations from the Pāli, Sanskrit, and French are my own unless otherwise indicated.

17. L. Feer, ed., *Saṃyutta Nikāya,* 5 vols. (London: Pali Text Society, 1884–98), 1:128; C. A. F. Rhys Davids and F. L. Woodward, trans., *The Book of the Kindred Sayings,* 5 vols. (London: Pali Text Society, 1917–30), 1:161–62.

18. Feer, ed., *Saṃyutta Nikāya* 1.37; C. A. F. Rhys Davids and Woodward, trans., *Kindred Sayings* 1:53.

19. Because I draw upon literature belonging to more than one Buddhist canon, I have found it convenient to use the term "post-Aśokan literature" as a catchall for referring to texts of various scholastic affiliations compiled after the reign of Aśoka and, for the most part, during the first half of the first millennium of the Common Era. The Sanskrit biographical sources I rely on here were composed in the centuries immediately preceding and succeeding the birth of Christ. The Pāli commentarial sources were redacted around the fifth century. For details on the composition of my sources, see the appendix.

20. "Hīnayāna" is a problematic term. It is a pejorative label meaning "the lesser or inferior vehicle" (Sanskrit, *hīna-yāna*) that is found in polemical contexts in Mahāyāna *Sūtra*s. It is unacceptable to substitute "Theravāda" for "Hīnayāna," as some scholars do when speaking of the variety of non-Mahāyāna schools extant around the time of Christ, since the present-day Theravāda may not be all that representative of the variety of schools that were labeled "Hīnayāna." Because there is no generally accepted alternative to the term "Hīnayāna," however, I use it here with no pejorative intent.

21. Jean-Paul Sartre, *Being and Nothingness: An Essay in Phenomenological Ontology,* trans. Hazel E. Barnes (New York: Citadel, 1969), pp. 228–78.

22. Elaine Scarry, *The Body in Pain: The Making and Unmaking of the World* (New York: Oxford University Press, 1985).

23. In a very suggestive passage on strictures against representing (and thus embodying) Yahweh in the Hebrew Bible, for example, Scarry argues that the emphatic embodiment of women in pornography and advertising imagery reflects (and contributes to) the relative powerlessness of women in contemporary society: "In discussions of power, it is conventionally the case that those with power are said to be 'represented'

whereas those without power are said to be 'without representation.' . . . But to have no body is to have no limits on one's extension out into the world; conversely, to have a body, a body made emphatic by being continually altered through various forms of creation, instruction (e.g., bodily cleansing), and wounding, is to have one's sphere of extension contracted down to the small circle of one's immediate physical presence. Consequently, to be intensely embodied is the equivalent of being unrepresented and (here as in many secular contexts) is almost always the condition of those without power. . . . Probably the most familiar contemporary instance of this phenomenon is the emphatic inequality in the representation of female and male bodies in Western art, film, and above all, magazine imagery. . . . It subverts women's autonomy over their own bodies; their power to determine the degree to which they will or will not reveal their own bodies is pre-empted by the prior existence of such images in the most public, most communal of spaces. . . . [Discussions of the aesthetic content of such public images miss the crucial] framing fact that, comparatively speaking, men have no bodies and women have emphatic bodies" (*The Body in Pain,* pp. 207, 359).

24. See John Berger, *Ways of Seeing* (London: Pelican, 1972), pp. 45–64. In *Gender Advertisements* (New York: Harper and Row, 1979); 1st ed., 1976), Goffman explores how contemporary advertising imagery instantiates and exploits for commercial purposes notions about how men and women differ. Goffman is particularly interested in how the artificial, "make-believe" world of advertising represents gender differences regarded as "natural" through framing techniques that subordinate and infantilize women.

25. The nine points of suppuration that break the surface of the boil are the nine orifices of the male body. Earlier layers of the Buddhist scriptural tradition (i.e., most of the *Aṅguttara, Saṃyutta, Majjhima,* and *Dīgha Nikāya*s) consistently gender the body as male in speaking of the nine openings of the human body. But when glossing these passages referring to the nine apertures of the (male) body, later commentaries consistently gender the body as female by identifying diseased, dying, or dead female bodies as the subjects of such passages, as I show in chapter 3. I believe that both genderings of the body stem from androcentrism—that of the *Nikāya*s because to consider the male body as normative for all humanity is the essence of androcentric thinking, and that of post-Aśokan commentaries because by identifying the grotesque body as feminine and using it as an object of meditation, men are provided with a solution to the male dilemma of how to resist the purportedly dangerous charms of women.

26. This expression is found in an English translation of a Mongolian Sūtra that is also extant in Tibetan. See Stanley Frye, trans., *The Sutra of the Wise and the Foolish (mdo bdzans blun) or the Ocean of Narratives (üliger-ün dalai)* (Dharamsala: Library of Tibetan Works and Archives, 1981), p. 71.

27. This subtitle is borrowed from the title of Paula Rabinowitz's review of feminist film theory published in *Feminist Studies* 16 (1990): 151–69.

28. Jane Tibbetts Schulenberg, "The Heroics of Virginity: Brides of Christ and Sacrificial Mutilation," in *Women in the Middle Ages and the Renaissance,* ed. M. B. Rose (Syracuse: Syracuse University Press, 1986).

29. Fran Dolan points out how often and how purposefully the pain of the female martyr is elided from early modern European accounts of death by torture. See " 'Gen-

tlemen, I Have Only One More Thing to Say': Women on the Scaffold in England, 1563–1680," *Modern Philology* 92 (1994): 157–78.

30. I am grateful to Wendy Doniger for pointing out the redundancy of Subhā's natural (female) eyes given the fact that she has learned to see herself and her world through the eyes of a male observer.

Chapter One

1. On the agitation of Chinese pilgrims upon seeing the holy sights of Buddhist India, see T. H. Barrett, "Explanatory Observations on Some Weeping Pilgrims," in *Buddhist Studies Forum,* vol. 1, *Seminar Papers, 1987–88,* ed. T. Skorupski (London: School of Oriental and African Studies, 1990), pp. 91–110.

2. The term *bhāvanā,* which might be translated as "coming into being," "realization," or "development," has traditionally been translated as "meditation." While the semantic range of this term leaves much to be desired, I have found no generally accepted, etymologically accurate alternative.

3. C. A. F. Rhys Davids, ed., *Visuddhimagga,* 2 vols. (London: Pali Text Society, 1920–21; reprint, Routledge and Kegan Paul, 1975), 1:189–94 (page references are to the 1975 edition). In South Asian monastic communities, the practice of contemplating corpses still goes on today in modified forms (see n. 6 above). Few lay meditators contemplate corpses, but there are a variety of lay meditation procedures that help contemporary Buddhists to conjure up images of the foulness of the body. On lay meditations in contemporary Sri Lanka, see "Despair and Recovery in Sinhala Medicine and Religion: An Anthropologist's Meditations," in *Healing and Restoring: Health and Medicine in the World's Religious Traditions,* ed. Lawrence E. Sullivan (New York: Macmillan, 1989).

4. C. A. F. Rhys Davids, ed., *Visuddhimagga,* 1:193–94.

5. There are many passages in the *Nikāya*s that prescribe the contemplation of foul things for those troubled by passion. The Buddha of the *Aṅguttara Nikāya* is unstinting in his praise of the practice. At *Aṅguttara Nikāya* 1:4, he says: "Monks, I know of nothing with the power to prevent sensual desire, if not already arisen, or to cause its eradication, if arisen, as the sign of foulness [*asubhanimittaṃ*]." See R. Morris and E. Hardy, eds., *Aṅguttara Nikāya,* 5 vols. (London: Pali Text Society, 1885–1900), 1:4. On another occasion, the Buddha is said to have stated: "Monks, when a monk lives much with the perception of the foul [*asubhasaññā*] heaped around [*paricita*] the mind, the mind draws back, bends back, turns back from the attainment of sexual intercourse [*methunadhammasamāpattiyā*] and is not distracted [*na sampasārīyati*] thereby" (4:46–47). At one point in the *Aṅguttara Nikāya,* the Buddha recommends "developing [*bhāvetabbā*] the foul [*asubhā*] in order to put away lust, developing friendliness in order to put away ill-will, developing mindful breathing [*ānāpānasati*] for [eliminating] distraction, and developing the perception of impermanence [*aniccasaññā*] for the abolishing of ego-ism [*asmimānasa*]." (4:357).

6. C. A. F. Rhys Davids, ed., *Visuddhimagga,* 1:179–80.

7. Ibid., 1:184.

8. Compare the excellent treatment of such Christian figures as Anthony and Augustine in Geoffrey G. Harpham, *The Ascetic Imperative in Criticism and Culture* (Chi-

cago: University of Chicago Press, 1987). Asceticism, Harpham argues, is "essentially a meditation on, even an enactment of, desire. . . . Asceticism fights fire with fire, supplanting erotic pleasure with an attenuated, 'profound,' and spiritual satisfaction" (pp. 45–46).

9. Aversion therapy suppresses undesirable compulsive behaviors by pairing stimuli conducive to such behaviors (such as violent pornography) with a noxious stimulus (such as electric shock). See N. H. Hadley, *The Foundations of Aversion Therapy* (New York: S. P. Medical and Scientific Books, 1985).

10. C. A. F. Rhys Davids, ed., *Visuddhimagga,* 1:77.

11. T. W. Rhys Davids and J. E. Carpenter, eds., *Dīgha Nikāya,* 3 vols. (London: Pali Text Society, 1889–1910), 2:141.

12. On the controversy surrounding Gandhi's experiments in celibacy, in which he concentrated on remaining celibate in mind as well as in body while sleeping with young female disciples, see Ved Mehta, *Mahatma Gandhi and His Apostles* (New Haven, CT: Yale University Press, 1993), pp. 190–213.

13. Where women's bodies frequently serve as object lessons on impermanence for men, we find in the *Therīgāthā* reports of *inanimate* objects serving the same function for women. For example, the very first entry in the *Therīgāthā* is a verse uttered by an anonymous woman whose husband would not consent to her leaving the world. Continuing in her domestic duties in a mindful fashion, this woman made a kitchen fire the basis for contemplating impermanence. As a result of this experience, she became a nonreturner (*anāgāmin*), a person who will not be reborn again. She stopped wearing jewels and ornaments to show her commitment to the Buddhist path and, her seriousness beyond all doubt, eventually succeeded in wresting consent from her husband. See *Therīgāthā* 1, trans. C. A. F. Rhys Davids, *Poems of Early Buddhist Nuns (Therīgāthā)* (Oxford: Pali Text Society, 1989; originally published as *Psalms of the Sisters,* Pali Text Society, 1909), p. 6 (page reference is to 1989 edition).

14. In the *Mahāvastu,* Ānanda admits to the monk Mahākāśyapa that he is a "foolish, womanish [*mātṛgrāma*], witless" man. This confession follows a rather heated exchange in which Mahākāśyapa upbraids Ānanda for irresponsible behavior and then a nun named Sthūlanandā comes to Ānanda's defense by attacking Mahākāśyapa's credentials. See É. Senart, ed., *Mahāvastu,* 3 vols. (Paris: Imprimerie Nationale, 1882–97), 3:50; J. J. Jones, trans., *The Mahāvastu,* 3 vols., Sacred Books of the Buddhists, vols. 16, 18, and 19 (London: Luzac and Company, 1949–56), 3:49.

15. In *West of Everything: The Inner Life of Westerns* (New York: Oxford University Press, 1992), Jane Tompkins describes the drive for total autonomy that, in Westerns, lures men to leave home and find solace in a life of wandering. In a chapter entitled "Landscape," Tompkins explores some of the parallels between the self-disciplined lives of early Christian ascetics of the Egyptian desert and the austere lives of Western heroes—men who thrive on physical ordeal in harsh desert landscapes, who are satisfied with a life of few creature comforts, and who are largely celibate. There is much that is problematic in her comparison of Western heroes and early Christian ascetics. Most problematic of all is Tompkins's assertion that heroism in Westerns is predicated on "a massive suppression of the inner life" (p. 66)—a goal that can scarcely be attributed to the highly introspective ascetics of the Egyptian desert. Tompkins's comparisons

are nevertheless worth exploring because of the light they shed on the link between nomadism and self-mastery.

16. Lord Chalmers, ed., *Sutta-Nipāta or Discourse Collection* (Cambridge, MA: Harvard University Press, 1932), pp. 10–12.

17. The Newar Buddhist population of Nepal is exceptional in this regard. Entering the courtyard of a Nepali monastery (*bahal*), one is likely to see diapers drying on clotheslines and an abundance of children due to the fact that celibacy is not required of the ritual specialists who serve the Newar Buddhist communities of Nepal's Kathmandu valley. See Michael Allen, "Buddhism without Monks: The Vajrāyana Religion of the Newars of the Kathmandu Valley," *South Asia* 3 (1973): 1-14.

18. Although contemporary Buddhists distinguish between higher and lower ordinations (called *upasampadā* and *pabbajjā*, respectively), no such distinction existed during the time of the Buddha. The Buddha gathered his disciples much in the manner of Jesus, by summoning them to follow him with the words, "Come, monk" (*ehi, bhikkhu*). See Richard Gombrich, *Theravāda Buddhism: As Social History from Ancient Benares to Modern Columbo* (London: Routledge and Kegan Paul, 1988), pp. 106–7.

19. The practice of temporary ordination is widespread today among Theravāda Buddhists in Burma and Thailand. Young men in those countries take lower ordination and live for a short time (usually one rainy season) as novices in a monastic setting, after which they typically return to the social world and seek marriage partners. The practice of temporary ordination has been seen as a *rite de passage* by many anthropologists. On temporary ordination as a rite of passage and an occasion for merit making in Burma, see Melford E. Spiro, *Buddhism and Society: A Great Tradition and Its Burmese Vicissitudes* (New York: Harper and Row, 1972), pp. 234–47. For a description of how temporary ordination figures in Thai constructions of manhood, see Charles F. Keyes, "Ambiguous Gender: Male Initiation in a Northern Thai Buddhist Society," in *Gender and Religion: On the Complexity of Symbols*, ed. Caroline Walker Bynum, Stevan Harrell, and Paula Richman (Boston: Beacon, 1986).

20. H. Oldenberg, ed., *Vinaya Piṭaka*, 5 vols. (London: Pali Text Society, 1879–83), 3:11–22.

21. Oldenberg, ed., *Vinaya Piṭaka*, 3:12.

22. Ibid., 3:13.

23. Ibid., 3:16.

24. The term Sudinna uses to express his delight with the celibate life (*abhirata*) can denote love and sexual enjoyment. Thus Sudinna's statement might aptly be translated, "I am in love with *brahmacariya*." The privative form *anabhirata* frequently occurs in the declarations of lovesick monks who are no longer in love with the practice of celibacy.

25. "Accharāyo yāsaṃ tvaṃ hetu brahmacariyaṃ carisi?" See Oldenberg, ed., *Vinaya Piṭaka*, 3:17. A type of female deity associated with lakes, rivers, and rainclouds who adorns the court of the god Indra in his paradise, the celestial nymphs of Indian mythology (Pāli, *accharā;* Sanskrit, *apsarās*, from *ap*√*sr̥*, "going into the water") may be seen as the personification of liquid flow. Such women can be won, according to Brahminical thought, by the householder who sponsors a thousand large-scale sacrifices. By sacrifice, the householder can conquer the celestial realm that Indra rules and assume the body

and activities of an Indra. See Wendy Doniger O'Flaherty, *Śiva: The Erotic Ascetic* (London: School of Oriental and African Studies, 1973; reprint, New York: Oxford University Press, 1981), pp. 64–68 (page references are to 1981 edition). But for Buddhists, cosmological upward mobility is not the point of practicing *brahmacarya.* To win celestial *apsaras*es and the body of Indra in which to enjoy them is to lose oneself in deceptive pleasures and to relinquish the opportunity to pursue the path of liberation in that celestial life span. The gods are the ultimate householders — in biographies of the Buddha, they appear as cheerleaders who can only stand at the sidelines and support the players but cannot themselves play the renouncer's game.

26. "Na kho ahaṃ bhagini accharānaṃ hetu brahmacariyaṃcarāmi" (Oldenberg, ed., *Vinaya Piṭaka,* 3:17).

27. Ibid.

28. Sudinna is said to reflect as follows: "Puttakaṃ pana labhitvā oramisassanti, tato ahaṃ yathā-sukhaṃsamaṇadhammaṃ karissāmi." See J. Takakusu and M. Nagai, *Samantapāsādikā: Buddhaghosa's Commentary on the Vinaya Piṭaka,* 7 vols. (London: Pali Text Society, 1924–47), 1:212.

29. Intercourse, along with theft, murder, and bragging falsely of superhuman powers, are the four offenses entailing defeat (*pārājikā dhammā*) that lead to immediate expulsion from the *sangha.*

30. Oldenberg, ed., *Vinaya Piṭaka,* 3:20.

31. Ibid., 1:43. John Strong discusses Indian Buddhist responses to such charges in "Filial Piety and Buddhism: The Indian Antecedents to a 'Chinese' Problem," in *Traditions in Contact and Change,* ed. Peter Slater and Donald Wiebe (Waterloo, Ontario: Wilfred Laurier Press, 1983), pp. 171–86.

32. In *The Position of Women in Hindu Civilization from Prehistoric Times to the Present Day* (1938; reprint, New Delhi: Motilal Banarsidass, 1978), Anant Sadashiv Altekar notes the erosion of women's autonomy from the Vedic Era to the beginning of the Christian Era; during this period, the institution and legitimization of customs such as adolescent marriage, widow burning (*sati*), and prohibitions against widow remarriage led to restrictions on female autonomy.

33. See O'Flaherty, *Śiva: The Erotic Ascetic,* pp. 68–82; see especially the story of the chaste sage Mandapāla (p. 69) who was denied the rewards of his austerities due to his lack of progeny.

34. In his preface to *Barabudur: Esquise d'une histoire du Bouddhisme fondée sur la critique archéologique des textes* (Hanoi: École Française d'Extreme Orient, 1935; reprint, New York: Arno Press, 1978), Paul Mus devotes a great deal of attention to the idea of the transmission of the father's legal and ritual personhood to the son in Brahminical culture as well as to Buddhist parallels.

35. One interpreter glosses defeat (*pārājika*) in this context as defeat by Māra, which amounts to moral failure. See Mohan Wijayaratna, *Buddhist Monastic Life according to the Texts of the Theravāda Tradition,* English translation by Claude Grangier and Steven Collins (New York: Cambridge University Press, 1990), p. 94.

36. Peter Brown, *The Making of Late Antiquity* (Cambridge, MA: Harvard University Press, 1978), p. 87.

37. As a biological instinct, sexual desire can lead to such antisocial behavior as incest. See, for example, Morris and Hardy, eds., *Aṅguttara Nikāya,* 3:66, on an inces-

tuous encounter between a mother and a son who spent too much time together after joining the *sangha.* But it is the social ramifications of sexuality that figure most prominently in Buddhist tradition. In the commentary to a story of sexual defeat in the *Vinayapiṭaka,* the following thoughts are attributed to a wayward monk dissatisfied with *brahmacariya*: "I remember my mother . . . I remember my father . . . I remember my brother . . . I remember my sister . . . I remember my son . . . I remember my daughter . . . I remember my wife . . . I remember my relations . . . I remember my friends . . . I remember the village . . . I remember the town . . . I remember my property . . . I remember my gold coins . . . I remember my crafts . . . I remember early laughter . . . chatter and amusement" (Oldenberg, ed., *Vinaya Piṭaka,* 3:25).

38. Cited by Brown, *The Making of Late Antiquity,* pp. 87–88. Even in traditions where marriage is given pride of place, as in Judaism, there can be conflict between a man's domestic obligations and the obligation to devote one's life to study. For tales typifying this conflict, see Daniel Boyarin, *Carnal Israel: Reading Sex in Talmudic Culture* (Berkeley and Los Angeles: University of California Press, 1993), chap. 5.

39. Tertullian, *Ad Uxorem,* cited in Katharina M. Wilson and Elizabeth Makowski, *Wykked Wyves and the Woes of Marriage: Misogamous Literature from Juvenal to Chaucer* (Albany: State University of New York Press, 1990), p. 39.

40. See especially Louis Dumont, "World Renunciation in Indian Religions," in *Homo Hierarchicus: The Caste System and Its Implications* (Chicago: University of Chicago Press, 1980).

41. See *The Rig Veda,* trans. Wendy Doniger (Harmondsworth: Penguin, 1983), pp. 29–32.

42. Steven Collins, "Monasticism, Utopias, and Comparative Social Theory," *Religion* 18 (1988): 104.

43. As Collins suggests, there are problems with Dumont's adoption of the emic Christian terms "world" and "worldly" as if they were universalizable. Nevertheless, if by "the world" one intends the social world constructed by karma and structured by caste duty, such terms as "world" and "worldly" do not violate the spirit of Buddhist monasticism.

44. 1 Cor. 7:9.

45. Prior to its being claimed as a technical term by the Mahāyāna, the term *bodhisattva* was used to refer to any one for whom—like Gotama Siddhartha before he achieved awakening (*bodhi*)—Buddhahood has been predicted but not yet achieved. I use the term *bodhisattva* here with that generic meaning; if the Mahāyāna usage is intended, I indicate that by use of capitalization (*Bodhisattva*).

46. That is the emerging consensus among scholars of the Mahāyāna. In his *Indo-Tibetan Buddhism: Indian Buddhists and Their Tibetan Successors,* 2 vols. (Boston: Shambhala, 1987), 1:63, David Snellgrove writes, "There would seem to be no doubt that the real protagonists of the Mahāyāna were monks, and the new scriptures were compiled by monks, some of whom were renowned as masters of philosophy. Also the career of the *Bodhisattva,* as described in the texts, assumes that the life of a monk and at least the life of celibacy are essential conditions for his progress. . . . However popular amongst the layfolk the cult of the great celestial *bodhisattvas* may be, there is no doubt that the teachings about the actual practice of the *bodhisattva* career are directed primarily towards monks." For a lucid review of the evidence against the widely

held theory of the Mahāyāna's lay origins, see Paul Williams's introduction to his *Mahāyāna Buddhism: The Doctrinal Foundations* (New York: Routledge, 1989).

47. The *Vimalakīrtinirdeśa Sūtra* is one text that appears to advocate living the life of a renouncer within the social world. The *Bodhisattva* Vimalakīrti is certainly portrayed as a man of the world in every possible respect. But in my view, Vimalakīrti's actions and statements must be seen in light of the metaphysically grounded antinomianism that undergirds the text. Knowing that one can only provisionally distinguish between good and bad conduct due to the ultimate emptiness (*śūnyatā*) of all *dharma*s or components of existence, the *Bodhisattva* Vimalakīrti lives as a wealthy householder fully engaged in the social world. Not only does Vimalakīrti visit brothels, gaming houses, and drinking halls, but he even advocates matricide, parricide, and the intentional wounding of Tathāgathas (7.1–5) in order to highlight the nondualism of the truth of emptiness. See *Vimalakīrtinirdeśa (The Teaching of Vimalakīrti),* French translation by Étienne Lamotte, rendered into English by Sara Boin, Sacred Books of the Buddhists, vol. 32 (London: Pali Text Society, 1976), pp. 173–80.

48. Senart, ed., *Mahāvastu,* 2:117. Compare the *Vinaya* passage quoted above reporting Sudinna's decision to renounce. Parallel passages in Pāli are to be found at several points in the *Majjhima Nikāya, Dīgha Nikāya,* and the *Vinaya Piṭaka.* See citations in I. B. Horner, *Women under Primitive Buddhism: Lay Women and Alms Women* (New York: E. P. Dutton, 1930), p. 166.

49. On Vedic precedents for the positive evaluation of open space and concomitant devaluation of closeness, see J. Gonda, "The Vedic Concept of *Amhas,*" *Indo-Iranian Journal* 1 (1957): 33–60; W. D. O'Flaherty, *The Rig Veda: An Anthology* (Harmondsworth: Penguin, 1983), p. 118. The Vedic terms that are most often opposed are *amhas* (cognate with "anxiety," "angst," and "anguish") are *pṛtu* and *varivas.* The Buddhist hybrid Sanskrit terms used in the *Mahāvastu* are *saṃbādha* and *abhyavakāśam.*

50. See Collins, "Monasticism, Utopias, and Comparative Social Theory."

51. In one past-life narrative immediately following the *Mahāvastu*'s account of the Great Renunciation, the Buddha explains that in a previous life he was not only indifferent to Yaśodharā, but nearly had to drown her in order to go forth on his own. He was a horse trader mistaken by a king for a robber and sentenced to death. She was a courtesan who, seeing him, fell in love with the horse trader and arranged with the king's executioner to have her present lover put to death in the horse trader's place. The horse trader is delighted with this turn of events until, dressed in costly garments and enjoying a sumptuous meal, he suddenly figures out how the courtesan obtained his release. He is so alarmed by the prospect that he will be destroyed just like the courtesan's previous lover that he throws up his food and begins to make plans to escape. The way he escapes, however, is as devious and nearly as violent as the way the courtesan acquired him as her lover: he attempts to drown her while pretending to be engaged in erotic love-play with her in a pool of water. See the *Syāmā Jātaka,* in Jones, trans., *Mahāvastu,* 2:162–70. Compare the Pāli *Kaṇavera Jātaka,* in *Jātakāṭṭhakathā* (The *Jātaka* Together with its Commentary) ed. V. Fausboll, 6 vols. (London: Pali Text Society, 1877–96; reprint Luzac and Co., 1962–64), 3:58–63 (page references are to the 1962–64 edition); R. Chalmers et al., trans., *The Jātaka or Stories of the Buddha's Former Births* (London: Pali Text Society, 1895–1907), 3:39–42.

52. Senart, ed. *The Mahāvastu,* 2:161–62. Whereas the *Mahāvastu* recommends

renouncing when things are going one's way, the *Mahābhārata*—an epic poem that is a touchstone of classical Hinduism—recommends renouncing when things are looking bleak: in times of distress, when overcome by old age, or when vanquished by the enemy. See *Mahābhārata* 12.10.17; cited in J. C. Heesterman, "Brahmin, Ritual, and Renouncer," in *The Inner Conflict of Tradition: Essays in Indian Ritual, Kingship, and Society* (Chicago: University of Chicago Press, 1985), p. 41.

53. John Strong, "The Family Quest in the *Mūlasarvāstivāda Vinaya*," (paper presented at the Buddhism in Asian Cultures Workshop at the University of Chicago Divinity School, April 1990).

54. Richard Gombrich, "Feminine Elements in Sinhalese Buddhism," *Wiener Zeitschrift für die Kunde Südasiens* 16 (1972): 74–75. Gombrich elsewhere characterizes the Sri Lankan Buddhist's image of the Buddha as that of a distant, dignified patriarch or king, not a nurturing mother with whom formality and reverential distance are unnecessary. See Richard Gombrich and Gananath Obeyesekere, *Buddhism Transformed: Religious Change in Sri Lanka* (Princeton, N.J.: Princeton University Press, 1988), pp. 400–401.

55. M. E. Lilley, ed., *Apadāna*, 2 vols. (London: Pali Text Society, 1925–27), 2: 532.

56. On the various bodies of the Buddha, see "Bodies of the Buddha," in *Guide to the Buddhist Religion*, ed. Frank Reynolds (New York: G. K. Hall, 1981); Louis de La Vallée Poussin," Notes sur les corps du Buddha," *Le Muséon* (1913), pp. 251–90; Nalinaksha Dutt, *Aspects of Mahayana Buddhism and Its Relation to Hinayana* (London: Luzac, 1930); Maryla Falk, *Nama-Rupa and Dharma-Rupa* (Calcutta: University of Calcutta, 1943); D. T. Suzuki, *Studies in the Lankavatara Sutra* (London: Routledge, 1930); Paul Mus, "Buddha Paré," *Bulletin de l'école française Extréme-Orient* 28 (1928): 147–278; Paul Demeiville, "Busshin," *Hobo-girin*, fasc. 2 (Tokyo: Maison Franco-Japanaise, 1930); Nagao Gadjin, "On the Theory of Buddha-Body," *Eastern Buddhist*, n.s., 6, no. 1 (May 1973): 25–53; John Makransky, "Controversy over *Dharmakāya* in India and Tibet: A Reappraisal of Its Basis, *Abhisamayālamkāra* Chapter 8," *Journal of the International Association of Buddhist Studies* 12 (1989): 45–78; Lewis Lancaster, "An Early Mahāyāna Sermon about the Body of the Buddha and the Making of Images," *Artibus Asiae* 36 (1974): 287–91; Frank Reynolds, "The Several Bodies of the Buddha: Reflections on a Neglected Aspect of Theravāda Tradition," *History of Religions* 16 (1977): 374–88.

57. The *Vimalakīrtinirdeśa Sūtra* describes a Buddhist paradise where all beings subsist only on the nutritive essence of the Dharma, which takes a very long time to digest if one is an advanced *Bodhisattva* but runs through novice practitioners like morning coffee. See Lamotte and Boin, trans., *Vimalakīrtinirdeśa (The Teaching of Vimalakīrti)*, pp. 204 ff. Compare Brian K. Smith on how in the *Brāhmaṇas* the hierarchy of the various Vedic sacrifices is expressed as a hierarchy of nutritive essences: "Gods and Men in Vedic Ritualism: Toward a Hierarchy of Resemblance," *History of Religions* 24 (1985): 305; "Eaters, Food, and Social Hierarchy in Ancient India: A Dietary Guide to a Revolution of Values," in *Journal of the American Academy of Religion* 58 (1990): 177–206.

58. In Sri Lanka, the motherhood of the Buddha is less likely to be established by denigrating worldly motherhood. As Gombrich points out in "Feminine Elements in

Sinhalese Buddhism," there is a Sinhalese saying, *ammā gedara Budun,* "The mother is the Buddha of the home," that suggests that not only is the Buddha considered a mother but mothers are comparable to Buddhas.

59. In recording the pathetic protestations of Vessantara's family upon being given away by King Vessantara and in showing the agony that such a difficult donation causes the king himself, the Pāli recension of the *Vessantara Jātaka* seems to acknowledge the conflict between transcendental religious values that encourage the giving up of wives and children and ordinary human values that discourage the abandoning of families.

60. See H. C. Norman, ed., *Dhammapadāṭṭhakathā* (The Commentary to the Dhammapada), 4 vols. (London: Pali Text Society 1906–14), 1:219 ff.

61. Buddhaghosa uses this medical analogy in his gloss on the four Noble Truths: "The truth of suffering is like a disease, the truth of the origin is like the cause of the disease, the truth of the cessation is like the allaying of disease, the truth of the path is like the medicine." Cited in Raoul Birnbaum, *The Healing Buddha* (Boulder, CO: Shambhala, 1979), p. 22.

62. Feer, ed., *Saṃyutta Nikāya,* 5:425.

63. In the *Dantabhūmi Sutta,* the untamed mind of the householder consumed by desire for the pleasures of the senses is compared to the wildness of the untamed elephant in whom the ways of the forest have not been subdued. See V. Trenckner and R. Chalmers, eds., *Majjhima Nikāya,* 3 vols. (London: Pali Text Society, 1888–1902), 3.129–38; I. B. Horner, trans., *The Middle Length Sayings,* 3 vols. (London: Pali Text Society, 1954–59), 3:175–83.

64. Michel Foucault describes a conversation with Peter Brown in which Brown suggests that sexuality functions as a "seismograph of our subjectivity" in Christian cultures. See "Sexuality and Solitude," in *On Signs,* ed. M. Blonsky (Baltimore: Johns Hopkins University Press, 1985), p. 368.

65. The lust-ridden disciple of an anonymous Desert Father suggests the value of encountering desire in declining the old man's offer to relieve him of his battle with lust: "Abba, I see that I am afflicted; but I see that this affliction is producing fruit in me. Therefore ask God to give me endurance to bear it." Sister Benedicta Ward, trans., *The Wisdom of the Desert Fathers: Apophthegmata Patrum* (Oxford: Fairacres, 1975), p. 9.

66. The *Buddhacarita* describes Māra as follows: "The one who in the world they call the love-god, with his various weapons, his flower-tipped arrows, likewise they call him Māra, the king of the way of desire, the enemy of liberation." See Johnston, ed., and trans., *The Buddhacarita, or Acts of the Buddha,* 1:145.

67. The quotation is given without citation in James Boyd, *Satan and Māra: Christian and Buddhist Symbols of Evil* (Leiden: E. J. Brill, 1975), p. 150.

68. Included in this army are ash-covered renouncers. In addition to serving as a possible sideswipe at Śaivism, the inclusion of renouncers among the demonic hosts suggests an affinity between those who dwell at the margins of society as renouncers and those who occupy the same position as demons preying on civilized humanity.

69. One account explains that Māra's daughters assume the forms of older women in order to arouse his desire. According to the *Saṃyutta Nikāya,* Māra's daughters echo the different-strokes-for-different-folks philosophy of the publishers of *Forty Plus* (a pornography magazine that features women over 40 whose bust size equals or exceeds

their age): "Men's tastes differ. What if each of us were now to assume the forms of one hundred women who have given birth once?' And so each of Māra's daughters, assuming the forms of one hundred women who have given birth once, approached the Blessed One and said: 'We're at your service, wanderer.' But the Blessed One paid them no mind, for he was liberated through the supreme destruction of the foundations [of rebirth]. So Māra's daughters went off to one side and reflected as follows: 'Men's tastes differ. What if each of us were now to assume the forms of one hundred women who have given birth twice?' . . . But the Blessed One paid them no mind. . . . So Māra's daughters went off to one side and reflected as follows: 'Men's tastes differ. What if each of us were now to assume the forms of one hundred middle-aged women . . . old women?'" See Feer, ed., *Saṃyutta Nikāya,* 1:125.

70. *Buddhacarita* 15.33–34; E. B. Cowell, ed., *The Buddhakarita of Asvaghosha* (Oxford: Clarendon, 1893), p. 130.

71. The Pāli version of this formula is: *Buddhaṃ saraṇaṃ gacchāmi; Dhammaṃ saraṇaṃ gacchāmi; sangham saraṇaṃ gacchāmi,* which translates as "I go to the Buddha for refuge; I go to the Dharma for refuge; I go to the Sangha for refuge." This formula also serves as a lay confession of faith.

72. Morris and Hardy, eds., *Aṅguttara Nikāya,* 3:68.

73. According to Hindu mythology, Śiva (the most ascetically inclined of the gods) resists the flower-tipped arrows of the god of love by scorching Kāma with an igneous ray from his third eye. But in many versions of the myth of Śiva and Kāma, it is Kāma who emerges victorious, for Śiva burns Kāma only to revive him later in a more potent form. See O'Flaherty, *Śiva: The Erotic Ascetic,* pp. 145–51.

74. Feer, ed., *Saṃyutta Nikāya,* 2:30.

Chapter Two

1. Feer, ed., *Saṃyutta Nikāya,* 5:320.

2. *Suttavibhaṅgha* 3.1.1; I. B. Horner, trans., *The Book of Discipline,* 5 vols., Sacred Books of the Buddhists, vols. 10, 11, 13, 14, 20 (London: Oxford University Press, 1938–52), 1:117. As we will see in chap. 4, the Buddha and members of his *sangha* are reported to have humiliated Māra on a number of occasions by magically outfitting him with a garland of carrion.

3. A number of Sanskrit texts refer to people called *saṃsāramocaka*s, or "liberators from *saṃsāra,*" who kill insects and sometimes humans in order to liberate them from their bad karma. On the theme of liberative murder, see Wilhelm Halbfass, "Tradition and Argument in Indian Ethics" (paper presented at the Workshop on Buddhist Intellectual Practice, University of Chicago Divinity School, January 31, 1992).

4. Among the other *dhutanga*s are restrictions on eating and dwelling places, such as living in the forest or at the foot of a tree. The *Majjhima Nikāya* lists—without labeling them as such—nine of the thirteen *dhutanga*s recognized by the commentarial tradition. For a discussion of the *dhutanga*s in Theravāda Buddhism, see Gombrich, *Theravada Buddhism,* p. 94. On the *dhutanga*s in Indian Buddhism generally, see Reginald Ray, *Buddhist Saints in India: A Study in Buddhist Values and Orientations* (New York: Oxford University Press, 1994), pp. 295–314.

5. Ibid.

6. Ibid. Robes made by patching together pieces of cloth in fidelity to the ascetic

tradition are also found in the Mahāyāna *sangha*s of Nepal and Tibet as well as other Asian *sangha*s.

7. On mindful breathing in the Theravāda tradition, see Paravahera Vajirañāṇa Mahāthera, *Buddhist Meditation in Theory and Practice: A General Exposition according to the Pāli Canon of the Theravāda School* (Colombo: M.D. Gunasena and Co., 1962), pp. 227–58. Vajirañāṇa cites the *Visuddhimagga* and the *Yogāvacara's Manual* on the status of mindful breathing as chief among meditative practices.

8. Medieval Hindu texts on renunciation also view disgust for transient things as a liberative state of mind. In the *Nāradaparivrājaka Upanishad* of the twelfth century C.E., the renouncer is advised to regard gold as a deadly poison, clarified butter as blood, hot water as urine, and the application of perfume as smearing oneself with filth. See Patrick Olivelle, *The Saṃnyāsa Upanishads: Hindu Scriptures on Asceticism and Renunciation* (New York: Oxford University Press, 1992), p. 214.

9. Feer, ed., *Saṃyutta Nikāya,* 2:30: "And what, monks, is the cause of liberation? Passionlessness [*virāga*] is the answer. I say, monks, that passionlessness is causally associated with liberation. And what, monks, is the cause of passionlessness? Aversion [*nibbidā*] is the answer. I say, monks, that aversion is causally associated with passionlessness. And what, monks, is the cause of aversion? The absolute knowledge of things as they really are [*yathābhūtañāṇadassana*] is the answer. Monks, I say that the absolute knowledge of things as they really are is causally associated with aversion."

10. Bhikkhu Khantipālo, *Bag of Bones: A Miscellany on the Body* (Kandy: Buddhist Publication Society, 1980), p. 8.

11. Feer, ed., *Saṃyutta Nikāya,* 2:98; F. L. Woodward and E. M. Hare, trans., *The Book of the Kindred Sayings,* 2:67 ff.

12. C. A. F. Rhys Davids, ed., *Visuddhimagga,* p. 342.

13. This practice of mixing up food is one of the *dhutanga*s undertaken at the monk or nun's option.

14. C. A. F. Rhys Davids, ed., *Visuddhimagga,* p. 344.

15. Ibid., p. 345. In Indic texts, digestion is generally understood as a process of cooking whereby matter is transformed through heat. In the *Upanishads,* where a variety of natural bodily processes like breathing are described as forms of Vedic sacrifice, digestion is attributed to the inner sacrificial fire, a microcosmic form of the fire god Agni that burns within all humans. Eating, therefore, is a sacrificial act, an oblation to the igneous mouth of Agni. While Buddhaghosa also understands digestion as a cooking process, his bubbling cesspool where outcastes throw their refuse is a far cry from the pure sacrificial space of the *Upanishad*ic stomach. As Olivelle (*Saṃnyāsa Upanishads*) notes, the Vedic construction of the body as a consecrated sacrificial space contrasts sharply with the renunciant construction of the body appearing at the end of the Vedic period—the renouncer sees the body as an abject collection of impurities. But if Heesterman is correct about the ritual impurity of the consecrated sacrificer (*dīkṣita*) in the preclassical system, then there is more continuity than conflict in the two cultural constructions of the body. See Heesterman, "Brahmin, Ritual, and Renouncer," pp. 27 ff.

16. "Just as when rice-gruel is being cooked, the chaff, husk-powder, rice-powder, and so on, boil over and smear the outer edge of the pot with scum, so when food, which has been eaten, is cooked [digested], giving rise to foam by means of the body's

heat which pervades the body, it rises up and smears the teeth with tartar, the tongue, palate, and so on, with saliva, phlegm, and so on; the eyes, ears, nose, the lower orifices, and so on, with eye-secretions, ear-wax, mucus, urine, feces, and so on, on account of which these openings are neither clean nor appealing though they be washed every day." See C. A. F. Rhys Davids, ed., *Visuddhimagga,* p. 346.

17. "After washing any one of these openings, the hand should be washed with water in its turn. After washing an opening the hand does not cease to be disgusting even if washed two or three times with cow-dung, clay, or aromatic powder" (ibid).

18. Ibid., pp. 345–46.

19. Feer, ed., *Saṃyutta Nikāya,* 2:94.

20. For a description of various meditations focusing on the body and an insightful discussion of Theravādan attitudes toward the body, see Steven Collins, "The Body in Theravāda Buddhist Monasticism," in *The Body in Religion: Comparative and Devotional Approaches,* ed. Sara Coakley (Berkeley and Los Angeles: University of California Press, forthcoming).

21. Trenckner and Chalmers, eds., *Majjhima Nikāya,* 3.90–91; Horner, trans., *Middle Length Sayings,* 3:131. On concepts of self and personhood in Theravāda Buddhist discourse, see Steven Collins, *Selfless Persons: Imagery and Thought in Theravāda Buddhism* (New York: Cambridge University Press, 1982).

22. In *Asceticism and Healing in Ancient India: Medicine in the Buddhist Monastary* (New York: Oxford University Press, 1991), Kenneth Zysk depicts Buddhist healers as empirically oriented anatomical theorists with fewer scruples about dissection than their Brahminical colleagues. Zysk finds it improbable that Brahminical practitioners would have originated dissection methods like that mentioned in the *Suśruta Samhitā*: a corpse is covered with bindings made of grass and netting, anchored down in a stream, and then dissected with branches when it is completely putrefied and malleable. See *Asceticism and Healing in Ancient India,* pp. 35–37. See also Francis Zimmermann's *The Jungle and the Aroma of Meats: An Ecological Theme in Hindu Medicine* (Berkeley and Los Angeles: University of California Press, 1987) on the low/outsider status of Ayurvedic physicians who must deceive their upper-caste vegetarian patients in order to get them to consume the meat and meat broths they need to recover from their illnesses.

23. Buddhaghosa regards *kāyagatāsatibhāvanā* as a uniquely Buddhist form of meditation "which did not occur except with the arising of the Buddhas, and which does not come within the scope of the adherents of various sects." See C. A. F. Rhys Davids, ed., *Visuddhimagga,* p. 275.

24. In the *Visuddhimagga,* for example, the heart is described as follows: "In its shape it is like a lotus-bud turned face downwards after the outer leaves have been removed. It is smooth outside, the inside is like the inside of a bitter gourd" (*Visuddhimagga,* p. 256). The intestines are precisely measured at "thirty-two cubits long in a man and twenty-eight cubits long in a woman, and folded up in twenty-one places. They are of a white color like that of a whitewash on gravel. In shape they resemble a beheaded snake folded up in a tub of blood" (p. 258).

25. One can either use this meditation as a means of cultivating insight (*vipassanā*) or as a means of cultivating tranquillity (*samatha*) (ibid., p. 277).

26. Khantipālo, *Bag of Bones,* p. 13.

27. C. A. F. Rhys Davids, ed., *Visuddhimagga,* p. 286.

28. Morris and Hardy, eds., *Aṅguttara Nikāya* 1:43–44; quoted in C. A. F. Rhys Davids, ed., *Visuddhimagga,* p. 241.

29. On beliefs about bodily impurity among contemporary rural Hindus of Rajasthan, see Morris G. Carstairs, *The Twice-Born: A Study of a Community of High-Caste Hindus* (Bloomington: Indiana University Press, 1958), pp. 77–88.

30. In the Hebrew Bible, for example, it is stated that all bodily discharges are defiling and those with discharges are disqualified from approaching the temple. See Mary Douglas, *Purity and Danger: An Analysis of the Concepts of Pollution and Taboo* (Routledge and Kegan Paul, 1979), pp. 51 ff. Jacob Neusner's *The Idea of Purity in Ancient Judaism* (Leiden: Brill, 1973) is a useful and historically nuanced survey that focuses on the period after the destruction of the temple.

31. Douglas, *Purity and Danger,* p. 53.

32. *Mānavadharmaśāstra* 5.132; J. Jolly, ed., *Mānavadharmaśāstra* (London: Trübner, 1887), p. 110.

33. *Mānavadharmaśāstra* 5.134–35; Jolly, ed., *Mānavadharmaśāstra,* ibid. The inclusion of bone marrow (*majjan*) in this list calls for an explanation. Although contemporary Western medical theory does not regard bone marrow as something that leaves the body while a person is alive, according to Indic medical theory bone marrow produces semen in men and milk in lactating women. So it is not inappropriate to classify it among those substances that are expelled from the body.

34. *Mānavadharmaśāstra* 5.133–34. The sacred elements of earth, water, and fire are used as purifying agents in many religions. Muslims, for example, wash with soil before facing Mecca to pray when water is not available. Although Brahminical and Zoroastrian purification rituals are strikingly similar in many respects due to their common Indo-Iranian cultural heritage, Zoroastrians take elaborate precautions that Hindus do not in order to avoid polluting the sacred elements of fire, water, and earth. For example, a preliminary application of bull urine is prescribed before water can be used to clean a garment polluted by bodily discharges. Zoroastrians also expose corpses rather than cremating or burying them so as to avoid polluting fire or earth. In Brahminical and Hindu thought, sacred purifying agents such as water, earth, and fire are not considered vulnerable to pollution. A Zoroastrian might well regard the Ganges River (which receives the remains of many cremated corpses) as miasmic in the extreme. But, to Hindus, the water of the Ganges is not only invulnerable to pollution from carrion—it is the Water of Heaven, the ultimate purifying agent. See Diana L. Eck, *Banaras: City of Light* (New York: Alfred A. Knopf, 1982), pp. 216–18. For a comparison of Zoroastrian and Hindu purity rituals, see Jamsheed K. Chomsky, *Purity and Pollution in Zoroastrianism: Triumph over Evil* (Austin: University of Texas Press, 1989), pp. 17–22.

35. *Mānavadharmaśāstra* 5.144.

36. Ibid., 5.83.

37. Ibid., 5.85; Jolly, ed., *Mānavadharmaśāstra,* p. 105.

38. Morris and Hardy, eds., *Aṅguttara Nikāya,* 4:377.

39. Ibid., 4:386–87.

40. That this passage on the body's putrescence is in no way atypical of the tradition

as a whole is suggested by the fact that in Buddhist scripture the body is frequently qualified as putrid (Pāli, *pūti*), as in the common compound *pūtikāya.*

41. C. A. F. Rhys Davids, ed., *Visuddhimagga,* pp. 342–43.

42. V. Trenckner, ed., *Milindapañha* (London: Williams and Norgate, 1880), pp. 73–74.

43. S. Sumangala, ed., *Dhammapada* (London: Pali Text Society, 1914), verse 147.

44. From Bhikkhu Nyāṇamoli, "A Thinker's Notebook," March 1956; cited in Khantipālo, *Bag of Bones,* p. 20.

45. The digestive process reminds Buddhaghosa of refuse decomposing in a sun-heated cesspool "at the gate of a village of outcastes [*caṇḍālagāmadvāre*]." See C. A. F. Rhys Davids, ed., *Visuddhimagga,* p. 345.

46. Ibid., p. 259.

47. Sue Hamilton, "From the Buddha to Buddhaghosa: Changing Attitudes towards the Human Body in Theravāda Buddhism," in *Religious Reflections on the Human Body,* ed. Jane Marie Law (Bloomington: Indiana University Press, 1995), p. 60.

48. The Buddha of the *Dīgha Nikāya* describes the body as "full of impurities [*asucino*] of various kinds, from the soles of the feet up and from the crown of the head down." See T. W. Rhys Davids and Carpenter, eds., *Dīgha Nikāya,* 2:293. The term for impurity used most frequently in Pāli materials is *asuci,* for which the Sanskrit cognate is *aśuci.*

49. Mary Douglas, *Natural Symbols: Explorations in Cosmology* (New York: Pantheon, 1982), p. 70.

50. Rules of etiquette often function like purity regulations in encoding a sense of social identity. After the dismantling of European sumptuary laws that prohibited members of lower social classes from imitating the sartorial and culinary fashions of the upper classes, it was largely good etiquette that set ladies and gentlemen apart from their social inferiors. For a fascinating account of the role of etiquette in the construction of eighteenth-century English bourgeoisie identity, see Peter Stallybrass and Allon White, *The Politics and Poetics of Transgression* (Ithaca, NY: Cornell University Press, 1986), pp. 80–124. See also Norbert Elias's monumental *Uber den Prozess der Zivilization* (Basel: Haus zum Falken, 1939), English ed., *The Civilizing Process: The History of Manners,* 2 vols., trans. Edmund Jephcott (New York: Urizen, 1978).

51. Because eating is an occasion where one aperture must be opened repeatedly for the purpose of admitting matter to the body, good etiquette generally prohibits the opening of other apertures for material exchange at such times. Thus picking one's nose at the table is in extremely bad taste. By the same logic, it is intuitively clear that to eat while sitting on the toilet (and thus to admit matter through the mouth while matter is being expelled through another orifice) would be a shocking departure from the standards of proper conduct.

52. C. A. F. Rhys Davids, ed., *Visuddhimagga,* p. 195. Emphasis mine.

53. Douglas, *Purity and Danger,* p. 124 ff.

54. "Grid" and "group" are terms that Douglas borrows from Basil Bernstein, "A Socio-Linguistic Approach to Socialization," in *Directions in Socio-Linguistics,* ed. J. Gumperz and D. Hymes (New York: Holt, Rinehart, & Winston, 1970). See *Natural Symbols,* pp. 54 ff. Although there is clear sexual segregation and differentiation based

on seniority in the *sangha,* it may be described as a low-grid society because it is organized around democratic principles. All decisions are based on the consensus of the majority. Authority does not radiate from a spiritual center through a hierarchy of command as in the ecclesiastical hierarchy of the Roman Catholic Church.

55. The *vetāla* is a supernatural being who possesses and reanimates dead bodies.

56. *Bodhicaryāvatāra* 4.48, 4.70; P. L. Vaidya, ed., *Bodhicaryāvatāra* (Dharbhanga: Mithila Institute of Post-graduate Studies and Research in Sanskrit Learning, 1960), pp. 145, 150.

57. The homologies between normal bodily emissions and the decay of the body in old age and death are made explicit in the commentary to *Dhammapada* verse 148, where the words *pabhaṅguraṃ rūpaṃ* ("perishable form") are glossed as follows: "Just as the jackal, even when it is young, is called *jarasigāla* [the aging jackal], and just as the *galoci* creeper, even when it is young, is called *pūtilatā* [the putrefying creeper], likewise [the human body], even on the day of its birth, even when it is golden hued, is [described as] perishable because it is [potentially] putrid owing to its constant dripping." See Norman, ed., *Dhammapadāṭṭhakathā* (The Commentary to the Dhammapada), 3:110–11. In Khantipālo, *Bag of Bones* (p. 54), Bhikkhu Khantipālo reminds the reader that "the body has a side which most of us don't want to see and know. We wish to hush up its dirt, stinks, belches and farts, to disregard and overlook them. Yet finally when laid low and near to death, these stenches and filths can be disguised no longer."

58. Elizabeth Baquedano Meza, "The Day of the Dead in Mixquic," in *The Skeleton at the Feast: The Day of the Dead in Mexico,* ed. Elizabeth Carmichael and Chloë Sayer (Austin: University of Texas Press, 1991), pp. 139, 143.

59. Interview with María Antonieta Sánchez de Escamilla, in Carmichael and Sayer, eds., *The Skeleton at the Feast,* p. 119.

60. See Lee Siegel, *Laughing Matters: The Comic Tradition in India* (Chicago: University of Chicago Press, 1990), p. 109.

61. On the conflation of the erotic and the horrific in Śaiva mythology and iconography, see O'Flaherty, *Śiva: the Erotic Ascetic,* pp. 236–51.

62. Michael Coulson, ed., *A Critical Edition of the Mālatīmādhava* (Delhi: Oxford University Press, 1989), pp. 100–101.

63. Siegel, *Laughing Matters,* pp. 43–44.

64. Paula Richman, *Women, Branch Stories, and Religious Rhetoric in a Tamil Buddhist Text* (Syracuse: Syracuse University Press, 1988), pp. 55–56 (translation is Richman's).

65. Ibid., p. 69.

66. Ibid. For a discussion of the Tamil poetic conventions that Cāttaṉār inverts for Buddhist rhetorical purposes, see pp. 63–77.

67. Ibid., p. 69.

68. Richman argues that for Cāttaṉār, the barren landscape called *pālai* "is the landscape that reveals the true nature of reality. The law of life's impermanence, summed up by the Buddhist doctrine of *anicca,* demonstrates itself most clearly in the *pālai* landscape. Cāttaṉār's story makes the case that the barren *pālai* is what really lies beneath outer appearance, even though our own ignorance leads us to view that appearance as real and permanent. All the passions and desires experienced in the landscapes of love lead ultimately to suffering and separation, the subject matter portrayed in both *pālai* and the cremation ground" (Ibid., pp. 70–71).

69. Compare the sentiments of Apyaya Dīkṣita (ca. sixteenth or seventeenth century): "People who have savored the joy of peace feel disgust for the joy of love, the highest enjoyment of lovers, just as those who have tasted pure food are revulsed by the garbage consumed by pigs" Siegel, *Laughing Matters,* p. 105 (translation is Siegel's).

70. For the Pāli edition, translated here, see Fausboll, ed., *Jātakāṭṭhakathā* (The Jātaka Together with Its Commentary), 5:278–312. A Sanskrit recension of this tale appears in Jones, trans., *The Mahāvastu,* 3 vols. (London: Luzac and Co., 1949–56), 2:372–442. For other South Asian versions of this *Jātaka* and its echoes in European folklore (i.e., "The Beauty and the Beast"), see H. T. Francis's introduction to his translation of the Pāli version in Chalmers et al., trans., *The Jātaka or Stories of the Buddha's Former Births,* 5:141. For an analysis of the *Kusa Jātaka* using Proppian categories and a comparison of the *Kusa Jātaka* with European versions of "The Beauty and the Beast," see Larry De Vries, "Literary Beauties and Folk Beasts: Folktale Issues in *Beauty and the Beast,*" appendix 1 to Betsy Hearn's *Beauty and the Beast: Visions and Revisions of an Old Tale* (Chicago: University of Chicago Press, 1989), pp. 155–88.

71. In an attempt to avoid marriage, the Buddha's disciple Mahākāśyapa reportedly used this statue ploy himself. He brought his parents a golden image made by skilled artists and told them that he would be happy to marry the girl who matches the statue in beauty. See verses 11–13 of the *Mahākāśyapāvadāna* in P. L. Vaidya, ed., *Avadānakalpalatā,* 2 vols. (Dharbhanga: Mithila Institute of Post-graduate Studies and Research in Sanskrit Learning, 1959), 2:449–53. Mahākāśyapa's story as related in the *Theragāthā* commentary is identical to that of prince Kusa in a number of particulars. See C. A. F. Rhys Davids, trans., *Psalms of the Early Buddhists,* vol. 2; *Psalms of the Brethren* (London: Pali Text Society, 1913), pp. 359–68.

72. Compare the comedy of errors found in the *Theragāthā* version of Mahākāśyapa's story, in C. A. F. Rhys Davids, trans., *Psalms of the Brethren,* pp. 359–60.

73. Fausboll, ed., *Jātakāṭṭhakathā,* 5:301. Here, King Madda is exercising his royal prerogative to determine punishments for transgressive behavior. Because Pabhāvatī has spurned Kusa, it seems, she is to receive the disfiguring punishment appropriate to an adulteress: those parts of her body most amenable to ornamentation and cosmetic decoration are to be cut off. The logic of punitive mutilation will be explored more fully in chapter 3 below.

74. Taking the variant reading *lambissati* for *lambahīti.*

75. Fausboll, ed., *Jātakāṭṭhakathā,* 5:302.

76. O'Flaherty, *Śiva: the Erotic Ascetic,* pp. 279–82.

77. The actual outcome of the *Kusa Jātaka* is decidedly less bloody than Pabhāvatī's fantasy would suggest. When Pabhāvatī returned to her father's kingdom, the ugly *bodhisattva* Kusa followed her there in order to win her back. First, Kusa went undercover as a minstrel in King Madda's court. He then took on a series of vocational disguises, working as a potter, a basket maker, etc. With each vocation he undertook, the ugly *bodhisattva* produced goods of such beauty that they were immediately purchased for Pabhāvatī and her sisters. Seeing his exquisite handiwork, Pabhāvatī deduces that the master craftsman supplying these goods could be none other than her husband Kusa. Although she resolves to keep Kusa's presence a secret, Pabhāvatī finally tells her mother that Kusa is in hiding nearby when, after King Madda has made arrangements for Pabhāvatī's execution and her mother has unsuccessfully attempted to inter-

vene on her daughter's behalf, the queen concludes that only King Kusa could possibly save Pabhāvatī now. As soon as they hear the news that Kusa is at hand, Pabhāvatī's parents insist that she go apologize to her husband, Kusa, thinking "today I will break down Pabhāvatī's pride and lay her low at my feet in the mud" (Fausboll, ed., *Jātakāṭṭhakathā,* p. 308), pours water on the ground at his feet, tramples the ground into a mass of mud, and makes Pabhāvatī fall to the ground and kiss his feet. After Pabhāvatī's show of contrition, Kusa prepares to wage war against the seven kings but then, in a stroke of genius, remembers that Pabhāvatī has seven unmarried sisters. These seven princesses are given in marriage to the seven kings and all live happily ever after.

78. A more condensed version of the harem scene is found in Pāli accounts of the Buddha's life, accounts which tend to have little to say about the *bodhisattva*'s youth and the events leading up to his renunciation. See the *Nidānakathā* portion of the *Jātaka,* translated by T. W. Rhys Davids, *Buddhist Birth Stories* (London: Trübner and Co., 1880), pp. 80–81.

79. Johnston, ed. and trans., *Buddhacarita,* chap. 2, verses 28–32 (1936 ed.), pp. 15–16 (1972 ed.). This and subsequent translations from Johnston's edition are my own. Suddhodana himself practices austerities while he encourages his son to play the sybarite. See *Buddhacarita,* 2:33–34.

80. In the Pāli accounts, the *bodhisattva* actually sees an old man, a sick man, a dead man, and a renouncer, while in the Sanskrit accounts, the gods conjure up these sights using psychic powers.

81. *Buddhacarita* 5.17; Johnston, ed. and trans., *Buddhacarita,* p. 47.

82. *Buddhacarita* 5.39; Johnston, ed. and trans., p. 50.

83. *Buddhacarita* 5.44–46; Johnston, ed. and trans., p. 51.

84. In his description of Rāvana's harem as seen by Hanumān in the *Rāmāyana,* the epic poet Vālmīki conveys a similar sense of amorous lethargy using many of the same tropes that Aśvaghoṣa uses in the *Buddhacarita.* In the *Rāmāyana,* however, the erotic *rasa* is not subverted by any suggestion of death or devastation. See Hari Prasad Shastri, trans., the *Rāmāyana of Vālmīki,* 3 vols. (London: Shantisadan, 1952–62), 2:356–57, 360–61.

85. *Buddhacarita* 5.50; Johnston, ed. and trans., *Buddhacarita,* p. 52.

86. *Buddhacarita* 5.56; Johnston, ed. and trans., *Buddhacarita,* p. 53.

87. *Buddhacarita* 5.57; Johnston, ed. and trans., *Buddhacarita,* p. 53.

88. *Buddhacarita* 5.58; Johnston, ed. and trans., *Buddhacarita,* p. 53. Johnston suggests that the reference is to dummies used in the training of elephants.

89. "*Gajabhagnā pratiyātanāṅganeva*"—the reference is probably to the use of dummies in training elephants for war.

90. Erotic manuals go into great detail in specifying how one should excite (and inscribe) one's lovers with bites and scratches—an ironic but inevitable result of subjecting erotic play to the exhaustive drive for categorization characteristic of Indic scholasticism. See *Vatsyayana Kama Sutra: The Hindu Ritual of Love* (New York: Castle, 1963), pp. 32–35. Such love-play could be (and was) taken for more violent forms of assault, as Lee Siegel's translation of verses from the *Subhāṣitaratnakoṣa* indicate: "The lady was embraced—she was scratched, she was bitten / in the battle of love—she was beaten, she was smitten. / This certainly should have meant her final expiration / were he not performing mouth-to-mouth resuscitation." See *Laughing Matters,* p. 103.

91. *Buddhacarita* 5.60; Johnston, ed. and trans., *Buddhacarita,* p. 53.

92. See the appendixed nontranslated portion of the Pāli *Vinaya* dealing with all the penetrable places that monks were wont to touch and penetrate (such as the mouths, vaginas, wounds, and even decapitated heads of bodies in the cremation ground), in Horner, trans., *The Book of Discipline,* 1:342.

93. *Buddhacarita* 5.61; Johnston, ed. and trans., *Buddhacarita,* p. 53.

94. *Buddhacarita* 5.63; Johnston, ed. and trans., *Buddhacarita,* p. 54. Johnston translates the phrase as "moved to disgust," but in my opinion this rendering fails to convey the mixture of aversion and disapproval or censure that the Sanskrit connotes.

95. The Sanskrit term *vikṛta* (from *vi* $\sqrt{kṛ}$) can denote a range of abnormal bodily states, from simple ugliness to deformation, the ravages of disease, accidental mutilation, and punitive disfiguration. I have chosen "monstrous" because in its etymology (from Latin *monere,* "to warn") this word suggests the didactic function that representations of bodily abnormality are often endowed with in religious contexts. The term "abominable" (from Latin *abominari,* "to loathe as of ill omen") might also suffice. On the display of monstrous feminine forms such as *sheela-na-gigs* on the exteriors of medieval cathedrals, see Jørgen Anderson, *The Witch on the Wall: Medieval Erotic Sculpture in the British Isles* (Copenhagen: Rosenkilde and Bagger, 1977). On gargoyles and other monstrosities displayed as a means of moral persuasion, see Michael Camille, *The Gothic Idol: Ideology and Image-Making in Medieval Art* (New York: Oxford University Press, 1989).

96. *Buddhacarita* 5.63; Johnston, ed. and trans., *Buddhacarita,* p. 54.

97. Samuel Beal, trans., *Fo-sh-hing-tsan-king: A Life of the Buddha by Aśvaghosa Bodhisattva,* Sacred Books of the East, vol. 19 (Oxford: Clarendon, 1883), p. 55 (emphasis mine).

98. Ibid., p. 55. Beal has "eunuchs" in a parenthetical qualification of "keepers." Fran Bantly was kind enough to look at the Chinese and ascertain that although (*a*) the allusion to "keepers" would seem to be an interpolation with scant textual support and (*b*) there is no textual support for Beal's parenthetical reference to eunuchs, it is clear that pain is being inflicted on the women. I am inclined to think that if anyone were there guarding the harem it would be women rather than eunuchs, given the fact that eunuchs were unknown in India before the introduction of Arab culture in the medieval period and also the fact that other Sanskrit biographies (the *Lalitavistara,* for example) refer to the presence of armed females in the women's apartments. I am indebted to Wendy Doniger for pointing out that Greek and other non-Indian women (called *yavanī*s, following the Sanskrit transcription of "Ionian") traditionally served martial functions in Indian courts.

99. In his *Avadāna Kalpalatā,* a collection of Buddhist hagiographic narratives, Kṣemendra provides a very clever example of this kind of wordplay. Kṣemendra's stanza can be read as an erotic description of a woman embracing her lover: "Swiftly stealing the heart of the still, love-sick man; showing her fondness for passion, she clasped his neck, decorated his face with scratches from her nails, parted his lips and marked them with wounds from her love-bites, and showed her superiority in inciting the pleasures of love." It can also be read as a disgusting scene of necrophagy: "Suddenly grabbing the heart of the fresh corpse which was lying still as if in a stupor, it displayed its fondness for blood; it attached itself to the corpse's throat, tore at its face with its claws, and gnawed at its mouth; showing its teeth, it ripped the corpse open and pulled apart

its limbs." Kṣemendra cites and explains this verse in his discourse on poetic decorum, the *Aucityavicāracarcā,* in *Kṣemendralaghukāvyasaṃgraha: Minor Works of Kṣemendra,* ed. Vidyaratna E. V. V. Raghavacharya and D. G. Pandye (Hyderabad: Osmania University Press, 1961), p. 31.

100. Beal, trans., *Fo-sh-hing-tsan-king,* p. 55.

101. S. Lefmann, ed., *Lalitavistara,* 2 vols. (Halle a. S.: Verlag der Buchhandlung des Waisenhauses, 1902–8), 1:205.

102. Ibid., 1:206.

103. Ibid., 1:206. A *rākṣasī* is a cannibalistic demoness hideous in her natural state but capable, when "man hunting," of taking on the shape of a beautiful young woman.

104. In this poem to a young girl, Hopkins asks: "Márgarét áre you gríeving / Over Goldengrove unleaving?" In the final lines he concludes that whatever the outward object of her pity, it is her own mortality the child is thinking of: "It ís the blight man was born for / It is Margaret you mourn for." See W. H. Gardner, ed., *Poems and Prose of Gerard Manley Hopkins* (London: Penguin, 1985), p. 50.

105. Lefmann, ed., *Lalitavistara,* 1:206.

106. Ibid., 1:207–8.

107. In the *Lalitavistara,* the *bodhisattva*'s mother instructs the women to light the lights, beat the drums, and stay up all night to keep an eye on Gotama. She also arms them with various weapons to ensure that her son does not get away undetected. See Gwendalyn Bays, trans., *The Voice of the Buddha,* pp. 201–2.

108. Lefmann, ed., *Lalitavistara,* 1:207–8.

109. For Western literary examples of the femme fatale theme, see Mario Praz, *The Romantic Agony,* trans. Angus Davidson (New York: Oxford University Press, 1970). For medieval vituperations against women's invincible powers of attraction that lead to the development of the femme fatale theme, see *Women Defamed and Women Defended: An Anthology of Medieval Texts,* ed. A. Blamires, K. Pratt, and W. W. Marx (New York: Oxford University Press, 1992). A thirteenth-century rule for cloistered women, for example, waxes at length on the perils of being seen by men. A woman should keep herself covered, if she must go about in public, because if a man should be smitten by her beauty, she would be guilty of inflaming his lust whether or not she intended to do so (or was even aware of his presence). The rule uses a passage from the Hebrew Bible (here called the "Old Law") to explain that the woman bears responsibility for the man's downfall: "For this reason it was commanded in God's name in the Old Law that a pit should always be covered; an if an animal fell into an uncovered pit, the man who had uncovered the pit had to pay the penalty. These are very terrible words for the woman who shows herself to men's sight. It is she who is represented by the man who uncovers the pit. The pit is her fair face, and her white neck, and her light eye, and her hand if she holds it out before his eyes; and further, her speech is a pit, if it is not controlled, and all other things whatsoever that belong to her, through which sinful love may be aroused. All this our Lord called a pit. . . . You uncover this pit, you who do anything by which a man is bodily tempted by you, even though you may be unaware of it. Have great fear of this judgement; and if the man is tempted in such a way that he commits mortal sin through you in any way, even though it is not with you, but with desire for you, or if he tries to yield with another person to the

temptation awakened in him through your doing, be quite sure of the judgement" (*Women Defamed and Women Defended,* pp. 96–97).

110. C. A. F. Rhys Davids, trans. *Psalms of the Early Buddhists,* vol. 2, *Psalms of the Brethren,* pp. 296–97.

111. E. H. Johnston, ed. and trans., *Saundarananda of Aśvaghoṣa* (Lahore, 1928; reprint, New Delhi: Motilal Banarsidass, 1975), p. 44 (page references are to the 1975 edition).

112. Ibid.

113. Ibid., p. 45.

114. In *Man and Superman,* one of G. B. Shaw's characters suggests an arachnoid image of woman as mantrap: "Why the whole world is strewn with snares, traps, gins, and pitfalls for the capture of men by women. . . . It is often assumed that the woman must wait, motionless, until she is wooed. Nay, she often does wait motionless. That is how the spider waits for the fly. But the spider spins her web. And if the fly . . . shews a strength that promises to extricate him, how swiftly does she abandon her pretence of passiveness, and openly fling coil after coil about him until he is secured for ever." Cited in Wolfgang Lederer, *The Fear of Women* (New York: Harcourt, Brace, and Jovanovich, 1968), p. 56.

115. Morris and Hardy, eds., *Aṅguttara Nikāya,* 3:68–69. See Siegel, *Laughing Matters,* p. 213.

116. In the Pāli *Jātaka,* the *bodhisattva*-horse is Gotama. In the *Siṃhalasārthabāhu Avadāna* and the *Avalokiteśvara Guṇa Karaṇḍavyūha Sūtra* (see notes 122–23 below), it is the *bodhisattva* Avalokiteśvara.

117. Fausboll, ed., *Jātakāṭṭhakathā,* 2:127. The framing of the *Mahāvastu* recension (the *Dharmalabhda Jātaka*) is of particular interest here. This story of a hero who knows in advance that he is going to encounter man-eating ogresses and thus easily outwits them along with his 500 merchants is a past-life tale told by the Buddha about himself when asked to explain why it was so easy for him to rebuff Māra's daughters after his awakening. The trader is identified as the *bodhisattva* and the ogresses are identified as Māra's daughters. See Senart, ed., *Mahāvastu* 3:286–300; Jones, trans., *Mahāvastu,* 3:274–87.

118. On this category of demonic beings, see Gail Hinich Sutherland, *The Disguises of the Demon: The Development of the Yakṣa in Hinduism and Buddhism* (Albany: State University of New York Press, 1991).

119. Fausboll, ed., *Jātakaṭṭhakathā,* p. 128.

120. Ibid.

121. Alan Sponberg argues that most Buddhists were psychologically sophisticated enough to distinguish between the external object of desire and the desirousness that is in the mind of the beholder. He notes a passage in the *Dṛdhādhyāṣayaparipṛccha Sūtra* in which the Buddha ridicules the idea that a man who has seen a beautiful woman must contemplate the foulness of her body in order to eliminate his desire for her. The problem lies in his mind, not her body, and only there will a solution be found. According to the metaphysics of emptiness that informs this text, "male" and "female" are not intrinsically existing entities. The man who is smitten by a woman he sees is thus no different from a man who falls in love with a female phantasm created

by a magician. Since in both cases the object of desire is a construct of the imagination without abiding essence, it makes no sense to meditate on the impurity of the woman as a remedy to lust since one is thereby contemplating the impurity of a nonexistent woman, an entity that has no existence outside the mind of the beholder. See Alan Sponberg, "Attitudes toward Women and the Feminine in Early Buddhism," in *Buddhism, Sexuality, and Gender,* ed. José Ignacio Cabezón (Albany: SUNY Press, 1992), pp. 23–24.

122. Holt is commenting on a version found in the *Avalokiteśvara Guṇa Karaṇḍavyūha Sūtra.* See John Holt, *Buddha in the Crown: Avalokiteśvara in the Buddhist Traditions of Sri Lanka* (New York: Oxford University Press, 1991), p. 51.

123. For a partial translation of this manuscript, see Todd Lewis, "Newar Tibetan Trade and the Domestication of the 'Siṃhalasārthabāhu Avadāna,'" *History of Religions* 33 (1994): 135–160.

124. Ibid., p. 148.

125. Wilson and Makowski, *Wykked Wyves and the Woes of Marriage,* p. 2.

126. Wendy Doniger has noted many levels on which renouncers and courtesans are brought together in Indic mythology. Not only is the seduction of ascetics by courtesans and heavenly dancing girls an ancient theme in Indic literature, but there is evidence of ritualized sex between *brahmacārin*s and courtesans. Commenting on the sociological determinants that would bring such strange bedfellows together, O'Flaherty suggests: "The necessity for a prostitute as the partner of the ascetic is not merely the result of the metaphysics of the conjunction of opposites, but is in part a consequence of the simple logistics of the necessary plot. After his experiences with the woman, the ascetic must be free to return to his yoga, in order to avoid the problems attendant upon the combination of asceticism and marriage. The one woman who can allow him to do this is the prostitute, who is sexually free just as he is, moving below the morals of conventional Hinduism just as he moves above them" O'Flaherty, *Śiva: The Erotic Ascetic,* p. 52.

127. *Chastity* (from the Latin *castus,* "pure") is the cessation of sexual activity, whereas *celibacy* (from the Latin *caelebs,* "single") has the primary meaning of singleness and has not always been understood as a chaste state. See Wilson and Makowski, *Wykked Wyves and the Woes of Marriage,* pp. 3–5.

128. The compound *artha-labdhā* may be a play on *Dharma-labdha* ("he who has achieved the Dharma")—the name of the hero of this tale.

129. Senart, ed., *Mahāvastu,* 3:291–92.

130. *Saundarananda* 18.63; Johnston, ed. and trans., *Saundarananda,* p. 141.

Chapter Three

1. Yasa joined the *sangha* after the five ascetics who had previously been Gotama's companions heard "the Wheel of the Dhamma set in motion" at Deer Park and became his disciples.

2. F. L. Woodward, ed., *Paramattha-Dīpanī-Theragāthā-aṭṭhakathā: The Commentary of Dhammapālācariya,* 3 vols, Pali Text Society Publications, vols. 129, 148, and 150 (London: Oxford University Press, 1940–59), 1:243. Compare the Buddha of the *Mahāvastu*'s statement: "I was delicately, most delicately brought up, monks [*Sukhumāro 'haṃ bhikṣavaḥ paramasukhumāro*]." See Senart, ed., *Mahāvastu,* 2:117.

3. The *Theragāthā* commentary describes Yasa as the son of a wealthy councillor; in the Pāli *Vinaya,* Yasa's father is said to be a wealthy merchant. Both accounts agree that Yasa was brought up in Varanasi (Benares).

4. This information is found in a relatively early account—the *Mahāvagga* or Great Division of the monastic code. See Oldenberg, ed., *Vinaya Piṭaka,* 1:15. Horner, trans., *The Book of Discipline,* 4:22.

5. Woodward, ed., *Paramattha-Dīpanī-Theragāthā-aṭṭhakathā,* 1:243.

6. Oldenberg, ed., *Vinaya Piṭaka,* 1:15.

7. These five men (Añña Koṇḍañña, Bhaddiya, Vappa, Mahānāma, and Assaji) were the *bodhisattva*'s companions when he practiced austerities after the Great Departure. See Horner, trans., *The Book of Discipline,* 1:10–19.

8. See, e.g., the *Dhammapadāṭṭhakathā* on the Arhatship of the laywoman Khemā, wife of Bimbisāra. After Khemā became an Arhat, the Buddha told King Bimbisāra: "Oh great king, Khemā should either go forth [*pabbajitun*] or go out [*parinibbāyitun*]." "By all means, Blessed One," her husband responds, "ordain her [literally, 'cause her to go forth'], but enough of going-out." See Norman, ed., *Dhammapadāṭṭhakathā* (The Commentary to the Dhammapada), 4:57-59. There was considerable controversy in the Indian Buddhist world over whether or not laypeople could become Arhats. André Bareau regards those Hīnayāna schools that accepted the possibility of Arhatship for laypeople as proto-Mahāyānist. See *Les sectes bouddhiques du petit vehicle* (Saigon: École Française d'Extreme Orient, 1955).

9. Yasa's mother Sujatā, it should be noted, is remembered for her very significant gift of food to Gotama: rice cooked in cream that she had churned from the milk of a thousand cows and given to the *bodhisattva* when he broke his fast on the eve of his awakening.

10. F. L. Woodward, ed., *Paramatthadīpanī: Dhammapāla*'s Commentary on the Theragāthā (London: Pali Text Society, 1893), 1:244.

11. Norman, ed., *Dhammapadāṭṭhakathā* (The Commentary on the Dhammapada), 1:99–100.

12. Ibid., 1:306–7.

13. That it was sleep that transformed Cittahatha's wife in this revealing way suggests an analogy between her and demonic shape-shifting women who are said to lose their disguises and assume their true forms when asleep or dead.

14. Norman, ed., *Dhammapadāṭṭhakathā* (The Commentary on the Dhammapada), 1:307.

15. "*Satthakanisādanapāsāṇadisaṃ tava sīsaṃ*" (ibid., 1:308).

16. Ibid. Cittahattha's rapid progression from the status of stream enterer to that of Arhat is significant—especially in light of Peter Masefield's problematic argument that in the Pāli *Nikāya*s this progression does not occur within a single lifetime. In an article entitled "Mind/Cosmos Maps in the Pāli *Nikāya*s," in *Buddhist and Western Psychology,* ed. Nathan Katz (Boulder, CO: Shambhala, 1983), Masefield argues that the Buddhist path as articulated in the Pāli *Nikāya*s does not consist of progressive stages within a single path culminating in Arhatship but, rather, consists of four separate attainments or realizations. Although the developed Theravāda tradition has generally regarded the four divisions of the path (the first three generally rendered in English as "stream winner," "once-returner," and "nonreturner,") as progressive stages,

Masefield questions the accuracy of this progressivist view of the path. He suggests that these divisions of the path refer to four specific attainments characterized by different durations of time. It takes the stream winner seven lifetimes (not counting the present) to work out his or her past karma. For the once-returner, the exhaustion of past karma will be accomplished in one more lifetime. The karmic residue of the nonreturner will cease after his or her death, while that of an Arhat expires while he or she is still alive. In *The Legend and Cult of Upagupta: Sanskrit Buddhism in North India and Southeast Asia* (Princeton, NJ: Princeton University Press, 1992), John Strong suggests that we speak of different soteriological "tracks" rather than soteriological "stages" (pp. 80 ff.). But he notes that characters in Sanskrit Buddhist literature often switch from a slower to a faster track, thus deviating from Masefield's schematization of the *Nikāy*ic path. In the Sanskrit *Avadāna*s, stream enterers often do go on to become Arhats within a single lifetime; they do not wait seven lifetimes for the cessation of their karma. As the example of Cittahattha suggests, post-Aśokan Pāli literature resembles Sanskrit Buddhist literature with respect to the switching of soteriological tracks.

17. Norman, ed., *Dhammapadāṭṭhakathā* (The Commentary to the Dhammapada), 1:308.

18. Ibid. Just after this incident, the Buddha overhears the monks commenting on how remarkable it was that someone destined to become an Arhat like Cittahattha would have been so agitated by afflictions (Pāli, *kilesā*; Sanskrit, *kleṣā*) as to return to the life of a householder seven times. The Buddha explains that in a past life he himself was an indecisive renouncer. He returned to the social world six times on account of the fact that each rainy season when the ground was wet he would remember that he had a small amount of seeds and a blunt spade at home and felt compelled to plant those seeds rather than let them go to waste. See E. W. Burlingame, trans., *Buddhist Legends,* 3 vols. (Cambridge, MA: Harvard University Press, 1921; reprint, London: Pali Text Society, 1990), 2:15–17 (page references are to the 1921 edition). Clearly, the *bodhisattva*'s indecision in this story parallels that of Cittahatha. Neither man delights in renunciation because both men are too engrossed in domestic affairs. But since Indic discourse constitutes wives as fields to be plowed by their husbands, the *bodhisattva*'s story resonates with that of Cittahattha in another respect: both men return home repeatedly to plant more seeds in their respective fields. On the concept of wife as field and husband as landlord in Indic juridical and ritual contexts, see *Manusmṛti* 3.175; 9.32–56, 145, 164, 180–81, 220; 10.269–72. On the classical Greek equation of women and fields, see Page duBois, *Sowing the Body: Psychoanalysis and Ancient Representations of Women* (Chicago: University of Chicago Press, 1988).

19. Norman, ed., *Dhammapadōṭṭhakathā* (The Commentary to the Dhammapada), 3:104–9. Except for the ending, the version found in the commentary to the *Vimānavatthu* is virtually identical to that of the *Dhammapada* commentary. See *Elucidation of the Intrinsic Meaning: The Commentary on the Vimāna Stories,* trans. Peter Masefield, assisted by N. A. Jayawickrama (Oxford: Pali Text Society, 1989), pp. 110–127.

20. Hired as a courtesan to entertain the husband of Uttarā, Sirimā becomes jealous of Uttarā and pours boiling hot oil on her. But Uttarā, a devoted lay follower of the Buddha, responds with kindness. Rather than defending herself physically, Uttarā suffuses herself with loving kindness and is therefore unaffected by the oil. Sirimā is so impressed by Uttarā's compassion and serenity that she begs to be forgiven. Uttarā

directs Sirimā to ask the Buddha, as her spiritual father, for forgiveness. This encounter leads to Sirimā's adoption of a new life of service to the *sangha.* See Uttarā's *Vimāna,* in Masefield and Jayawickrama, trans., *Elucidation of the Intrinsic Meaning,* pp. 90–109.

21. The text is specific in its reference to the gender of those who enjoy Sirimā's generosity, specifying that Sirimā feeds eight monks (*aṭṭha bhikkhū*) per day. This textual indication that the order of nuns may not have been as well supported as the male monastic order is echoed by texts that praise those who give donations to monks more than those who give donations to nuns. For example, a hierarchy of possible donations to the *sangha* is specified in *Majjhima Nikāya* 3.255–56. The best donation is one given to the entire *sangha* with the Buddha as its head; next comes a gift to the entire *sangha* after the Buddha has passed away. If one cannot afford to give gifts to the entire *sangha,* a donation to the *bhikkhu sangha* would be the next best option. Gifts to the *bhikkhunī sangha* come in fourth in this ranking of donations. The subordination of nuns to monks is reduplicated in the lowest tier of donations—gifts to selected individuals. Here again, giving to selected monks is better than giving to selected nuns. See Horner, trans., *Middle Length Sayings,* 3:303.

22. The relations between monks and laywomen (many of whom were widely acclaimed as generous supporters of the *sangha*) were of great interest to Sanskrit satirists. In *Laughing Matters,* pp. 212–13, Lee Siegel shows that Sanskrit satirists viewed women's service to the Buddhist *sangha* as an often-exploited opportunity for sexual gratification on the part of ostensibly chaste monks. In one satire, a monk visits a brothel in order to "comfort Miss Server-of-Monks (*Sangha-dāsā*) with the words of the Buddha—she is suffering from the death of her mother. It is insinuatingly ambiguous as to just what 'to comfort' means, just as it is ambiguous as to just how the girl 'serves' the brotherhood." Ironically, anti-Buddhist satirists may have gotten their inspiration from Buddhist texts, which are often quite frank about the abuses perpetrated by charlatans in monk's clothing. See, for example, the *Vinaya*'s extensive account of the exploits of Udāyin, the archetypal licentious monk. Udāyin is reported to have solicited sex from a widow as a form of alms; see Horner, trans., *The Book of Discipline,* 1:222 ff. On another occasion (1:234–36), Udāyin served as a pimp. The fact that Udāyin is always handy with a lewd double entendre as he carries out his exploits suggests that those Buddhists who composed the Pāli *Vinaya* texts had a well-developed sense of humor. On humor in Pāli literature generally, see Walpola Rahula, "Humour in Pāli Literature," *Journal of the Pali Text Society* 9 (1981): 156–73.

23. The English word "charm," derived from the Latin *carm(en)* ("song, magical formula"), suggests the quasi-magical power to enchant the spectator that is often (if erroneously, given the Buddhist understanding of causality) attributed to beautiful women. The word "glamour," like "charm," once had magical connotations. Derived from the word "grammar" in its archaic sense of occult learning, the term "glamour" occurs in the seventeenth-century *Malleus Malificarum* (a tract on witchcraft by the ever-vigilant Dominican Inquisitors Heinrich Kramer and Johann Sprenger) in the following passage: "Here is declared the truth about the diabolical operations with regard to the male organ. And to make plain the facts in this matter, it is asked whether witches can with the help of devils really and actually remove the member, or whether they only do so apparently by some glamour or illusion." See M. Summers, trans., *The*

Malleus Malificarum of Heinrich Kramer and Johann Sprenger (London: John Rodker, 1948; reprint, New York: Dover, 1971), p. 58 (page reference is to the 1971 edition).

24. Norman, ed., *Dhammapadāṭṭhakathā* (The Commentary to the Dhammapada), 3:106.

25. Here, Sirimā the food provider has herself come to resemble food.

26. Peter Masefield takes a variant reading of *geharakkhake dārake* to refer to young children who should be looked after at home. See Masefield and Jayawickrama, trans., *The Elucidation of Intrinsic Meaning,* p. 111.

27. Norman, ed., *Dhammapadāṭṭhakathā* (The Commentary to the Dhammapada), 3:106–7.

28. That the nuns are relegated to standing with the laypeople while the monks stand on the other side with the Buddha suggests the subordinate status of the *bhikkhunī sangha.*

29. Norman, ed., *Dhammapadāṭṭhakathā* (The Commentary to the Dhammapada), 3:108.

30. Ibid., 3:108–9.

31. Some of the physical symptoms of lovesickness most frequently mentioned in post-Aśokan literature are depression, sluggishness, sallow skin, haggard features, and prominent veins.

32. The importance of swift therapeutic action is illustrated in a parable discussed below (see chap. 4) — the parable of the poisoned arrow (*Cūlamāluṅkya Sutta*); Horner, trans., *Middle Length Sayings,* 2:97–101.

33. In one case, a monk saw a dead body that had a genital sore (*aṅgajātasāmantā vaṇo hoti*). "Thinking 'this is not a breach of the discipline,' he put his member in the genitals (*aṅgajāte aṅgajātaṃ pavesetvā*) and ejaculated by means of the sore [*vaṇena nīhari*]." See Horner, trans., *The Book of Discipline,* 1:49, 349.

34. Members of the *sangha* practicing *asubhabhāvanā* were encouraged to notify the authorities of their presence in a particular cremation ground so that they would not be taken for criminals hiding out there.

35. Woodward, ed., *Paramatthadīpanī: Dhammapāla's Commentary on the Theragāthā,* 2:167. The entire narrative is found on pages 167–69.

36. Ibid., 2:167.

37. Ibid. The term translated here as "body" (*samussayaṃ, from* $\sqrt{si}$, "to raise up") might also be translated as "construct" or "compound." Compare C. A. F. Rhys Davids's translation of this stanza: "Behold the foul compound, Kulla, diseased, / Impure, dripping, exuding, pride of fools." See C. A. F. Rhys Davids, trans., *Psalms of the Early Buddhists,* vol. 2; *Psalms of the Brethren,* p. 212.

38. Woodward, ed., *Paramatthadīpanī: Dhammapāla's Commentary on the Theragāthā,* 2:167. C. A. F. Rhys Davids (*Psalms of the Brethren,* p. 211) condenses the entire episode of magical transformation into this bromidic statement: "And when even this [*asubhabhāvanā*] sufficed not, he himself went with him and bade him to mark the process of putrefaction and dissolution. The Exalted One then sent out a glory, producing in him such mindfulness that he discerned the lesson, attained the first *jhāna,* and on that basis developed insight, won Arahantship."

39. Woodward, ed., *Paramatthadīpanī: Dhammapāla's Commentary on the Theragāthā,* 2:133–36.

40. Ibid., 2:134.
41. Ibid.
42. Ibid.
43. Ibid.
44. On the courtesan as gold digger, see Siegel, *Laughing Matters,* pp. 121–26. Drawing on interviews with retired courtesans in Lucknow, Veena Talwar Oldenburg provides some useful information on the lifestyles of various types of courtesans in colonial Lucknow. Oldenburg focuses on the waning prestige of courtesans in the middle of the nineteenth century and the colonial tendency to lump all the members of what was formerly a fairly stratified profession (from the elite *gaṇikā* to the least prestigious *raṇḍī*) together under the catch-all category of "prostitute." See *The Making of Colonial Lucknow, 1856–1877* (Princeton, NJ: Princeton University Press, 1984), pp. 132–44.
45. It is not clear, however, whether the irony of this situation was apparent to Rājadatta himself. Although the commentary to the *Theragāthā* clearly indicates that the dead body Rājadatta encountered was that of the courtesan who had fleeced him, it does not state whether or not Rājadatta *recognized* the dead woman as his former lover. There is, however, another story involving a venal courtesan brought to justice and left in the cremation ground, and in this case the element of recognition is very much to the fore. After being punished for her misdeeds, the courtesan Vāsavadattā is actively sought out as an object of meditation by Upagupta, a man she had repeatedly tried to seduce. Because it develops a number of interesting themes, I have chosen to devote a separate section (see below, this chapter) to the analysis of Upagupta's encounter with Vāsavadattā rather than tell it here, although it could very appropriately be compared to Rājadatta's story.
46. Norman, ed., *Dhammapadāṭṭhakathā* (The Commentary on the Dhammapada), 3:111–13.
47. Peter Brown, *The Body and Society: Men, Women, and Sexual Renunciation in Early Christianity* (New York: Columbia University Press, 1988).
48. Norman, ed., *Dhammapadāṭṭhakathā* (The Commentary to the Dhammapada), 1:66–77.
49. Mahākāla's name seems significant on a number of levels. It is an epithet of the Hindu god of death as well as of horrific forms of the Hindu god Śiva and his Buddhist equivalents. That the cremation-ground keeper's name (Kālī) is a feminine version of the name that Mahākāla shares with his brother (*kāla,* meaning "dark one") suggests an affinity between Mahākāla and the cremation-ground keeper Kālī. Her name may also be significant in that the earliest references to Kālī, the fearsome goddess so popular in Bengal, appear within a century of the *Dhammapadāṭṭhakathā*'s redaction.
50. This bloodthirsty threat strikes me as another clue to the latent divinity of the cremation-ground keeper (see n. 49 above), since Kālī is often asked to trample, dismember, and mutilate the bodies of the enemy.
51. Norman, ed., *Dhammapadāṭṭhakathā* (The Commentary to the Dhammapada), 1:70.
52. Ibid.
53. Ibid., pp. 70–71.
54. Ibid., p. 71.

55. Ibid.

56. Ibid., p. 72.

57. It is interesting to compare Hindu and Buddhist treatments of the theme of the renounced wife, the woman whose husband has broken the bonds of marriage in renouncing the world. Both Hindu and Buddhist treatments of this theme tend to celebrate the renounced wife's ability to stay connected to her husband by taking up his ascetic vocation, much as a "football widow" will make it her business to familiarize herself with the finer points of football trivia so as to enter into her husband's world. In Buddhist accounts of the life of the Buddha's renounced wife Yaśodharā, she is often said to practice meditation in the palace after the departure of her husband. Likewise Śiva's wife Parvatī is said to practice austerities in order to be a good wife to her ascetically inclined husband. Judging from their literary traditions, I would surmise that South Asian Hindus and Buddhists are less likely to honor the renounced wife who actively opposes her husband's renunciant lifestyle and attempts to persuade him to rejoin her. In the *Yogavāsiṣṭha,* however, the sage Vāsiṣṭha tells a tale that exalts a queen named Cūḍālā who opposes her husband's renunciation and wins him back using magical powers. Although the shape-shifting powers Cūḍālā employs to win her husband back are reminiscent of the magical ploys used by Māra's daughters to attack the sons of the Buddha and by the celestial nymphs that are the downfall of Hindu sages, Queen Cūḍālā is in no way demonized in this tale. Indeed, this is a tale of a king whose enlightenment comes at the hands of his queen. Informed by traditions of nondualistic thought with roots in both Hindu monism and the Buddhist philosophy of emptiness, the tale that the sage Vāsiṣṭha tells can be read as a sustained critique of sexism. Queen Cūḍālā achieves spiritual awakening before her husband and tries to lead him to awakening too. But he resists her teaching, dismissing his wife's statements as the prattle of a young, uneducated woman dabbling in philosophy. So Queen Cūḍālā uses her yogically enhanced powers of perception and determines that her husband will listen to what she has to say if she assumes the forms of young male fellow travelers on the celibate path her husband has chosen for himself. By assuming male forms that metamorphose at night into desirable female forms, Queen Cūḍālā teaches her husband that all forms are illusory and that austerities are meaningless without the ultimate renunciation: the renouncing of one's own deluded constructions of reality. See Swami Venkatesananda, *The Concise Yogavāsiṣṭha* (Albany: SUNY Press, 1984), pp. 333–83.

58. Karen C. Lang, "Lord Death's Snare: Gender-Related Imagery in the 'Theragāthā' and 'Therīgāthā,' " pp. 63–79.

59. Woodward, ed., *Paramatthadīpanī: Dhammapāla's Commentary on the Theragāthā,* 2:110.

60. Ibid., 2:111.

61. Ibid., 2:110.

62. Ibid., 3:36. The narrative is found on pages 33–41.

63. Ibid., pp. 34–35. In his commentary, Dhammapāla explains the shift from the singular to the plural in this verse by suggesting that once one clever deer has managed to eat the bait without springing the trap, others follow. Dhammapāla also takes pains to point out that the deer eating the bait in the middle of the trap set for it is a metaphor for Raṭṭhapāla's eating the alms given to him by his family with the intention of trapping him and returning him to the lay life. "The precious things and the harem of

women" offered to Raṭṭhapāla are like the deer hunter's baited snare, Raṭṭhapāla's family are like the deer hunters, and Raṭṭhapāla, of course, is the clever deer who escapes the trap. See Woodward, ed., *Paramatthadīpanī: Dhammapāla's Commentary on the Theragāthā,* 3:36.

64. It is ironic that this and other caustic fulminations against women in the *Brahmavaivarta Purāṇa* are placed in the mouth of the supreme Goddess; see Cheever Mackenzie Brown, *God as Mother: A Feminine Theology in India; An Historical and Theological Study of the Brahmavaivarta Purāṇa* (Hartford, VT: Claude Stark and Co., 1974), pp. 181 ff.

65. I have relied on two primary and two secondary sources in my exposition here. The fullest account is found in the *Divyāvadāna,* ed. E. B. Cowell and R. A. Neil (Cambridge: Cambridge University Press, 1886), pp. 353–56, and a more abbreviated version is given in Kṣemendra's *Avadānakalpalatā,* ed. Vaidya, 2:449–51. John Strong's *The Legend of King Aśoka* (Princeton, NJ: Princeton University Press, 1983) includes a complete translation of the *Divyāvadāna* account on pp. 179–84; Strong's *The Legend and Cult of Upagupta,* pp. 76–79, includes translated portions of both the *Divyāvadāna* and the *Avadānakalpalatā* versions.

66. The expression *alakṣaṇako buddho* first occurs in the context of a prediction by the Buddha. See Cowell and Neil, eds., *Divyāvadāna,* pp. 348–49. It is certainly significant that Upagupta's name ("hidden") implies concealment. Developing Strong's comments on the mythic models for one who is an *alakṣaṇaka buddha* (*The Legend and Cult of Upagupta,* p. 91), I would suggest that Upagupta's marks are like those of Maitreya and the saving *Bodhisattva*s of the Mahāyāna *Sūtra*s in being hidden by the ornaments that laypeople wear. In "Le Buddha paré: son origine indienne: Sakyamuni dans le Mahayanisme moyen," *Bulletin de l'École Française d'Extreme Orient* 28 (1928): 153–278, Paul Mus reflects on the dynamics of concealment and exposure entailed by the various traditions of representing the Buddha's body in sculpted images.

67. Cowell and Neil, eds., *Divyāvadāna,* p. 353.

68. Ibid.

69. *Upagupta uvāca, akālas te bhagini maddarśanāyeti* (ibid). On the liturgical meanings of the term *darśana* (Hindi, *darśan*), see Diana L. Eck, *Darśan: Seeing the Divine Image in India* (Chambersburg, PA: Anima Books, 1981).

70. According to the *Avadānakalpalatā* (Vaidya, ed., pp. 449–50), Vāsavadattā poisons the man herself. The *Divyāvadāna* (Cowell and Neil, eds., p. 353) uses causative verbs suggesting that she hired assassins to kill him.

71. Cowell and Neil, eds., *Divyāvadāna,* p. 353. A grammatically preferable alternate reading for *hastapādau karṇanāsaṃ* is *hastapādakarṇanāsāñ ca.*

72. Ibid., pp. 353–54. I read *gatamānarāgaharṣāyāḥ* and *niśitāsivikṣatāyāḥ* as ablatives.

73. Ibid., p. 354.

74. Strong, *The Legend and Cult of Upagupta,* p. 77.

75. Vaidya, ed., *Avadānakalpalatā,* 2:450. To restate Kṣemendra's aside in less metaphorical terms, one could say that if penetration is Upagupta's goal, he would not be all that particular as to Vāsavadattā's outer appearance.

76. Ibid.

77. Although I am setting up something of a contrast between the modest Vāsava-

dattā who does not want to be the sexualized object of Upagupta's gaze and the vain Vāsavadattā who does not want Upagupta's gaze to fall on those parts of her that are not fit to be seen, Anne Hollander's argument in *Seeing through Clothes* (New York: Viking, 1978) would suggest that the dichotomy should not be drawn too rigidly. Hollander concludes from her wide-ranging study of the role of clothing in portrayals of the human body that the truly erotic body is clothed, not nude. Sartorial fashions dictate what is seen as erotic in any given historical era. It is the suggestion of fashionably erotic bodies—bodies with the impossibly high, rounded breasts favored in the Renaissance, for example—produced by foundation garments and clothing that appeals to the eye. The anatomically correct female, endowed with what by Renaissance standards would be unfashionably large, pendulous breasts, is at a distinct disadvantage without her clothes on, since it is foundation garments that create the impression of fashionably high, spherical breasts. The female nudes that are most highly valued by art lovers are rarely anatomically correct. Thus Victorian nudes often display the ample derriere that bustles imparted to the profile of fashionable Victorian ladies.

78. Cowell and Neil, eds., *Divyāvadāna,* p. 354.

79. Ibid.

80. C. A. F. Rhys Davids, ed., *Visuddhimagga,* 1:190.

81. Compare Śāntideva's image of the living body as a corpse animated by a ghost (*vetāla*) or a *revenant,* a vampire in the early folkloric sense of a reanimated corpse. The word *revenant* bears an appropriate double meaning in the French, connoting a pleasant appearance that revives the spirits of the viewer—a "sight for sore eyes"—and also a dead person who has been revived. See Paul Barber, *How Shall the Dead Arise? The Folklore of Vampires, Burial, and Death* (New Haven, CT: Yale University Press, 1988).

82. Cowell and Neil, eds., *Divyāvadāna,* pp. 354–55.

83. In Rabindranath Tagore's retelling of this story, Upagupta goes out of compassion to comfort Vāsavadattā when she, abandoned by her friends and family, is dying of the plague. Instead of using her ulcerated body as an object lesson on impermanence, he bathes her sores with cool water while she dies in his arms. Rabindranath Tagore, *The Collected Poems and Plays of Rabindranath Tagore* (New York: Macmillan, 1937), pp. 154–55. Piyadassi Thera summarizes Tagore's version of the story in *The Virgin's Eye: Women in Buddhist Literature* (Colombo: Buddhist Publication Society, 1980), pp. 31–33.

84. Cowell and Neil, eds., *Divyāvadāna,* p. 354.

85. Woodcut illustrations from the Kashmir valley show Vāsavadattā's arms cut off above the elbow. She is depicted sitting upright listening to Upagupta's sermon. See *Buddhist Tales of Kashmir in Tibetan Woodcuts (Narthang series of the woodcuts of Kṣemendra's Avadana-kalpalata*), ed. Sharada Rani (New Delhi: Sharada Rani, 1977), *Avadāna* 72, plate 22.

86. Perhaps a better metaphor for Vāsavadattā's condition would be that she is laid out on a dissection table undergoing an autopsy. The original sense of the term "autopsy" can be discerned in its etymology: it is from the Greek *auto-opsis,* "a seeing with one's own eyes." In "The Pathology Lesson," *Granta* 39 (Spring 1992):96, Michael Dibdin notes that ancient Roman officials displayed the bodies of murder victims "so that the public could personally satisfy themselves of the fact and manner of the crime."

Likewise, early English law "required coroners and juries to view the bodies of those who had died in suspicious circumstances."

87. Take, for example, the ancient Roman culture whose linguistic practices were responsible for transmuting the Greek term *kosmos* (the primary meaning of which is "order") into the Latin term from which the English word "cosmetic" is derived. Like several other Indo-European peoples (such as those who, calling themselves Aryans, migrated into the Indian subcontinent), the Romans legislated what decorations and decorum were appropriate for the different orders or estates of society. Since the structure of society was thought to be grounded in a cosmic order, the practice of decoratively outfitting oneself in a manner suitable to one's social station was truly a cosmic as well as a cosmetic act. Within and without the Indo-European world (e.g., in many European countries during the Renaissance and in early modern Japan), sumptuary laws prohibited persons of one social class from wearing the distinctive insignia and imitating the personal adornment typical of other social classes. But the codes that indicate a person's social location and social status are not always codified in a juridical sense. Within subcultures, especially, such codifications of style generally fall outside the purview of dominant cultural groups and thus escape detection and juridical prohibition. In the American gay subculture of the 1960s and 1970s, for example, sexual preferences were often signaled by the placement of scarves and keys in pants pockets. Contemporary American inner-city gang subculture outpaces Madison Avenue in promoting status competitions characterized by the reverential imitation of the fashions of the powerful by the powerless and the continual redefining of what is fashionable so as to prevent imitation and enforce status differentiation. Especially noteworthy in this regard is the tradition of competitive sartorial displays in New Orleans in which African American youth styling themselves "Indians" show off elaborate and laboriously produced outfits. These competitions seem to enact through masquerade the status differentiation battles that youth gangs in other cities tend to act out more violently.

88. See Thorsten Veblen, *The Theory of the Leisure Class: The Economic Study of Institutions* (New York: Macmillan, 1899; reprint, New York: Modern Library, 1934), on the role of personal adornment in signaling wealth and freedom from the necessity for productive labor. The long fingernails of ancient Chinese aristocrats and modern Western women are conspicuous signs of leisure, as are the fringed shawls of the priest or hierophant.

89. "The penal ceremony had the effectiveness of a long public confession. . . . There was the use of 'symbolic' torture in which the forms of execution referred to the nature of the crime: the tongues of blasphemers were pierced, the impure were burnt, the right hand of murderers was cut off; sometimes the condemned man was made to carry the instrument of his crime—thus Damiens was made to hold in his guilty right hand the famous dagger with which he had committed the crime, hand and dagger being smeared with sulphur and burnt together. As Vico remarked, this old jurisprudence was 'an entire poetics'. . . . We have come full circle: from the judicial torture to the execution, the body has produced and reproduced the truth of the crime—or rather constitutes the element which, through a whole set of rituals and trials, confesses that the crime took place, admits that the accused did indeed commit it, shows that he bore it inscribed in himself and on himself, supports the operation of punishment and manifests its effects in a most striking way. The body, several times tortured, provides

the synthesis of the reality of the deeds and the truth of the investigation, of the documents of the case and the statements of the criminal, of the crime and the punishment. It is an essential element, therefore, in a penal liturgy." See Michel Foucault, *Discipline and Punish: The Birth of the Prison,* trans. Alan Sheridan (New York: Vintage, 1979), pp. 44–45, 47.

90. This example, taken from George Ryley Scott's *The History of Corporal Punishment: A Survey of Flagellation in Its Historical, Anthropological, and Sociological Aspects* (London: Luxor, 1959), p. 42, dates to a transitional period in which the spectacle of the scaffold became a survivable ordeal that precedes imprisonment. The example is from England, where the new and old regimes of punishment coexisted in interesting ways. Foucault comments (*Discipline and Punish,* pp. 14–15) on the tenacity of the logic of corporal punishment in early nineteenth-century Britain even as a new era with its own logic was being ushered in with the birth of the prison. By depriving people of their liberty and disciplining their bodies in prisons that were (along with schools, asylums, and factories) patterned after the monastery, the architects of the new system of humane punishment were no longer interested in inscribing the criminal's body for the edification of the populace. They had, Foucault argues, discovered that it is more effective to use the body as a window onto, and means of transforming, the soul.

91. *Mānavadharmaśāstra* 8.281–3; Jolly, ed., *Mānavadharmaśāstra,* p. 178. In Hindu and Buddhist hells (as in the nightmarish portion of Hieronymus Bosch's *The Garden of Earthly Delights,* where musicians are being beaten inside drums, crucified on harps, and sodomized by flutes), the punishment represents the nature of the crime in ingeniously specific ways.

92. Foucault, *Discipline and Punish,* pp. 108, 58.

93. Given the importance of punitive display in Upagupta's life, it may be significant that the young merchant goes on to become the spiritual adviser to King Aśoka, a man whose religious conversion occurred while he was engaged in torturing a monk.

94. In listening to Upagupta's anatomy lesson, Vāsavadattā becomes a stream winner. Thus she also achieves a level of understanding that puts her on the path, but her attainment puts her on a different level or slower track than Upagupta.

95. Strong, *The Legend and Cult of Upagupta,* pp. 126–27.

96. See Édouard Huber, trans., *Sūtrālaṃkāra* (Paris: Ernest Leroux, 1908), pp. 330–41.

97. "The Struggle for Liberation in the 'Therīgāthā,'" (master's thesis, McMaster University, Department of Religious Studies, 1990), pp. 72–77.

98. Norman, ed., *Dhammapadāṭṭhakathā* (The Commentary to the Dhammapada); on the date of the text and the identity of the commentator, see Burlingame's introduction to his translation of this commentary, *Buddhist Legends,* 1:57–60.

99. Norman, ed., *Dhammapadāṭṭhakathā* (The Commentary to the Dhammapada), 3:100–33. For the most comprehensive edition of the *Dhammapada,* see John Ross Carter and Mahinda Palihawadane, trans. and ed., the *Dhammapada* (New York: Oxford University Press, 1987); for the chapter on decay, see pp. 214–22.

100. Piyadassi (Thera), *The Virgin's Eye,* pp. 33–49.

101. The incident is recounted in the *Shardūlakarṇa* [Tiger's Ear] *Avadāna* of Cowell and Neil, eds., *Divyāvadāna,* pp. 611–55. The *Shardūlakarṇa Avadāna* was partly

translated by Eugene Burnouf in his *Introduction a l'histoire du buddhisme indien,* 3 vols. (Paris: Imprimerie Royale, 1844), 1:205–210. Prakṛti's name is significant due to the fact that in the ancient philosophical system called Sāṃkhya (which undergirds the practice of Yoga) *prakṛti* is one of two primordial principles, one male and one female. The practitioner identifies with *puruṣa,* the male spiritual principle inherent in all beings but held in bondage by *prakṛti,* the feminine psychomaterial principle whose many manifestations constitute the world. *Puruṣa* is compared to a mesmerized spectator watching *prakṛti* dance the world into existence. *Puruṣa* is so transcendent as to be without qualities, so he is unable to move or shut his eyes to the spellbinding spectacle of *prakṛti*'s dance. Only when *prakṛti* has completed her dance and left the stage can *puruṣa* realize his inherent spiritual perfection. See G. J. Larson, *Classical Samkhya: An Interpretation of Its Meaning* (New Delhi: Motilal Banarsidass, 1979).

102. Cowell and Neil, eds., *Divyāvadāna,* pp. 613. Where the *mantra*s of Prakṛti's mother have the semantic vagueness and incantatory quality of repeated sounds common to many *mantra*s (e.g., she begins "*amale vimale kuṇkume sumane*"), what the Buddha utters to break her spell is more readily translatable and may be rendered into English as: "There is a lake [i.e., nirvana] that is pure, beautiful, calm, and completely secure where all dangers, fears, and instabilities are stilled; by the power of this declaration of truth may Ānanda the monk be well." This "Buddha *mantra*" follows the classic formula of a speech act common in South Asian literature whereby a declaration of truth has efficacious consequences for the person who makes the claim. See W. Norman Brown, "The Metaphysics of the Act of Truth (Satyakriyā)," in *Mélanges d'indianisme à la mémoire de Louis Renou* (Paris: E. de Boccard, 1968), pp. 171–77.

103. Piyadassi Thera, *The Virgin's Eye,* p. 45.

104. T. W. Rhys Davids and Carpenter, eds., *Dīgha Nikāya,* 2:141.

105. Piyadassi Thera, *The Virgin's Eye,* p. 51.

106. See Thomas Watters, *On Young Chwang's Travels to India,* 2 vols. (New York: AMS, 1971), 1:302.

107. According to the *Saṃyutta Nikāya,* the stout (*thulla*) nun Thullatissā came to Ānanda's defense when he was thoroughly dressed down and addressed as "boy" (*kumāra*) by Mahākassapa for associating with a large band of ill-behaved monks. Out of fidelity to her friend, Stout Tissā attacked Mahākassapa's credentials, reminding him that he was once the leader of a rival sect. See Feer, ed., *Saṃyutta Nikāya,* 2:219; trans. C. A. F. Rhys Davids and Woodward, trans., *Kindred Sayings,* 2:148.

108. The *Mahāvastu* reports that the nun who defended Ānanda was named Sthūlanandā (Stout Nandā). According to this account, Sthūlanandā exposes herself to Mahākāśyapa, dies, and is reborn in one of the lowest hells. See Jones, trans., *Mahāvastu,* 3:46–56.

109. "Three things, O monks, have power when they are concealed. What three are these? Concealed, O monks, women have power, but not when they are exposed. The *mantra*s of Brahmins, O monks, have power when they are concealed [kept secret], but not when they are exposed. False views have power when they are concealed, but not when they are exposed. Three things, O monks, shine when exposed but not when they are concealed. What three are these? The moon shines when it is exposed, not when it is concealed. The sun shines when it is exposed, not when it is concealed. And the Dharma and monastic discipline of the Buddhas, O monks, shines when it is ex-

posed, not when it is concealed." See Morris and Hardy, eds., *Aṅguttara Nikāya,* 1: 282–83.

Chapter Four

1. A number of essays and monographs have been written about Māra. Among the most important are: B. M. Barua, "Māra," *Buddhist Review* 7 (1915): 194–211; James W. Boyd, *Satan and Māra: Christian and Buddhist Symbols of Evil* (Leiden: E. J. Brill, 1975); B. C. Law, "The Buddhist Conception of Māra," in *Buddhistic Studies,* ed. B. C. Law (Calcutta: Thacker, Spink, and Co., 1931), pp. 259–83; T. O. Ling, *Buddhism and the Mythology of Evil* (London: George Allen and Unwin, 1962); L. de La Vallée Poussin, "Māra," *Encyclopedia of Religion and Ethics* 8 (1955): 406–7; Alex Wayman, "Studies in Yama and Māra," *Indo-Iranian Journal* 3 (1959): 4–73, 112–31. Unlike many of those who have analyzed Māra's legends, John Strong has shown great sensitivity to the affinities between Māra and the Buddha. See *The Legend and Cult of Upagupta,* pp. 93–117.

2. The most developed version of Nanda's story is found in the commentary to the *Dhammapada* (*Dhammapadāṭṭhakathā* 1.9.b); Norman, ed., *Dhammapadāṭṭhakathā* (The Commentary to the Dhammapada), 1:115–25. A more abbreviated version is found in the Pāli *Jātakas*; see the *Saṅgāmāvacara Jātaka,* in Fausboll, ed., *Jatakāṭṭhakathā* (The Jātaka Together with Its Commentary), 2:92. A poetic version of Nanda's tale is attributed to Aśvaghoṣa; see Johnston, ed. and trans., *Saundarananda.*

3. Nanda's betrothed is named Janapāda Kalyāṇī in the *Dhammapada* commentary but is called Sundarī elsewhere.

4. The verb form that the Buddha uses to instruct the monks to ordain Nanda, once he has obtained Nanda's nominal consent, is a causative imperative form of *pabbajjituṃ,* "to go forth," which literally translates as "you [plural] make him go forth." When banishing subjects from the realm, kings use the same verb form to instruct their men. I am grateful to my Pāli teacher, Jonathan Walters, for pointing out to me this and other rich nuances of post-Aśokan Pāli literature.

5. Norman, ed., *Dhammapadāṭṭhakathā* (The Commentary to the Dhammapada), 1:116.

6. Ibid., 1:116.

7. Fausboll, ed., *Jātakāṭṭhakathā* (The Jātaka Together with Its Commentary), 2:92.

8. Norman, ed., *Dhammapadāṭṭhakathā* (The Commentary to the Dhammapada), 1:119.

9. "*Samaṇadhammaṃ katvā bhante imā accharā labhantīti*"; Fausboll, ed., *Jatakāṭṭhakathā* (The Jātaka Together with Its Commentary), 2:93.

10. Ibid.

11. Norman, ed., *Dhammapadāṭṭhakathā* (The Commentary to the Dhammapada), 1:118. Reading *paluddhamakkatiṃ* with the Burmese manuscript for *paluṭṭhamakkatiṃ.* The same variant reading is found in Burmese manuscripts of the *Saṅgāmāvacara Jātaka.*

12. Ibid., 1:119.

13. Ibid.

14. "*Yadā tvaṃ arahattaṃ patto, tadā yevāhaṃ paṭissavā mutto,*"; Fausboll, ed., *Jatakāṭṭhakathā* (The Jātaka Together with Its Commentary), 2:94.

15. Shundo Tachibana, *The Ethics of Buddhism* (London: Oxford University Press, 1926; reprint, New York: Barnes and Noble, 1975).

16. In *Skilful Means* (London: Duckworth, 1978), Michael Pye draws on a wide range of Buddhist texts illustrating what he regards as a pragmatic soteriological orientation that is common to all schools of Buddhism. Drawing on early passages in the Pāli *Nikāya*s, he demonstrates that the idea that the Buddha's teachings are only provisionally true (i.e., provided for the solution of a particular problem) is not unique to Mahāyāna or proto-Mahāyāna texts.

17. Trenckner and Chalmers, eds., *Majjhima Nikāya,* 2:426–32.

18. Ibid., p. 431.

19. Compare Zimmermann, *The Jungle and the Aroma of Meats,* on the salutary duplicity of Brahminical physicians who must disguise the meat and meat broth they feed their patients for their patients' own good.

20. U. Wogihara and C. Tsuchida, eds., *Saddharmapuṇḍarika-sūtra* (Tokyo: Sankibo Buddhist Book Store, 1958), p. 70.

21. Ibid., p. 72.

22. One reason that is often given for the prominence of skillful means in Mahāyāna discourse is that the notion of expedient means serves to reconcile discrepancies between the teachings of the Buddha as recorded in the canons of different schools. In the *Lotus,* it is argued that the Buddhas appear to teach various doctrines but in fact teach only one. The apparent variety of doctrinal statements is due to skillful means. Thus the Buddhas teach one (*eka*) path or vehicle (*yāna*) in the guise of three different sectarian orientations. According to the *ekayāna* doctrine of the *Lotus,* we are all riding in one vehicle (*yāna*) whether we would identify our spiritual lineage as belonging to the Hīnayāna or the Mahāyāna. Although there is a polemical edge to the teaching of the *ekayāna* in the *Lotus,* it is important not to regard teaching by means of expedients as a consolation to the spiritually retarded. Mahāyāna texts, as Pye argues *Skilful Means,* pp. 4–5), tend to identify their own distinctive teachings as provisional truths with no ontological foundation. Seminal early Mahāyāna texts such the *Vimalakīrtinirdeśa Sūtra* and other *Sūtra*s that are inspired by the philosophical perspective associated with the perfection of wisdom (*prajñaparamitā*) declare the Buddhas and *Bodhisattva*s who teach the Dharma and the beings to whom this teaching is directed to be phantoms with no intrinsic nature. Thus there is no teaching that is not an expedient means—not even the Mahāyānist doctrine of the *Bodhisattva* is exempt.

23. Vishnu S. Sukthankar et al., eds., *Mahābhārata,* 5 vols. (Poona: Bhandarkar Oriental Research Institute, 1971–76), 3:1922.

24. See Lamotte and Boln, trans., *Vimalakīrtínirdesá* (The Teaching of Vimalakīrti), pp. 176–69.

25. Garma C. C. Chang, trans., *A Treasury of Mahāyāna Sūtra*s: *Selections from the Mahāratrakūṭa Sūtra* (University Park: Pennsylvania State University Press, 1983), p. 433. The woman is identified as Gopā, the chief wife of Gotama (otherwise known as Yaśodharā). In this *Sūtra,* there are a number of curious details about the *bodhisattva*'s birth (such as his entering his mother's body in the form of a white elephant and exiting from her right side rather than from her vagina) that are explained as skillful means. Likewise, the marriage of Gotama and Yaśodharā is explained as a means of ensuring that people would know Gotama to be a human being (p. 447). The genera-

tion of Gotama's son Rāhula by means of sexual intercourse is described (p. 477) as an *upāya.* Rāhula was not born from the union of a man and a woman but was, like his father, consciously seeking birth as a human being in order to fulfill a *bodhisattva* vow.

26. Ibid., p. 456.

27. Trenckner and Chalmers, eds., *Majjhima Nikāya,* 1:130–42.

28. Ibid., p. 135.

29. T. W. Rhys Davids and Carpenter, eds., *Dīgha Nikāya,* 3:134.

30. Animal husbandry has left its mark on many terms for life in the *sangha.* The word that is often translated as "family" or "lineage" (*gotra*) is more literally translated as "fold," specifically, a fold for cows (*go*), as David Snellgrove notes on p. 67 of the first volume of his *Indo-Tibetan Buddhism.* The term *gaṇa* ("flock" or "herd") was used by Jains and Buddhists alike as a term for groups of homeless renouncers traveling together.

31. Fausboll, ed., *Jātkāṭṭhakathā* (The Jātaka Together with Its Commentary), 2: 94–95.

32. *Dantabhūmi Sutta* (Discourse on the Tamed Stage), in Trenckner and Chalmers, ed., *Majjhima Nikāya,* 3:128–38. See esp. pp. 136–38.

33. Feer, ed., *Saṃyutta Nikāya,* 1:124. Māra's daughters say to their father, "Having bound (*bhandhitvā*) this one by means of the snare of passion like a forest elephant, we'll procure him (*ānayissāma*) and he will be a vassal to you (*vasago te*)."

34. Ibid., 2:226.

35. The expression "hook of the Dharma" is found in an English translation of a Mongolian *Sūtra* that is also extant in Tibetan. See Frye, trans., *The Sutra of the Wise and the Foolish,* p. 71.

36. Norman, ed., *Dhammapadāṭṭhakathā* (The Commentary to the Dhammapada), 1:122.

37. In a sense, the Buddha redirects Nanda's affection toward himself as the King of the Dharma. Relief sculptures from a recently discovered pillar at Mathurā show one scene in which Nanda is making an *añjali* or reverential gesture in adoration of his fiancée and another scene in which he and another monk are venerating the Buddha with the same gesture. See Klaus Fischer, "Hidden Symbolism in Stūpa-Railing Reliefs: Coincidentia Oppositorum of Māra and Kāma," in *The Stupa: Its Religious, Historical, and Architectural Significance,* ed. Anna Libera Dallapiccola in collaboration with Stephanie Zingel-avé Lallemant (Wiesbaden: Franz Steiner, 1980), p. 92.

38. Norman, ed., *Dhammapadāṭṭhakathā* (The Commentary to the Dhammapada), 1:122–23.

39. The term *ukkaṇṭhita* is standardly used of monks who are dissatisfied with *brahmacariya* on account of a woman.

40. Norman, ed., *Dhammapadāṭṭhakathā* (The Commentary to the Dhammapada), 1:124.

41. Ibid., 1:125.

42. For a discussion of the role of dream and illusion in various accounts of the Buddha's life, see Wendy Doniger O'Flaherty, *Dreams, Illusion, and Other Realities* (Chicago: University of Chicago Press, 1984), pp. 149–56.

43. In its entry under the term "insight," the *Oxford English Dictionary* (compact

ed., New York: Oxford University Press, 1971) describes some interesting phases in the evolution of the English word "insight." In its medieval usages, it was (akin to the Middle English "inwit") a term for internal sight, an inner capacity for seeing that is both of the mind and of the eyes. By the sixteenth century, it had come to be analyzed as seeing into a thing or subject by "penetrating into things or seeing beneath their surface with the eyes of the understanding." Wordsworth (cited in the *Oxford English Dictionary,* S. V. "insight") used the term in this way in speaking of the insight into the character of one's wife that comes with marriage: "When the closer view of wedded life / Hath shown that nothing human can be clear / From frailty, for that insight may the Wife / to her indulgent Lord become more dear."

44. On the gold-digging courtesan in Sanskrit satire, see Siegel's *Laughing Matters.*

45. *Upāyakauśalya Sūtra,* in Chang, ed., *A Treasury of Mahāyāna Sūtras,* p. 434.

46. Ibid.

47. Ibid.

48. P. Anujan Achan, ed., *Bhagavadajjukīya* (Trichur: Mangalodayam Press, 1925), p. 71.

49. On the epithets of Māra, see Wayman, "Studies in Yama and Māra," pp. 51–52.

50. Feer, ed., *Saṃyutta Nikāya,* 1:103 ff.

51. M. Walleser and H. Kopp, eds., *Manorathapūraṇī: Buddhaghosa's Commentary on the Aṅguttara Nikāya,* 5 vols. (London: Pali Text Society, 1924–57), 1:397–98.

52. I take the alternate reading *sakabhāve andhāretuṃ asakkonto* for *sakabhavena ṭhātuṃ asakkonto.*

53. I take the alternate reading *tumhādisānaṃ* for *tādisānaṃ.*

54. Walleser and Kopp, eds., *Manorathapūraṇi,* p. 398.

55. I take the alternate reading *ārabdho* for *arabdhaṃ.*

56. Cowell and Neil, eds., *Divyāvadāna,* p. 357.

57. The Hindu goddess Kālī is also represented wearing earrings made of human corpses (sometimes said to be aborted fetuses). Corpses, in fact, furnish a considerable portion of Kālī's attire (at least in her fierce manifestations). She wears a garland of dismembered heads around her neck, a girdle of hands around her waist, in addition to corpse-earrings.

58. Cowell and Neil, eds., *Divyāvadāna,* pp. 357–58.

59. Strong, *The Legend and Cult of Upagupta,* p. 97.

60. A Pāli formula (*vandanā gāthā,* "verses of worship") that is common in South Asia is: "I worship the Buddha with this flower, and by this merit of mine may there be release [*Pūjemi buddhaṃ kusumenānena / puññena m'etena ca hotu mokkhaṃ*]. As the flower withers away, so too this body of mine goes to a state of destruction [*Pupphaṃ milāyāti yathā idan me / kāyo tathā yāti vināsabhāvam*]."

61. Cowell and Neil, eds., *Divyāvadāna,* p. 358.

62. Ibid., p. 360.

63. On the role of the dog in mythology as the bestial alter ego to humans, see David Gordon White, *Myths of the Dog-Man* (Chicago: University of Chicago Press, 1991).

64. The term *śravaka* (literally, "listener") is used in Mahāyānist contexts to refer to Buddhists outside the Mahāyāna fold.

65. Translation by Frye, *The Sutra of the Wise and the Foolish,* p. 234.

66. As John Strong notes, the phrase "by Upagupta Māra was bound" (*Upaguttena badho Māro*) is standardly used in Pāli grammars to illustrate the instrumental case. See *The Legend and Cult of Upagupta,* p. 93.

67. Translated by Frye, *The Sutra of the Wise and the Foolish,* p. 233.

68. In *The Varieties of Religious Experience,* William James suggests that "the truth of which asceticism has been the faithful champion" is "the metaphysical mystery, thus recognized by common sense, that he who feeds on death that feeds on men possesses life supereminently and excellently, and meets the secret demands of the universe." See *The Varieties of Religious Experience* (New York: Collier, 1961), p. 288.

69. Senart, ed., *Mahāvastu,* 2:276–78.

70. That Māra's son Sārthavāha understands the Dharma that his father cannot comprehend is indicated in the *Mahāvastu* by his long discourse on the mortality, impurity, and frailty of the body. Throughout his monologue, Sārthavāha contrasts the sublime body of the Buddhas with the grotesque human body, as in this passage (ibid., 2:326–27): "The person with little understanding who generates a craving for sensual pleasures is swept away and deluded by forms. Like a jackal enjoying a corpse in the cemetery, he himself takes comfort in the source of the malady that causes dis-ease [*duḥkhakararogamūlaṃ*]. Don't try to delude me, friend of Darkness, in praising sensual pleasures that are condemned by the wise. The *bodhisattva* should stay away from the pleasures of sense just as one avoids a bed full of burning coals. For if he had pursued such pleasures he would not have gained this place which is crowded with birds and full of trees; nor would he have attained a body covered with the marks [of a *mahapuruṣa,* or potential Buddha] if he had pursued pleasures."

71. Huber, trans., *Sūtrālaṃkāra,* pp. 105–116; the English translation is mine.

72. Ibid., pp. 105, 106.

73. Ibid.

74. Ibid., p. 107.

75. Ibid., pp. 109–10.

76. Ibid., pp. 110–111.

77. Ibid., p. 111.

78. Ibid., p. 114–116.

79. Oldenberg, ed., *Vinaya Piṭaka,* 2:110–12. On the ambivalence with which Piṇḍola Bhāradvāga is regarded in Indian Buddhist texts, see Ray, *Buddhist Saints in India,* pp. 151–62.

80. Mahā Moggallāna is renowned for his psychic powers. It is perhaps for this reason that he is closely associated with Māra. In the *Majjhima Nikāya,* Mahā Moggallāna announces that he was once the Māra called Dūsin who encouraged householders to revile and abuse monks. See the *Māratajjaniya Suttanta,* in Treckner and Chalmers, eds., *Majjhima Nikāya,* 1:332–38; Horner, trans., *Middle Length Sayings,* 1:395–403.

81. Oldenberg, ed., *Vinaya Piṭaka,* 2: 112.

82. On knowledge of others obtained by psychic means, see Morris and Hardy, eds., *Aṅguttara Nikāya* 3:69; and Feer, ed., *Saṃyutta Nikāya,* 5:268.

83. Oldenberg, ed., *Vinaya Piṭaka,* 2:112. Horner reckons the value of a *māsaka* as very low: "Five *māsaka*s apparently constitute the lowest commercial value that an object can have, and anything less is presumably commercially valueless and therefore

negligible." See her introduction to *The Book of the Discipline,* 1:xxii. By this reckoning, Piṇḍola Bhāradvāga sold himself very cheap indeed.

84. C. A. F. Rhys Davids, ed., *Visuddhimagga,* 1:20–21.

85. I take the variant reading *vipallatthacittā* for *vipallattacittā.*

86. C. A. F. Rhys Davids, ed., *Visuddhimagga,* p. 21.

87. Woodward, ed., *Paramattha-Dīpanī-Theragāthā-aṭṭhakathā,* 2:195–98.

88. Ibid., p. 196.

89. Strong, *The Legend and Cult of Upagupta,* pp. 83–84.

Chapter Five

1. Foley, "The Women Leaders of the Buddhist Reformation as Illustrated by Dhammapāla's Commentary on the *Therīgāthā,*" 1:348.

2. In *Women in Buddhism: Images of the Feminine in the Mahayana Tradition* (pp. ix–x), Diana Paul suggests the androcentrism of Buddhist scripture in arguing that her materials "reveal as much about men's self-concept in relation to women" as they do about what women might think of themselves. Karen Lang ("Lord Death's Snare," p. 64) asserts that: "Monks wrote and compiled virtually all of the texts included in the early Buddhist canon. Much of this material reflects their ambivalent attitudes toward women. Women were considered physically and spiritually weaker, less intellectual and more sensual than men. The community of monks feared women as potential seducers." For a recent attempt to grapple with the androcentric aspects of Buddhism while suggesting a feminist revalorization of Buddhism, see Rita M. Gross's *Buddhism after Patriarchy: A Feminist History, Analysis, and Reconstruction of Buddhism* (Albany: State University of New York, 1993).

3. Jonathan Walters, "A Voice from the Silence: The Buddha's Mother's Story," *History of Religions* 33 (1994): 358–79.

4. Ibid., p. 378.

5. Dhammapāla's preface to the commentary on the *Therīgāthā* states: "Now it came thereafter to pass, while the Master was staying at the Hall of the Gabled House near Vesālī, that King Suddhodana attained Arhatship and passed away. Then in Great Pajāpatī arose the thought of renouncing the world." See C. A. F. Rhys Davids, trans., *Psalms of the Brethren* (London: Pali Text Society, 1913), p. 4. The *Aṅguttara Nikāya* suggests that it was her son Nanda's ordination that prompted Gotamī to renounce. See *Aṅguttara Nikāya,* Morris and Hardy, eds. 4:276; Woodward and Hare, trans., *The Book of Gradual Sayings,* 4:183.

6. In the *Mūlasarvāstivāda Vinaya,* the conception of Rāhula is said to take place on the eve of the Great Departure, while the birth of the child comes much later. Due to the miraculously long six-year gestation period in which Yaśodharā carried him in her womb, Rāhula was born on the day of the Buddha's awakening at Bodhgaya. See John Strong, *The Legend and Cult of Upagupta,* p. 221 ff.

7. Carol Gilligan, *In a Different Voice: Psychological Theory and Women's Development* (Cambridge, MA: Harvard University Press, 1982).

8. *Manusmṛti* 5.147; Wendy Doniger with Brian K. Smith, trans., *The Laws of Manu* (Harmondsworth: Penguin, 1991), p. 115.

9. Lilley, ed., *Apadāna,* 2:530.

10. Falk, "The Case of the Vanishing Nuns," p. 215.

11. Ibid., p. 216.

12. In "The Female Mendicant in Buddhist Srī Laṇkā," in *Buddhism, Sexuality, and Gender,* edited by José Ignacio Cabezon (Albany: State University of New York Press, 1985), p. 51, Tessa Bartholomeusz reports that a majority of the quasi-monastic "ten-precept mothers" (*dasa sil mātāvo*) she interviewed in Sri Lanka "do not rally behind the scholars and other lay people who are trying to reestablish the order of nuns with the help of the Chinese [i.e., Chinese *bhikṣunsīs* who would be necessary in order to ordain Srī Lankan women]. Many of them expressed a desire to remain free of the control of the monks, which would be impossible with the advent of the *bhikkhunī saṇgha* in Laṇkā. They relate their autonomy with power, declaring that if they were granted *pabbajjā,* they would lose the independence they have gained by renouncing lay life. In other words, as one *dasa sil mātā* related to me, they would go from 'one oppressive situation to another' if they became ordained members of the *saṇgha.*"

13. For this equation of the Buddha as father and his Dharmically constituted sons in the history of Buddhism subsequent to the death of the Buddha, see Strong, *The Legend of King Aśoka,* p. 82 ff.

14. Nina Auerbach, *Woman and the Demon: The Life of a Victorian Myth* (Cambridge, MA: Harvard University Press, 1982), p. 8.

15. Morris and Hardy, eds., *Aṇguttara Nikāya,* 4:277. This passage may be a later interpolation added by a misogynistic editor. A passage found later in the same *Nikāya* indicates that the Buddha knew directly after attaining Buddhahood that his order would include nuns as well as monks. See Morris and Hardy, eds., *Aṇguttara Nikāya,* 4:310.

16. I. B. Horner infers from scriptural accounts that several nuns addressed mixed lay audiences. See her *Women under Primitive Buddhism,* pp. 254–56. In present-day Sri Lanka, some lay nuns speak at public gatherings in which monks are in attendance. But this is a novel departure, according to Richard Gombrich and Gananath Obeyesekere, for public preaching "has hitherto always been a male prerogative." See their *Buddhism Transformed: Religious Change in Sri Lanka* (Princeton, NJ: Princeton University Press, 1988), p. 285.

17. E. Muller, ed., *Paramatthadīpanī: Dhammapāla's Commentary on the Therīgāthā* (London: Pali Text Society, 1893), p. 40.

18. Woodward, ed., *Paramatthadīpanī: Dhammapāla's Commentary on the Therīgāthā,* 1:213.

19. In his commentary on this stanza, Dhammapāla underscores the fact that mindfulness is only destroyed when the mind fixes on pleasing characteristics. The solution is simply to focus the mind on the foul characteristics that are also present in all bodies (ibid., p. 214).

20. Ibid.

21. For Ambapālī's story, see Dhammapāla's commentary on *Therīgāthā* 64 in Muller, ed., *Paramatthadīpanī: Dhammapāla's Commentary on the Therīgāthā,* pp. 206–14.

22. Ibid., p. 207.

23. Ibid., pp. 207–9.

24. Ibid., pp. 76–78.

25. Ibid., p. 76.

26. The *Therīgāthā* refers the reader to the account of Moggallāna given at *Theragāthā* 263. See Woodward, ed., *Paramatthadīpanī: Dhammapāla's Commentary on the Therīgāthā,* 3:162–80.

27. *Dhammapāla's Commentary on the Theragāthā* (p. 167) explains this line, in words ascribed to Moggallāna, "You treat as your own [literally, "you make mineness," *mamattan karosi*] that body [*kaḷebare*] consisting of limbs which is not one's own place [*aṇṇasmin padese*] but that of dogs, jackals, families of worms, etc." In other words, due to the fact that the body is violated by worms in life and carrion-eating animals at death, it cannot be considered one's own property but the property of all those creatures living in symbiosis with human bodies. Current biological theory supports this Buddhist notion that the body is not really one's own, that it is rented, not owned, as it were. Without the various microorganisms that are vital to digestion and other processes, the human body would not be able to function.

28. Woodward, ed., *Paramatthadīpanī: Dhammapāla's Commentary on the Therīgāthā,* 3:163.

29. Vimalā identifies herself as achieving *avitakka,* a term for the second *jhana,* a state of trance or concentration characterized by the cessation of reflective thinking.

30. Muller, ed., *Paramatthadīpanī: Dhammapāla's Commentary on the Therīgāthā,* p. 131.

31. On hair as an emblem of sexuality and shaving the head as symbolic of castration (due to the unconscious device of the upward displacement of the genitals), see Charles Berg, *The Unconscious Significance of Hair* (London: Allen and Unwin, 1951); on the shaved head as indicative of general social status but not necessarily individual behavior, see E. R. Leach, "Magical Hair," *Journal of the Royal Anthropological Institute* 88 (1958): 147–68; for a discussion of Leach's argument in light of data gleaned from case studies of Indian men and women, see Gananath Obeyesekere, *Medusa's Hair: An Essay on Personal Symbols and Religious Experience* (Chicago: University of Chicago Press, 1981), pp. 33–40.

32. Obeyesekere states (*Medusa's Hair,* p. 38) that "the Buddhist monk is sexless, a neuter. And this idea is represented in the castration symbolism of shaven head."

33. The insights of Leach and Obeyesekere are somewhat problematically applied to women, since women are obviously not susceptible to castration. In a presentation entitled "Shaved Heads and Loose Hair" given at the American Academy of Religion's 1990 annual meeting, New Orleans, Karen Lang has pointed out that long flowing hair is not always associated with sexual activity in Indic contexts. While loose hair can connote sexual receptivity, women also wear their hair loose during the nonreceptive portions of their menstrual periods. See Lang's contribution to *Off with Her Head,* ed. Howard Eilberg-Schwartz and Wendy Doniger (Berkeley: University of California Press, 1995).

34. See Goffman, *Gender Advertisements;* and Iris Young, "Throwing Like a Girl: A Phenomenology of Feminine Body Comportment, Motility and Spaciality," *Human Studies* 3 (1980): 137–56.

35. Laura Mulvey, "Visual Pleasure and Narrative Cinema," *Screen* 16 (1975): 6–18; see also Mary Ann Doane, "Film and Masquerade: Theorising the Female Spectator," *Screen* 23 (1982): 74–88.

36. Berger, *Ways of Seeing,* p. 47.

37. Frigga Haug, ed., *Female Sexualization,* trans. Erika Carter (London: Verso, 1987). In *The Sadeian Woman and the Ideology of Pornography* (New York: Pantheon, 1978), Angela Carter makes a similar argument about the commodification of beauty in her analysis of the Marquis de Sade's writings: "The Sadeian paradise is a model of the world, in its cash-sale structure" (p. 83).

38. E. Lynn Linton, *Modern Women* (New York, 1889), pp. 253–54; cited in Bram Dijkstra, *Idols of Perversity: Fantasies of Feminine Evil in Fin-de-Siecle Culture* (New York: Oxford University Press, 1986), p. 135.

39. For Freud, the female character is one that gravitates toward exhibitionistic self-display for sexual gratification, while males tend to be voyeurs, seeking gratification in the visual display of others. Although most documented cases of exhibitionism in fact involve males exposing themselves to females (Harold I. Kaplan and Benjamin J. Sadock, *Synopsis of Psychiatry: Behavioral Sciences Clinical Psychiatry,* 6th ed. [Baltimore: Williams and Wilkins, 1991], p. 445), nevertheless Freud's observations ring true in the realm of cultural productions in which women are frequently exhibited in eroticized ways that cater to the ego of the male viewer/voyeur.

40. Linton, *Modern Women,* p. 135.

41. That women make the world a mirror in which to view themselves implies that women do not engage with objects in the world as conscious subjects. Women's lack of subjectivity in turn encourages men to project their own subjective wishes and agendas onto women, allowing them to forgo, in Susanne Keppeler's view, many of the considerations one would normally accord a conscious subject whose needs and wishes do not a priori mirror one's own. When a man meets a woman's gaze, it is often to lose himself in the pellucid beauty of eyes that, seeing nothing but reflections, do not engage him as one subject to another like the gaze of a man. See Susanne Keppeler, *The Pornography of Representation* (Minneapolis: University of Minnesota Press, 1986), pp. 49–63.

42. See Dijkstra, *Idols of Perversity,* pp. 127–59; and Philip Ariés, *Images of Man and Death,* trans. Janet Lloyd (Cambridge, MA: Harvard University Press, 1985), pp. 200–203.

43. In a strict sense, these phantom bodies are not doubles of the nuns who perceive them. They are, for example, often more beautiful than the vain nuns for whom they were created. But since the phantom females seem to serve as stand-ins for the bodies of vain nuns who *ought* to be using their own bodies as objects of meditation, they may be considered doubles of those bodies.

44. Norman, ed., *Dhammapadāṭṭhakathā* (The Commentary to the Dhammapada), 3:113–19.

45. Rūpa Nandā's worry is doubly well founded. Her body is indeed inferior to his, as we shall see shortly, since it does not even approach his in beauty. But what Rūpa Nandā may not be aware of at this point, although her language suggests it, is the natural putrescence of her body. The Pāli word *dosa* (Sanskrit, *doṣa*) not only denotes something faulty or inferior, but something in a corrupt or rotten state. See *The Pali Text Society's Pali-English Dictionary,* T. W. Rhys Davids and William Stede, eds. (London: Pali Text Society, 1986), s.v. *dosa.*

46. If her brother's beauty is so ineffable, Rūpa Nandā must be thinking, then a point-by-point contrast in which her own body is found wanting compared to his might

engage the mouth of the Tathāgata the whole day long. Here Rūpa Nandā shows herself to be utterly subject to narcissistic thought processes.

47. Norman, ed., *Dhammapadāṭṭhakathā* (The Commentary to the Dhammapada), 3:114.

48. Ibid., p. 115.

49. In talking about how best to approach Rūpa Nandā with a teaching appropriate (*sappāyā*) for her, the Buddha here uses a Pāli term related to the technical term *upāya* used in Mahāyāna literature.

50. Norman, ed., *Dhammapadāṭṭhakathā* (The Commentary to the Dhammapada), 3:114. I am grateful to Jonathan Walters for this perfectly apt translation of *solasavassuddesikaṃ*. But I am not convinced by his unprecedented interpretation of the rest of the passage, by which the Buddha and not the spectral woman holds the fan. This requires what is in my view an unlikely use of *vījamānaṃ* as an adverb ("fanningly," i.e., with the brush of a fan as a dramatic flourish) modifying the action of the Buddha in conjuring up the woman. In my view, all the components of the sentence that refer to fans and fanning must refer to the phantom woman as they are in the accusative.

51. Ibid., 3:116.

52. Ibid., 3:113–19. Literally, "Karma-state or work-state," a *kammaṭṭhāna* may be understood either as an occasion for contemplating the effects of karma or an occasion for engaging in contemplative work.

53. The term translated here as "body" (*samussayaṃ*, from $\sqrt{}$*si*, "to raise up) might also be translated as "construct" or "compound."

54. Norman, ed., *Dhammapadāṭṭhakathā* (The Commentary to the Dhammapada), 3:117.

55. Ibid., 3:118.

56. Ibid., 3:119.

57. Lilley, ed., *Apadāna*, 2:572–76.

58. Since the word *nanda* means "joy," this phrase could mean "being joyless." But from the variant readings, it is clear that Kalyāṇī Nandā's middle brother Nanda is intended here. Thus she is living at home without a male guardian, since her brothers have renounced and by this time her father Suddhodana has died.

59. Sri is a goddess associated with beauty and prosperity.

60. Lilley, ed., *Apadāna*, 2:573–74.

61. For a description of the buds and blossoms of the celestial coral tree, see Morris and Hardy, eds., *Aṅguttara Nikāya*, 4:117.

62. I have taken the variant reading *vaṇitakibbisṇā* instead of the problematic *nītakibbisā*.

63. The term for impurity (*abhejja*) has as its literal meaning "that which cannot be sacrificed" (Sanskrit, *amedhya*). Excrement, as the most vile, impure thing imaginable, is often referred to as *abhejja*.

64. Norman, ed., *Dhammapadāṭṭhakathā* (The Commentary to the Dhammapada), 3:574–75.

65. Ibid., 3:576.

66. Muller, ed., *Paramatthadīpanī: Dhammapāla's Commentary on the Therīgāthā*, pp. 272–300.

67. Buddhaghosa explains in the *Visuddhimagga* that the body is full of corpses be-

cause the food one has swallowed festers in one's stomach like dead bodies thrown into a cesspool. See *The Path of Purity,* trans. Pe Maung Tin (London: Pali Text Society, 1922–31; reprint, 1975), p. 399.

68. Dhammapāla's commentary suggests that Sumedhā's parents have no power to give Sumedhā in marriage since her body is already the property of worms. See Muller, ed., *Paramatthadīpanī: Dhammapāla's Commentary on the Therīgāthā,* p. 284.

69. Ibid., p. 276.

70. Ibid., pp. 245–60.

71. Ibid., pp. 246–47.

72. Ibid., p. 247.

73. Ibid., p. 248.

74. Ibid., pp. 248–49.

75. As Keven Trainor notes in "In the Eye of the Beholder: Nonattachment and the Body in Subhā's Verses (*Therīgāthā* 71)," *Journal of the American Academy of Religion* 61 (1992): 57–79, Subhā's reference to a decorated plaything whose movements are controlled by the manipulation of a puppeteer may be an allusion to the subservient role that she would play were she to go off with the young man as his consort.

76. Muller, ed., *Paramatthadīpanī: Dhammapāla's Commentary on the Therīgāthā,* p. 249.

77. Ibid. For an understanding of how such images function in Indian discourse on illusion, see Wendy Doniger O'Flaherty, *Dreams, Illusion, and Other Realities,* chap. 6.

78. Muller, ed., *Paramatthadīpanī: Dhammapāla's Commentary on the Therīgāthā,* p. 249. Dhammapāla's commentary (p. 259) explains that the eye consists of seven membranes of various colors.

79. Ibid., pp. 249–50.

80. Oldenberg, ed., *Vinaya Piṭaka,* 3:20.

81. Cited in Mary Lefkowitz, *Women in Greek Myth* (Baltimore: Johns Hopkins University Press, 1990), p. 131. The twentieth-century Indian guru Sri Muktānanda used to tell a story reminiscent of Subhā's tale. A young woman plagued by the unwanted attention of a persistent male admirer agrees one day, quite uncharacteristically, to see him. She invites him to come to her third-floor flat to visit. On the appointed day, the woman takes a liberal quantity of laxative and leaves a trail of excrement on the stairs of her apartment building. When her suitor comes to visit, she explains that this—her essence—is his for the taking. I am grateful to Karen Anderson for sharing this story—and many insightful remarks on things Indological—with me.

82. Muller, ed., *Paramatthadīpanī: Dhammapāla's Commentary on the Therīgāthā,* p. 250.

83. E. W. Burlingame, trans., *Buddhist Parables* (New Delhi: Motilal Banarsidass, 1991), p. 332.

84. Ibid., pp. 333–34.

85. Schulenberg, "The Heroics of Virginity," pp. 51–55.

86. Ibid., p. 53.

87. Lewis, I. M., *Ecstatic Religion: An Anthropological Study of Spirit Possession and Shamanism* (Harmondsworth: Penguin, 1971), esp. pp. 186, 191, 200.

88. Gonzague de Ray, *Les saints del église de Marseille* (Marseille: Société anonyme

de l'imprimerie Marseillaise, 1885), pp. 225–38; cited in Schulenberg, "The Heroics of Virginity," pp. 46–47.

89. Roger of Wendover, *Flowers of History: Comprising the History of England from the Descent of the Saxons to A.D. 1235,* trans. J. A. Giles (London: H. G. Bohn, 1849), pp. 191–92, cited in Schulenberg, "The Heroics of Virginity," pp. 47–48.

90. Fray Antonio de Yepes, *Cronica general de la Orden de San Benito* (Madrid: Ediciones Atlas, 1959), 1:137–38, translated by Victoria J. Meyer in Schulenberg, "The Heroics of Virginity," p. 48.

91. Schulenberg, "The Heroics of Virginity," pp. 48–49.

92. Ibid., p. 55.

93. *Palladius: The Lausiac History,* trans. R. T. Meyer (New York: Newman Press, 1964; reprint, London: Longmans, Green, and Co., 1965), pp. 146–47.

94. *Anonymous Apophthegmata* 172, cited in Peter Brown, *Body and Society,* p. 242.

95. *The World of the Desert Fathers: Stories and Sayings from the Anonymous Series of the Apophthegmata Patrum,* trans. Columba Stewart (Fairacres: SGL Press, 1986), pp. 14–15.

96. Ibid.

97. Ibid., p. 15.

98. Palladius: *The Lausiac History,* pp. 36–37.

99. Saint Jerome, *Regula Monacharum,* P.L. 30:414–15, translated by Sara Richards in Schulenberg, "The Heroics of Virginity," p. 42.

100. See Peter Brown, *Body and Society.*

101. Marina Warner, *Alone of All Her Sex: The Myth and Cult of the Virgin Mary* (New York: Random House, 1983), p. 73.

102. *Regula Monacharum,* cited in Schulenberg, "The Heroics of Virginity," p. 42.

103. Although Buddhist cultures do feature cults dedicated to the worship of virginal girls (e.g., the Kumāri cult of Nepalese Buddhism), such cultic practices are related to the widespread North Indian practice of *kanyā-pūjā,* or the worship of prepubescent girls. Such cultic practices can be seen, as Michael Allen suggests, as marking the liminal position of the immature North Indian bride who wears the marks of a married woman (as do Nepal's highly venerated virgins) for a protracted period (sometimes years) before her marriage is consummated. Such young women are sacred by virtue of their liminality, which is a temporary state. They are not destined for a life of permanent virginity, and they cease to be venerated as sacred beings once they reach puberty. See Michael Allen, "Girls' Prepubertal Rites amongst the Newars of the Kathmandu Valley," in *Women in India and Nepal* (New Delhi: Sterling Publishers, 1990), pp. 190–91.

104. According to Schulenberg, Saint Jerome advocates an extremist position, viewing suicide as a valid means of preserving virginity threatened by sexual assault. Those virgins whose sexual purity is corrupted will be turned away from Christ's bridal chamber to feed the goats at his left hand, for "He has no power to crown one who has been corrupted." See Jerome, *The Letters of St. Jerome: Ancient Christian Writers,* 2 vols. trans. Christopher Mierow (Westminister, MD: Newmann Press, 1963), 1:138; see Schulenberg, "The Heroics of Virginity," pp. 32–33.

105. One who engages in intercourse against his or her will is not subject to expul-

sion. The Pāli *Vinaya* suggests that Buddhist men dedicated to the celibate life were vulnerable to rape by women, warning monks to beware of women who mount sleeping monks and otherwise force themselves on the unwary. See Horner, trans., *The Book of Discipline,* 1:58–63.

106. Medieval Christian theologians such as Peter Abelard understood Aristotelian theory to imply that the female body is by nature more permeable than the male body. Thus Abelard argues that there is no reason why nuns should be denied the opportunity to partake of wine during the Mass when they are less likely to become inebriated than monks, to whom the cup was not denied: "The woman's body is pierced with many holes. . . . By these holes the vapour of the wine is speedily released. On what ground then is that allowed to monks which to the weaker sex is denied?" Cited in Prudence Allen, *The Concept of Woman: The Aristotelian Revolution, 750 B.C. to A.D. 1250* (Montreal: Eden Press, 1985), pp. 281–82.

107. See Mikhail Bakhtin, *Rabelais and His World,* trans. Helene Iswolsky (Bloomington: Indiana University Press, 1984), chap. 5.

108. See François Rebelais, *The Histories of Gargantua and Pantagruel,* trans. J. M. Cohen (Harmondsworth: Penguin, 1955).

109. On miraculous exudings by women saints of the high Middle Ages, see Carolyn Walker Bynum, *Holy Feast and Holy Fast: The Religious Significance of Food to Medieval Women* (Berkeley and Los Angeles: University of California Press, 1985), pp. 122–29.

Conclusion

1. Sartre, *Being and Nothingness,* p. 234.

Appendix

1. See Gregory Schopen, "Two Problems in the History of Indian Buddhism: The Layman/Monk Distinction and the Doctrines of the Transference of Merit," *Studien zur Indologie und Iranistik* 10 (1985): 9–47.

2. I am grateful to Charlie Hallisey for suggesting this interpretation to me at a time when the explanatory framework I had in mind was rather unwieldy.

3. There has been considerable controversy over what Aśoka meant by the term Dharma, a term used by Hindus as well as by Buddhists. The great French Buddhologist Étienne Lamotte, for example, argues that Aśoka used the term Dharma to mean something much more generic than the truth discovered by the Buddha; see *Histoire du bouddhisme indien* (Louvain: Institut Orientalist de Louvain, 1958), p. 333. But whether Aśoka should be considered a Hindu or a Buddhist, it is clear that he was a generous patron of the Buddhist *sangha* and that it was under Aśoka that Buddhism gained a foothold throughout the subcontinent.

4. J. Takakusu, trans., *A Record of the Buddhist Religion as Practiced in India and the Malay Archipelago (A.D. 671–689),* by I-Tsing (Oxford: Clarendon, 1896), pp. 177-78.

5. Adolph von Harnack, "Das Mönchtum: Seine Ideale und Geschichte," in *Reden und Aufsätze* (Giessen: A. Topelmann, 1911–30), 1:101.

6. Translation by Thoman Watters as cited by Kanai Lal Hazra in *Buddhism in India as Described by Chinese Pilgrims, A.D. 399–689* (New Delhi: Munishiram Manoharlal, 1983), p. 46.

7. In "Hīnayāna and Mahāyāna in Indian Buddhist History," *Journal of the American Academy of Religion* 63 (1995): 1–25, Richard Cohen has recently argued that attempts to "save appearances" by positing semi-Mahāyānic or proto-Mahāyānic forms of Buddhism that preexist the origins of the Mahāyāna as such have little heuristic use. It contributes little to our understanding of Indian Buddhism's institutional history to invoke a long period of that history in which the Mahāyāna existed as a body of thought and practice but had not yet "emerged" as such. In order to save appearances, the origins of the Mahāyāna are thus placed outside of history and "we are left with the Mahāyāna/Hīnayāna distinction as a mere structural dualism devoid of specific content, a mere nominalism" (p. 21).

8. On the evidence that Aśvaghoṣa wrote under the auspices of Kaniṣka, see Johnston, ed. and trans., *Buddhacarita,* pp. xiii–xvi.

9. The Sanskrit biographies, with the exception of the *Buddhacarita,* are composite sources and, as such, difficult to date with any accuracy. Like much of the material in the Pāli *Khuddaka Nikāya,* very early and very late passages have been woven together in the Sanskrit biographies.

10. The *Buddhacarita* does contain an epilogue that cannot be ascribed to Aśvaghoṣa, but the rest of the work is clearly the product of a single author.

11. See Johnston, ed. and trans., pt. 2, *Buddhacarita,* pp. xxviii–xxxv.

12. K. R. Norman, *Pāli Literature Including the Canonical Literature in Prakrit and Sanskrit of All the Hindyana Schools of Buddhism* (Wiesbaden: Harrassowitz, 1983); Maurice Winternitz, *A History of Indian Literature,* 2 vols. (New Delhi: Motilal Banarsidas, 1983), 2:186–90; Eugene Watson Burlingame, "Buddhaghosa's Dhammapada Commentary," *Proceedings of the American Academy of Arts and Sciences* 45 (1910): 467–550.

13. See "Buddhaghosa, the Harmonizer," in *A History of Buddhist Philosophy: Continuities and Discontinuities,* by David Kalupahana (Honolulu: University of Hawaii Press, 1992).

14. Winternitz, *A History of Indian Literature,* 2:197, cites one such passage in the *Sumaṅgalavilāsinī* (Buddhaghosa's commentary to the *Dīgha Nikāya*) where the Buddha emits rays of light in six colors from his body as his surroundings are transformed into the paradisiacal condition of matter in the Pure Lands.

15. See Cohen, "Hīnayāna and Mahāyāna in Indian Buddhist History."

Selected Bibliography

Allen, Michael. "Girls' Prepubertal Rites amongst the Newars of the Kathmandu Valley." In *Women in India and Nepal.* New Delhi: Sterling Publishers, 1990.

Altekar, Anant Sadashiv. *The Position of Women in Hindu Civilization from Prehistoric Times to the Present Day.* 1938. Reprint, New Delhi: Motilal Banarsidas, 1978.

Anderson, Jørgen. *The Witch on the Wall: Medieval Erotic Sculpture in the British Isles.* Copenhagen: Rosenkilde and Bagger, 1977.

Aṅguttara Nikāya. Edited by R. Morris and E. Hardy. 5 vols. London: Pali Text Society, 1885–1900.

Apadāna. Edited by M. E. Lilley. 2 vols. London: Pali Text Society, 1925–27.

Aśokāvadāna. In *Divyāvadāna.* Edited by E. B. Cowell and R. A. Neil. Cambridge: Cambridge University Press, 1886.

Bakhtin, Mikhail. *Rabelais and His World.* Translated by Helene Iswolsky. Bloomington: Indiana University Press, 1984.

Barber, Paul. *How Shall the Dead Arise? The Folklore of Vampires, Burial, and Death.* New Haven, CT: Yale University Press, 1988.

Barrett, T. H. "Explanatory Observations on Some Weeping Pilgrims." In *Buddhist Studies Forum.* Vol. 1, *Seminar Papers, 1987–88,* edited by T. Skorupski. London: School of Oriental and African Studies, 1990.

Barua, B. M. "Māra." *Buddhist Review* 7 (1915): 194–211.

Bassein, Beth Ann. *Women and Death: Linkages in Western Thought and Literature.* Westport, CT: Greenwood Press, 1984.

Berger, John. *Ways of Seeing.* London: Pelican, 1972.

Bergler, Edmund. *Fashion and the Unconscious.* Madison, WI: International Universities Press, 1987.

Bhagavadajjukīya of Mahendravikramavarman. Edited by P. Anujan Achan. Trichur: Mangalodayam Press, 1925.

Buddhacarita of Aśvaghoṣa. Edited and translated by E. H. Johnston. Lahore: University of Punjab, 1936. Reprint, New Delhi: Oriental Books Reprint Corporation, 1972.

Birnbaum, Raoul. *The Healing Buddha.* Boulder, CO: Shambhala, 1979.

Blackstone, Katherine Rennie, "The Struggle for Liberation in the 'Therīgāthā.'" Master's thesis, McMaster University, Department of Religious Studies, 1990.

Blamires, A., K. Pratt, and C. W. Marx, eds. *Women Defamed and Women Defended: An Anthology of Medieval Texts.* New York: Oxford University Press, 1992.

Bodhicaryāvatāra of Śantideva. Edited by P. L. Vaidya. Darbhanga: Mithala Institute of Post-graduate Studies and Research in Sanskrit Learning, 1960.

Boisvert, Mathieu. "The Use of Death for Meditation Purposes in Theravāda Buddhism." *Buddhist Studies Review.* Forthcoming.

Bond, George. "Theravāda Buddhism's Meditations on Death and the Symbolism of Initiatory Death." *History of Religions* 19 (1980): 237–58.

Boyarin, Daniel. *Carnal Israel: Reading Sex in Talmudic Culture.* Berkeley and Los Angeles: University of California Press, 1993.

Boyd, James W. *Satan and Māra: Christian and Buddhist Symbols of Evil.* Leiden: E. J. Brill, 1975.

Brown, Cheever Mackenzie. *God as Mother: A Feminine Theology in India: An Historical and Theological Study of the Brahmavaivarta Purāṇa.* Hartford, VT: Claude Stark and Co., 1974.

Brown, Peter. *The Making of Late Antiquity.* Cambridge, MA: Harvard University Press, 1978.

———. *The Body and Society: Men, Women, and Sexual Renunciation in Early Christianity.* New York: Columbia University Press, 1988.

Brown, W. Norman. "The Metaphysics of the Act of Truth (Satyakriyā)." In *Mélanges d'indianisme à la mémoire de Louis Renou.* Paris: E. de Boccard, 1968.

Brundage, James. *Law, Sex, and Christian Society in Medieval Europe.* Chicago: University of Chicago Press, 1987.

Burlingame, Eugene Watson. "Buddhaghosa's Dhammapada Commentary." *Proceedings of the American Academy of Arts and Sciences* 45 (1910): 467–550.

Burnouf, Eugene. *Introduction a l'histoire du buddhisme indien.* 3 vols. Paris: Imprimerie Royale, 1844.

Bynum, Carolyn Walker. *Holy Feast and Holy Fast: The Religious Significance of Food to Medieval Women.* Berkeley and Los Angeles: University of California Press, 1985.

Camille, Michael. *The Gothic Idol: Ideology and Image-Making in Medieval Art.* New York: Oxford University Press, 1989.

Carmichael, Elizabeth, and Chloë Sayer, eds. *The Skeleton at the Feast: The Day of the Dead in Mexico.* Austin: University of Texas, 1991.

Carstairs, Morris G. *The Twice-Born: A Study of a Community of High-Caste Hindus.* Bloomington: Indiana University Press, 1958.

Chomsky, Jamsheed K. *Purity and Pollution in Zoroastrianism: Triumph over Evil.* Austin: University of Texas Press, 1989.

Cohen, Richard. "Hīnayāna and Mahāyāna in Indian Buddhist History." *Journal of the American Academy of Religion* 63 (1995): 1–25.

Collins, Steven. *Selfless Persons: Imagery and Thought in Theravāda Buddhism.* New York: Cambridge University Press, 1982.

———. "Monasticism, Utopias, and Comparative Social Theory." *Religion* 18 (1988): 101–35.

———. "The Body in Theravāda Buddhist Monasticism." In *The Body in Religion: Comparative and Devotional Approaches,* edited by Sara Coakley. Berkeley and Los Angeles: University of California Press. Forthcoming.

Coomaraswami, Ananda. "*Saṃvega:* Aesthetic Shock." In *Coomaraswami 1: Selected Papers on Traditional Art and Symbolism,* edited by Roger Lipsey. Bollingen Series 89. Princeton, NJ: Princeton University Press, 1977.

Das, R. M. *Women in Manu and His Seven Commentators.* Bodh-Gaya: Kanchana Publications, 1962.

Demeiville, Paul. "Busshin." In *Hobo-girin.* Fasc. 2. Tokyo: Maison Franco-Japonaise, 1930.

Dhammapada. Edited by S. Sumangala. London: Pali Text Society, 1914.

Dhammapadāṭṭhakathā (The Commentary to the Dhammapada). Edited by H. C. Norman. 4 vols. London: Pali Text Society, 1906–14.

Dibdin, Michael. "The Pathology Lesson." *Granta* 39 (Spring 1992): 91–101.

Dīgha Nikāya. Edited by T. W. Rhys Davids and J. E. Carpenter. 3 vols. London: Pali Text Society, 1889–1910.

Dijkstra, Bram. *Idols of Perversity: Fantasies of Feminine Evil in Fin-de-Siecle Culture.* New York: Oxford University Press, 1986.

Doane, Mary Ann. "Film and Masquerade: Theorising the Female Spectator." *Screen* 23 (1982): 74–88.

Doniger, Wendy (see also Wendy Doniger O'Flaherty), and Brian K. Smith, trans. *The Laws of Manu.* Harmondsworth: Penguin Books, 1991.

Douglas, Mary. *Purity and Danger: An Analysis of the Concepts of Pollution and Taboo.* New York: Routledge and Kegan Paul, 1979.

———. *Natural Symbols: Explorations in Cosmology.* New York: Pantheon, 1982.

duBois, Page. *Sowing the Body: Psychoanalysis and Ancient Representations of Women.* Chicago: University of Chicago Press, 1988.

Dumont, Louis. *Homo hierarchicus: Le systeme des castes et ses implications.* Paris: Editions Gallimard, 1966.

———. *Homo Hierarchicus: The Caste System and Its Implications,* translated by Mark Sainsbury, Louis Dumont, and Basia Gulati. Complete rev. ed. Chicago: University of Chicago Press, 1980.

Dutt, Nalinaksha. *Aspects of Mahayana Buddhism and Its Relation to Hinayana.* London: Luzac, 1930.

Eck, Diana L. *Darśan: Seeing the Divine Image in India.* Chambersburg, PA: Anima Books, 1981.

———. *Banaras: City of Light.* New York: Alfred A. Knopf, 1982.

Elias, Norbert. *Über den Prozess der Zivilisation.* Basel: Haus zum Falken, 1939; English ed., *The Civilizing Process: The History of Manners.* 2 vols. Translated by Edmund Jephcott. New York: Urizen Books, 1978.

Encyclopedia of Religion and Ethics. Edited by James Hastings. New York: Scribner's, 1917–27. S.v. "Māra," by L. de La Vallée Poussin.

Falk, Maryla. *Nama-Rupa and Dharma-Rupa.* Calcutta: University of Calcutta, 1943.

Falk, Nancy Auer. "The Case of the Vanishing Nuns: The Fruits of Ambivalence in Ancient Indian Buddhism." In *Unspoken Worlds: Women's Religious Lives and Non-western Cultures,* edited by Nancy Auer Falk and Rita M. Gross. Belmont, CA: Wadsworth, 1989.

Fischer, Klaus. "Hidden Symbolism in Stūpa-Railing Reliefs: Coincidentia Oppositorum of Māra and Kāma." In *The Stupa: Its Religious, Historical, and Architectural Significance,* edited by Anna Libera Dallapiccola in collaboration with Stephanie Zingel-avé Lallemant. Wiesbaden: Franz Steiner Verlag, 1980.

Foley, Caroline A. "The Women Leaders of the Buddhist Reformation as Illustrated by Dhammapāla's Commentary on the Therī-gāthā." In *Tnansactions of the Ninth International Congress of Orientalists.* Vol. I (Indian and Aryan Sections). Edited by E. Delmar Morgan. London: Committee of the Congress, 1893.

Fo-sh-hing-tsan-king: A Life of the Buddha by Aśvaghosa Bodhisattva. Translated by Samuel Beal. Sacred Books of the East, vol. 19. Oxford: Clarendon Press, 1883.

Foucault, Michel. *Discipline and Punish: The Birth of the Prison.* Trans. Alan Sheridan. Vintage Books, 1979.

———. "Sexuality and Solitude." In *On Signs,* edited by Marshall Blonsky. Baltimore: Johns Hopkins University Press, 1985.

Goffman, Erving. *Gender Advertisements.* New York: Harper and Row, 1979.

Gonda, Jan. "The Vedic Concept of *Amhas.*" *Indo-Iranian Journal* 1 (1957): 33–60.

Gombrich, Richard. "Feminine Elements in Sinhalese Buddhism." *Wiener Zeitschrift für die Kunde Südasiens* 16 (1972): 69–93.

———. *Theravāda Buddhism: A Social History from Ancient Benares to Modern Columbo.* London: Routledge and Kegan Paul, 1988.

Gombrich, Richard, and Gananath Obeyesekere, *Buddhism Transformed: Religious Change in Sri Lanka.* Princeton, NJ: Princeton University Press, 1988.

Gregg, Robert, trans. *Athanasius: The Life of Anthony and the Letter to Marcelinus.* New York: Paulist Press, 1980.

Hadley, N. H. *The Foundations of Aversion Therapy.* New York: S. P. Medical and Scientific Books, 1985.

Halbfass, Wilhelm. "Tradition and Argument in Indian Ethics." Paper presented at the Workshop on Buddhist Intellectual Practice, University of Chicago Divinity School, January 31, 1992.

Hamilton, Sue. "From the Buddha to Buddhaghosa: Changing Attitudes towards the Human Body in Theravāda Buddhism." In *Religious Reflections on the Human Body,* edited by Jane Marie Law. Bloomington: Indiana University Press, 1995.

Harpham, Geoffrey G. *The Ascetic Imperative in Criticism and Culture.* Chicago: University of Chicago Press, 1987.

Heesterman, J. C. "Brahmin, Ritual, and Renouncer." In *The Inner Conflict of Tradition: Essays in Indian Ritual, Kingship, and Society.* Chicago: University of Chicago Press, 1985.

Hollander, Anne. *Seeing through Clothes.* New York: Viking Press, 1978.

Holt, John. *Buddha in the Crown: Avalokiteśvara in the Buddhist Traditions of Sri Lanka.* New York: Oxford, 1991.

Horner, I. B. *Women under Primitive Buddhism: Lay Women and Alms Women.* New York: E. P. Dutton, 1930.

James, William. *The Varieties of Religious Experience.* New York: Collier Books, 1961.

Jātakāṭṭhakathā (The Jātaka Together with its Commentary). Edited by V. Fausboll. 6 vols. London: Pali Text Society, 1877–96. Reprint, London: Luzac and Co., 1962–64.

———. (The Jātaka or Stories of the Buddha's Former Births). Translated by R. Chalmers, W. H. D. Rouse, H. T. Francis, and R. A. Neil. 6 vols. London: Pali Text Society, 1895–1907.

Kane, P. V. *History of Dharmasastra.* 6 vols. Second edition. Poona: Bhandarkar Oriental Institute, 1974.

Keppeler, Susanne. *The Pornography of Representation.* Minneapolis: University of Minnesota, 1986.

Kayser, Wolfgang. *The Grotesque in Art and Literature.* Bloomington: Indiana University Press, 1963.

Khantipālo (Bhikkhu). *Bag of Bones: A Miscellany on the Body.* Kandy: Buddhist Publication Society, 1980.

King, Winston. "Practicing Dying: The Samurai-Zen Death Techniques of Suzuki-Shosan." In *Religious Encounters with Death: Insights from the History and Anthropology of Religions.* University Park: Pennsylvania State University Press, 1977.

Kṣemendra. *Kṣemendralaghukāvyasaṃgraha: Minor works of Kṣemendra.* Edited by Vidyaratna E. V. V. Raghavacharya and D. G. Pandye. Hyderabad: Osmania University Press, 1961.

———. *Avadānakalpalatā of Kṣemendra.* Edited by P. L. Vaidya. 2 vols. Dharbhanga: Mithila Institute of Post-graduate Studies and Research in Sanskrit Learning, 1959.

Lalitavistara. 2 vols. Edited by S. Lefmann. Halle a.S.: Verlag der Buchhandlung des Waisenhauses, 1902–8.

Lancaster, Lewis. "An Early Mahāyāna Sermon about the Body of the Buddha and the Making of Images." *Artibus Asiae* 36 (1974): 287–91.

Lang, Karen C. "Lord Death's Snare: Gender Related Imagery in the 'Theragāthā' and the 'Therīgāthā.'" *Journal of Feminist Studies in Religion* 2 (1986): 63–79.

———. "Shaven Heads and Louse Hair: Buddhist Attitudes toward Hair and Sexuality." In *Off with Her Head! The Denial of Women's Identity in Myth, Religion, and Culture,* edited by Howard Eilberg-Schwartz and Wendy Doniger. Berkeley: University of California Press, 1995.

Larson, G. J. *Classical Samkhya: An Interpretation of Its Meaning.* New Delhi: Motilal Banarsidass, 1979.

The Lausiac History of Palladius. Translated by R. T. Meyer. New York: Newman Press, 1964. Reprint, London: Longmans, Green, and Co., 1965.

La Vallée Poussin, Louis de. "Notes sur les corps du Buddha." *Le Muséon* (1913): 251–90.

Law, B. C. "The Buddhist Conception of Māra." In *Buddhistic Studies.* Edited by B. C. Law. Calcutta: Thacker, Spink, and Co., 1931.

Lederer, Wolfgang. *The Fear of Women.* New York: Harcourt, Brace, and Jovanovich, 1968.

Leslie, Julia. *The Perfect Wife: The Orthodox Hindu Woman according to the Strīdharmapaddhati of Tryambakayajvan.* New York: Oxford University Press, 1989.

Lewis, Todd. "Newar Tibetan Trade and the Domestication of the 'Siṃhalasārthabāhu Avadāna.'" *History of Religions* 33 (1994): 135–60.

Ling, T. O. *Buddhism and the Mythology of Evil.* London: George Allen and Unwin, 1962.

Long, J. Bruce. "Death as a Necessity and as a Gift in Hindu Mythology." In *Religious Encounters with Death: Insights from the History and Anthropology of Religions.* University Park: Pennsylvania State University Press, 1977.

Mahābhārata. Edited by Vishnu S. Sukthankar et al. 5 vols. Poona: Bhandarkar Oriental Research Institute, 1971–76.

Majjhima Nikāya. Edited by V. Trenckner and R. Chalmers. 3 vols. London: Pali Text Society, 1888–1902.

Makransky, John. "Controversy over *Dharmakāya* in India and Tibet: A Reappraisal of Its Basis, *Abhisamayālamkāra* Chapter 8," *Journal of the International Association of Buddhist Studies* 12 (1989): 45–78.

Mālatīmādhava of Bhavabhūti. Edited by Michael Coulson. Delhi: Oxford University Press, 1989.

Malleus Malificarum of Heinrich Kramer and Johann Sprenger. Translated by M. Summers. London: John Rodker, 1948. Reprint, New York: Dover, 1971.

Mānavadharmaśāstra. Edited by J. Jolly. London: Trübner, 1887.

Manorathapūraṇī: Buddhaghosa's Commentary on the Aṅguttara Nikāya. Edited by M. Walleser and H. Kopp. 5 vols. London: Pali Text Society, 1924–57.

Mahāvastu. Edited by É. Senart. 3 vols. Paris: Imprimerie Nationale, 1882–97.

———. Translated by J. J. Jones. 3 vols. Sacred Books of the Buddhists, vols. 16, 18, and 19. London: Luzac and Co., 1949–56.

Masefield, Peter. "Mind/Cosmos Maps in the Pāli *Nikāya*s." In *Buddhist and Western Psychology,* edited by Nathan Katz. Boulder, CO: Shambhala, 1983.

Mbo bdzans blun. Sutra of the Wise and the Foolish or the Ocean of Narratives (üliger-ün dalai). Translated by Stanley Frye. Dharamsala: Library of Tibetan Works and Archives, 1981.

Mehta, Ved. *Mahatma Gandhi and His Apostles.* New Haven, CT: Yale University Press, 1993.

Miles, Margaret R. *Carnal Knowing: Female Nakedness and Religious Meaning in the Christian West.* New York: Beacon Press, 1989.

Milindapañha. Edited by V. Trenckner. London: Williams and Norgate, 1880.

Mullin, Glen. *Death and Dying: The Tibetan Tradition.* London: Arkana, 1986.

Mulvey, Laura. "Visual Pleasure and Narrative Cinema." *Screen* 16 (1975): 6–18.

Mus, Paul. "Buddha Paré." *Bulletin de l'école française Extrême-Orient* 28 (1928): 147–278.

———. Preface to *Barabudur: Esquise d'une histoire du Bouddhisme fondée sur la critique archéologique des textes.* Hanoi: École Française d'Extreme Orient, 1935. Reprint, Arno Press, 1978.

Nagao, Gadjin. "On the Theory of Buddha-Body (Buddha-kāya)." *Eastern Buddhist,* n.s., 6, pt. 1 (May 1973): 25–53.

Neusner, Jacob. *The Idea of Purity in Ancient Judaism.* Leiden: Brill, 1973.

Norman, K. R. *Pāli Literature Including the Canonical Literature in Prakrit and Sanskrit of All the Hinayana Schools of Buddhism: A History of Indian Literature.* Vol. 7. Fasc. 2. Edited by Jan Gonda. Wiesbaden: Harrassowitz, 1983.

Obeyesekere, Gananath. *Medusa's Hair: An Essay on Personal Symbols and Religious Experience.* Chicago: University of Chicago Press, 1981.

———. "Despair and Recovery in Sinhala Medicine and Religion: An Anthropologist's Meditations." In *Healing and Restoring: Health and Medicine in the World's Religious Traditions,* edited by Lawrence E. Sullivan. New York: Macmillan, 1989.

O'Flaherty, Wendy Doniger (see also Doniger, Wendy). *Śiva: The Erotic Ascetic.* New York: Oxford University Press, 1973. Reprint, New York: Oxford University Press, 1981.

———. *Women, Androgynes, and Other Mythical Beasts.* Chicago: University of Chicago Press, 1980.

———, trans. *The Rig Veda.* Harmondsworth: Penguin, 1983.

——— *Dreams, Illusion, and Other Realities.* Chicago: University of Chicago Press, 1984.

Oldenburg, Veena Talwar. *The Making of Colonial Lucknow, 1856–1877.* Princeton, NJ: Princeton University Press, 1984.

Olivelle, Patrick. *The Saṃnyāsa Upanishads: Hindu Scriptures on Asceticism and Renunciation.* New York: Oxford University Press, 1992.

Oxford English Dictionary, Compact Edition. 2 vols. New York: Oxford University Press, 1971. S.v. "Insight."

Paramattha-Dīpanī-Theragāthā-aṭṭhakathā: The Commentary of Dhammapālācariya. Edited by F. L. Woodward. 3 vols. Pali Text Society Publications. London: Oxford University Press, 1940–59.

Paramattha-Dīpanī-Therīgāthā-aṭṭhakathā: The Commentary of Dhammapālācariya. Edited by E. Muller. Pali Text Society Publications, vol. 30. London: Pali Text Society, 1893.

Paul, Diana. *Women in Buddhism: Images of the Feminine in Mahayana Tradition.* Berkeley: Asian Humanities Press, 1979. Second ed., Berkeley and Los Angeles: University of California Press, 1985.

Piyadassi (Thera). *The Virgin's Eye: Women in Buddhist Literature.* Colombo: Buddhist Publication Society, 1980.

Praz, Mario. *The Romantic Agony.* Translated by Angus Davidson. New York: Oxford University Press, 1970.

Pye, Michael. *Skilful Means.* London: Duckworth and Co., 1978.

Rahula, Walpola. "Humour in Pāli Literature." *Journal of the Pali Text Society* 9 (1981): 156–73.

Rāmāyana of Vālmīki. Edited by J. M. Mehta and others. Baroda: Oriental Institute, 1960.

———. Translated by Hari Prasad Shastri. 3 vols. London: Shantisadan, 1957–62.

Ray, Reginald. *Buddhist Saints in India: A Study in Buddhist Values and Orientations.* New York: Oxford University Press, 1994.

Reynolds, Frank. "The Several Bodies of the Buddha: Reflections on a Neglected Aspect of the Theravāda Tradition." *History of Religions* 16 (1977): 374–89.

———. "Death as Threat, Death as Achievement: Buddhist Perspectives with Particular Reference to the Theravāda Tradition." In *Death and Afterlife: Perspectives of World Religions,* edited by Hiroshi Obayashi. New York: Praeger, 1992.

Reynolds, Frank E., and Earle H. Waugh, eds. *Religious Encounters with Death: Insights from the History and Anthropology of Religions.* University Park: Pennsylvania State University Press, 1977.

——— *Guide to the Buddhist Religion.* New York: Hall, 1981.

Richman, Paula. *Women, Branch Stories, and Religious Rhetoric in a Tamil Buddhist Text.* Syracuse: Syracuse University Press, 1988.

Saddharmapuṇḍarika-sūtra. Edited by U. Wogihara and C. Tsuchida. Tokyo: Sankibo Buddhist Book Store, 1958.

Said, Edward. *Orientalism.* New York: Vintage Books, 1979.

Samantapāsādikā: Buddhaghosa's Commentary on the Vinaya Piṭaka. Edited by J. Takakusu and M. Nagai. 7 vols. London: Pali Text Society, 1924–47.

Saṃyutta Nikāya. Edited by L. Feer. 5 vols. London: Pali Text Society, 1884–98.

Sartre, Jean-Paul. *Being and Nothingness: An Essay in Phenomenological Ontology.* Translated by Hazel E. Barnes. New York: Citadel Press, 1969.

Saundarananda of Aśvaghoṣa. Edited and translated by E. H. Johnston. Lahore, 1928. Reprint, New Delhi: Motilal Banarsidass, 1975.

Scarry, Elaine. *The Body in Pain: The Making and Unmaking of the World.* New York: Oxford University Press, 1985.

Schulenburg, Jane Tibbetts. "The Heroics of Virginity: Brides of Christ and Sacrificial Mutilation." In *Women in the Middle Ages and the Renaissance.* Edited by M. B. Rose. Syracuse: Syracuse University Press, 1986.

Scott, George Ryley. *The History of Corporal Punishment: A Survey of Flagellation in Its Historical, Anthropological, and Sociological Aspects.* London: Luxor Press, 1959.

Siegel, Lee. *Laughing Matters: Comic Tradition of India.* Chicago: University of Chicago Press, 1987.

Sikṣasamuccaya of Śantideva. Edited by C. Bendall. St. Petersburg: Russian Bibliotheca Buddhica, 1897.

Smith, Brian K. "Gods and Men in Vedic Ritualism: Toward a Hierarchy of Resemblance." *History of Religions* 24 (1985): 291–307.

———. *Reflections on Resemblance, Ritual, and Religion.* New York: Oxford University Press, 1989.

———. "Eaters, Food, and Social Hierarchy in Ancient India: A Dietary Guide to a Revolution of Values." *Journal of the American Academy of Religion* 58 (1990): 177–206.

Snellgrove, David. *Indo-Tibetan Buddhism: Indian Buddhists and Their Tibetan Successors.* 2 vols. Boston: Shambhala, 1987.

Spiro, Melford E. *Buddhism and Society: A Great Tradition and Its Burmese Vicissitudes.* New York: Harper and Row, 1972.

Spivak, Gayatri. "Can the Subaltern Speak? Speculations on Widow-Sacrifice." *Wedge* 7/8 (1985): 120–30.

Sponberg, Alan. "Attitudes toward Women and the Feminine in Early Buddhism." In *Buddhism, Sexuality, and Gender,* edited by José Ignacio Cabezón. Albany: SUNY Press, 1992.

Stallybrass, Peter, and Allon White. *The Politics and Poetics of Transgression.* Ithaca, NY: Cornell University Press, 1986.

Strong, John. "Filial Piety and Buddhism: The Indian Antecedents to a 'Chinese' Problem." In *Traditions in Contact and Change,* edited by Peter Slater and Donald Wiebe. Waterloo, Ontario: Wilfred Laurier Press, 1983.

———. *The Legend of King Aśoka.* Princeton, NJ: Princeton University Press, 1983.

———. "The Family Quest in the *Mūlasarvāstivāda Vinaya.*" Paper presented at the Buddhism in Asian Cultures Workshop, University of Chicago Divinity School, April 1990.

———. *The Legend and Cult of Upagupta: Sanskrit Buddhism in North India and Southeast Asia.* Princeton, NJ: Princeton University Press, 1992.

Sutherland, Gail Hinich. *The Disguises of the Demon: The Development of the Yakṣa in Hinduism and Buddhism.* Albany: State University of New York Press, 1991.

Sutta-Nipāta or Discourse Collection. Edited by Lord Chalmers. Cambridge, MA: Harvard University Press, 1932.

Sūtrālaṃkāra. Translated by Édouard Huber. Paris: Ernest Leroux, 1908.

Suzuki, D. T. *Studies in the Lankavatara Sutra.* London: Routledge, 1930.

Tachibana, Shundo. *The Ethics of Buddhism.* London: Oxford University Press, 1926. Reprint, New York: Barnes and Noble, 1975.

Tagore, Rabindranath. *The Collected Poems and Plays of Rabindranath Tagore.* New York: Macmillan, 1937.

Tompkins, Jane. *West of Everything: The Inner Life of Westerns.* New York: Oxford University Press, 1992.

Upāyakauśalya Sūtra. In *A Treasury of Mahāyāna Sūtras: Selections from the Mahāratrakūṭa Sūtra.* Translated by Garma C. C. Chang. University Park: Pennsylvania State University Press, 1983.

Vajirañāṇa, Paravahera (Mahāthera). *Buddhist Meditation in Theory and Practice: A General Exposition according to the Pāli Canon of the Theravāda School.* Colombo: M. D. Gunasena and Co., 1962.

Veblen, Thorsten. *The Theory of the Leisure Class: The Economic Study of Institutions.* New York: Macmillan, 1899. Reprint, New York: Modern Library, 1934.

Vessantara Jātaka. Translated by Margaret Cone and Richard Gombrich. Oxford: Clarendon Press, 1977.

Vimalakīrtinirdeśa (The Teaching of Vimalakīrti). French translation by Étienne Lamotte, rendered into English by Sara Boin. Sacred Books of the Buddhists, vol. 32. London: Pali Text Society, 1976.

Vimānavatthu. Translated by Peter Masefield and N. A. Jayawickrama. Oxford: Pali Text Society, 1989.

Vinaya Piṭaka. Edited by H. Oldenberg. 5 vols. London: Pali Text Society, 1879–83.

———. Translated by I. B. Horner. 5 vols. Sacred Books of the Buddhists, vols. 10, 11, 13, 14, and 20. London: Oxford University Press, 1938–52.

Visuddhimagga of Buddhaghosa. Edited by C. A. F. Rhys Davids. 2 vols. London: Pali Text Society, 1920–21.

———. Translated by Pe Maung Tin, *The Path of Purity.* London: Pali Text Society, 1922–31. Reprint, London: Pali Text Society, 1975.

Wadley, Susan S., ed. *The Powers of Tamil Women.* South Asia Series, vol. 6. Syracuse, NY: Syracuse University, 1980.

Walters, Jonathan. "A Voice from the Silence: The Buddha's Mother's Story." *History of Religions* 33 (1994): 358–79.

Warner, Marina. *Alone of All Her Sex: The Myth and Cult of the Virgin Mary.* New York: Random House, 1983.

Watters, Thomas. *On Young Chwang's Travels to India.* 2 vols. New York: AMS Press, 1971.

Wayman, Alex. "Studies in Yama and Māra." *Indo-Iranian Journal* 3 (1959): 4–73, 112–31.

Weinberger-Thomas, Catherine. "Cendres d'immortalité: La crémation des veuves en Inde." *Archives de Sciences Sociales des Religions* 67 (1989): 9–52.

White, David Gordon. *Myths of The Dog-Man.* Chicago: University of Chicago Press, 1991.

Wijayaratna, Mohan. *Buddhist Monastic Life according to the Texts of the Theravāda Tradition.* Translated by Claude Grangier and Steven Collins. New York: Cambridge University Press, 1990.

Wildridge, T. Tindall. *The Grotesque in Church Art.* London: William Andrew, 1899. Reprint, Detroit: Gale Research, 1969.

Williams, Paul. *Mahāyāna Buddhism: The Doctrinal Foundations.* New York: Routledge, 1989.

Willis, Janice. "Nuns and Benefactresses: The Role of Women in the Development of Buddhism." In *Women, Religion, and Social Change,* edited by Yvonne Yazbeck Haddad and Ellison Banks Findly. Albany: SUNY Press, 1985.

Wilson, Katharina M., and Elizabeth Makowski. *Wykked Wyves and the Woes of Marriage: Misogamous Literature from Juvenal to Chaucer.* Albany: State University of New York Press, 1990.

Winternitz, Maurice. *A History of Indian Literature.* 2 vols. New Delhi: Motilal Banarsidas, 1983.

The Wisdom of the Desert Fathers: Apophthegmata Patrum. Translated by Sister Benedicta Ward. Fairacres: Fairacres Press, 1975.

Zimmerman, Francis. *The Jungle and the Aroma of Meats: An Ecological Theme in Hindu Medicine.* Berkeley and Los Angeles: University of California Press, 1987.

Zysk, Kenneth. *Asceticism and Healing in Ancient India: Medicine in the Buddhist Monastery.* New York: Oxford University Press, 1991.

Index